Praise for *The Cross in the Midst of Creation*

"Perhaps, like me, you barely recognize the Christian faith in the evangelical caricatures that dominate our public life. This book is a powerful guide to the actual, difficult, beautiful, and empowering gospel story, and a bridge back to a real faith for those with the courage to follow."
—Bill McKibben, author of *The Flag, the Cross, and the Station Wagon: A Graying American Looks Back at His Suburban Boyhood and Wonders What the Hell Happened*

"With a theological move to the heart of things, Sharon Delgado builds from her previous works on global economy and climate crisis to offer a coherent biblical ethic—a primer costly and right on time. Like the gospel writers and Paul, she cannot speak of the cross or its way without calling by name the powers of domination that wield it. *The Cross in the Midst of Creation* explicates the freedom of the resurrection in resistance, transformation, and so in hope."
—Bill Wylie-Kellermann, author of *Principalities in Particular: A Practical Theology of the Powers That Be*

"With radical fidelity to the ancient gospel, Sharon Delgado unleashes the timeliness of the cross amid current systems of social and ecological destruction. Through her spirited rendition we learn, we sense, we practice the rising up that is possible. Even now."
—Catherine Keller, professor of constructive theology, Drew University's graduate division of religion

"In the wake of the last quarter-century's numerous (and necessary) deconstructions of a millennium of problematic atonement theologies, many social justice–oriented Christians have become wary of, or ambivalent about, the New Testament proclamation of Christ crucified. Delgado's literate and readable study is a reliable guide to reconstruction. It offers a contextual, liberationist, and intersectional approach that restores the cross to the center of the Christian story—and the church's engagement in peacemaking, racial-social equity, and reparative justice work today."
—Ched Myers, coauthor of *Healing Haunted Histories: A Settler Discipleship of Decolonization*

"With translucent prose, provocative storytelling, and trustworthy biblical scholarship, Sharon Delgado restores to Christians the cross of our salvation in the era of climate's uncreation. We cannot get to the new creation without walking the way of the cross—though our way be littered with fear-based belief systems, deterministic notions of atonement, false ideologies, bad Bible study, religious preaching antithetical to the gospel, and devilish enticements to side with a victorious empire.

"We certainly need salvation, *The Cross in the Midst of Creation* reminds us, but what does our salvation look like? To great effect, Delgado puts William Stringfellow's powers theology in necessary conversation with Dorothee Soelle's *Suffering*, not only adding significantly to the theological canon on principalities and powers but forging a new understanding of the nature of our struggle and the practices for our redemption.

"For post-evangelical Christians longing for a deeper incarnation, look no farther. The apostle Paul's word of the cross (1 Cor 1:18) demands to be heard now, because suffering brooks no neutrality."

—Rose Marie Berger, senior editor at *Sojourners* magazine
and author of *Bending the Arch: Poems*

"Finally, a book that I can say should be read by every preacher, minister, priest, and teacher of theology. In a Scripture-based and well-balanced presentation, Sharon Delgado has managed to put to rest the idea of a punishing and vindictive god who doesn't know how to forgive without demanding his pound of flesh. This book does that and so much more. *The Cross in the Midst of Creation* is a timely book meant to be read slowly and pondered over, so the fruits of digesting it are passed on to others. Well done!"

—Mary Anne Muller, theology instructor,
St. John's University, Queens, New York

"This book is a powerful answer to the terrifying times in which we are living. Sharon Delgado has given voice to the cross that it might speak to the anxieties, confusion, and despair of this moment and point the way toward new life. I pray this book lands in the hands of all those who are longing for its urgent message."

—Nichola Torbett, activist and coeditor of *Resipiscence:
A Lenten Devotional to Dismantle White Supremacy*

"What does it mean to truly take the loving and just transformative engagement of Jesus with the world seriously in the midst of the global challenges of

our time? Sharon Delgado's *The Cross in the Midst of Creation* provides one of the most comprehensive, creative, and powerful answers to this question that I have witnessed. Biblically grounded, engaged with tradition, scientifically sound, and informed by the wisdom of Delgado's significant experience working for social and economic justice, this important work points the way in a realistic and practical manner toward the hope for beloved community and warns us clearly of the chaos that will surely come if we do not take up the urgent and sacrificial work that is required for such a time as this."
—Mark Davies, Wimberly Professor of Social and Ecological Ethics, and director of the World House Institute at Oklahoma City University

"The Christian cross has been fraught with problematic projections and co-opted by white nationalists. Yet, for so many, it remains a powerful symbol of faith.

"Grappling with the danger and challenges of these times and grounded in an unwavering commitment to justice and creation, Sharon Delgado masterfully weaves Christian history, multiple liberation theologies, story, and contemplative practices into a work that redeems the cross as a symbol of inclusive love, collective liberation, and transformative praxis.

"This book is for followers of Jesus who are looking for ways to articulate and embrace their faith in face of the challenges and critique of Christian hegemony, and for those outside the Christian tradition who want to meaningfully and knowledgeably engage with the tradition and its symbols.

"*The Cross in the Midst of Creation* lives up to the promise of its subtitle: *Following Jesus, Engaging the Powers, Transforming the World.*"
—Beth Johnson, minister, activist, and public theologian, Palomar Unitarian Universalist Fellowship; cochair, California Poor People's Campaign

"Eight centuries ago, Thomas Aquinas wrote that every virtue is found in the cross. Today Sharon Delgado revives that truth and applies it to our current times of climate change, political division, violence, injustice, and racism. Delgado draws from the vast reservoirs of Christian spirituality and activism: Archbishop Oscar Romero, Marcus Borg, Dorothee Soellee, Elizabeth Johnson, Dietrich Bonhoeffer, James Cone, Jürgen Moltmann, William Stringfellow, M. Shawn Copeland, and many others. She points to the cross as source of what our world needs most—courage, humility, and compassion."
—Daryl Grigsby, author, and presenter at Jesuit School of Theology Sabbatical Renewal Program

THE CROSS IN THE MIDST OF CREATION

THE CROSS IN THE MIDST OF CREATION

FOLLOWING JESUS, ENGAGING THE POWERS, TRANSFORMING THE WORLD

SHARON DELGADO

FORTRESS PRESS
MINNEAPOLIS

THE CROSS IN THE MIDST OF CREATION
Following Jesus, Engaging the Powers, Transforming the World

Cover image: Abstract yellow cross on blue background/Thoom/Shutterstock
Cover design: Laurie Ingram Art + Design.com

Print ISBN: 978-1-5064-7169-3
eBook ISBN: 978-1-5064-7170-9

To the young people who are living through
these troubling times, in hope that they may
know and follow the One who brings light
out of darkness and life out of death

Naturally one can develop a theology that no longer has the somber cross at its center. Such an attempt deserves criticism not because it bids farewell to Christianity as it has been, but because it turns aside from reality, in the midst of which stands the cross.

CONTENTS

PREFACE

CALLED TO PREACH CHRIST CRUCIFIED

THE WEEKEND BEFORE I submitted this manuscript to Fortress Press, I spent three days in silent retreat. My plan was to read it through prayerfully and edit it one more time. I wanted to focus on the overall spirit of the book, to make sure that it was consistently aligned with the vision that had inspired it so many years ago.

When I arrived at the retreat center, one of the first things I did was walk the labyrinth on the grounds.[1] I entered the labyrinth and walked slowly, pausing, balancing, and breathing deeply with each step as I followed the inlaid brick path that led to the center. I was reminded of my life, at times moving forward and at times doubling back, a circuitous route with unexpected twists and turns. I couldn't see the labyrinth's overall pattern and could only focus on the section of the path right in front of me, but I kept putting one foot in front of the other, slowly, mindfully. I finally reached the center circle, an inlaid mosaic with a pattern of the Trinity. From there, I looked out in the different directions and could see the unity of the overall pattern. So is the journey of life, and so is the story of my journey of bringing this work to completion.

____

1. "Labyrinth walking is an ancient practice used by many different faiths for spiritual centering, contemplation, and prayer. Entering the serpentine path of a labyrinth, you walk slowly while quieting your mind and focusing on a spiritual question or prayer." Wendy Bumgardner, "Walking a Labyrinth as Spiritual Exercise," July 17, 2021, *Very Well Fit*, accessed February 2, 2022, https://www.verywellfit.com/walking-the-labyrinth-3435825.

As I look back at the pattern of my life, which informs the writing of this book, I see influences from childhood, including my Methodist grandmother, who introduced me to Jesus and told me she prayed for me every day. As a young adult, I considered myself a spiritual seeker, but as it turned out, Christ found me. This took place during a crisis in my marriage, bringing the love of my life and me back together and giving us a solid foundation for the raising of our kids. It's as if the Spirit of Jesus, his teachings, and the story of his life, death, and resurrection broke my heart of stone and gave me a heart of flesh and continue to do so today.

Some ten years later, I had a profound spiritual experience in which the cross was central. I had just finished reading the first two chapters of 1 Corinthians, which are rich in imagery related to the concept in 1:18 of "the word of the cross" (RSV) and close with the words "but we have the mind of Christ" (2:16 NRSV). I was practicing a form of prayer that Saint Ignatius taught by imaginatively employing all my senses to bring a biblical scene to life. I knelt, placing myself (in my imagination) at the foot of the cross. I pictured the sky outside, overcast and dark, as I imagined it was on the day that Jesus was crucified. I heard a few birds singing outside my window—the barrier between the real and imagined was suddenly crossed—I could hear their occasional, perhaps mournful cries. I asked myself, "If I were really there, what would I smell?" I imagined an acrid, smoky smell—it seemed so present, so real. "And what would I taste?" Immediately, the thought and taste came at the same time: vinegar!

In that moment, I found myself not at the foot of the cross but looking out from the vantage point of the cross, completely disoriented and confused. My first response was "No! This is sacrilegious." Nevertheless, there I stayed. I was gradually calmed and reassured, as words of Scripture comforted me: "I have been crucified with

Christ; and it is no longer I who live, but it is Christ who lives in me" (Gal 2:19–20); "So if anyone is in Christ, there is a new creation" (2 Cor 5:17); "But we have the mind of Christ" (1 Cor 2:16). Such words, which I had internalized through years of reading and reflecting on Scripture, put the experience in perspective, enabled me to accept what was happening, and oriented me spiritually.

Little by little, I became acclimated to the change in perspective. I saw people—all of humanity, it seemed—and I felt deep compassion and unconditional love for all. Most striking was that I had no sense of separation. Everything was colored with familiar impressions and textures, but there was no separate "me." I saw that at my deepest core, who I am is not an isolated individual but all that I have ever loved, an interwoven network of relationships and continuous movement of life that will go on regardless of whether I live or die. That realization set me free from the fear of death. Fear was replaced by a tremendous sense of courage and strength. Months and even years after the vividness of the experience had faded, a strong sense of fearlessness, compassion, and spiritual strength remained, motivating me to continue seeking "God's wisdom, secret and hidden" (1 Cor 2:7) and to challenge the "wisdom of this age or . . . the rulers of this age" (1 Cor 2:6) as Jesus did in his day, although it led them to crucify him (1 Cor 2:8). As time went by, I came to understand these passages more deeply, as is reflected in this book.

This visionary experience propelled me directly into formal preparations in the United Methodist Church for ordained ministry with a specialized focus on peace, justice, and the healing of creation. But it wasn't until I was in seminary that a spiritual director pointed out that the profound spiritual experience that had so completely transformed my perspective "sounds like an experience of call to ministry." I recognized immediately that this was true, and words from the Corinthians passages were illuminated in a new way: "Consider your own call, brothers and sisters: not many of you were wise by human standards, not many were powerful, not many were of noble birth" (1 Cor 1:26). I knew that in my case, these words were an understatement.

One morning years later, while pastoring a church, I was silently praying through these familiar passages, which were now deeply ingrained in my memory, when a new realization came to me. I realized that my call to ministry was not a one-time thing and that these passages define and limit my call in an ongoing way, for Christ sent me "to proclaim the gospel, and not with eloquent wisdom, so that the cross of Christ might not be emptied of its power" (1 Cor 1:17). When this dawned on me, I laughed out loud at how long it had taken me to catch on and at how God had been calling me, gently leading me, and waiting patiently for me to understand from the beginning. By contrast, my awareness unfolds over time, as I am ready, able, and willing to see and understand. As with the labyrinth, I don't usually see the unity and overall pattern in life but simply take it one step at a time.

Over the years, my life has taken many twists and turns, some of which from this vantage point I would not repeat. I have gone through various trials, times of repentance, reversals, and transformations, yet I still remain confident in the God who "was pleased to reveal his Son *in me*" (Gal 1:15–16).[2]

Although the roots of this work extend back through many years, the process of writing largely took place during the Covid-19 pandemic. I wrote the first draft during the pandemic's early stages. My husband, Guari, and I were home alone much of the time, and I am grateful for our focused conversations that led to the initial

---

2. This passage can be translated as "in me" or "to me." I chose the former to reflect my experience.

draft. He is always my best supporter and critic. Our grown children dropped off essentials and brought the grandkids by for short visits outside. The solitude came at great cost, especially for others, but I used the time to write.

One person who knew what I was working on from the beginning was my longtime spiritual director, Jane Swan, who knows the significance of the cross in my life. She reflects back to me in my own words what she hears the Spirit saying to me. She encouraged me to follow the Spirit's lead in the writing of this book.

I am grateful for the encouragement, support, and feedback from trusted friends who read early drafts of the manuscript. I am always grateful for the insights of Bill Wylie-Kellermann, whose work on the powers and principalities has strengthened my own. Daryl Grigsby, another friend and early reader, gave me invaluable insight into the importance of the Black church as an expression of faithfulness to the gospel and as a counterweight to the Christian nationalism of much of US Christianity. Others who read drafts of the manuscript and gave me valuable feedback include the Reverend David Bunje, Jaydee Hanson, Barbara Dean, Becky Gillespie, Mary Anne Muller, the Reverend Richenda Fairhurst, Ruth Stacy, and Jolie Pardew. My book is stronger for having taken their suggestions seriously. I am also grateful to those who found this work worthy to endorse, whose names and endorsements are listed on the back cover or inner front pages of this book.

The team at Fortress Press that facilitated publication did a remarkable job. Beth Gaede, senior acquisitions editor for professional and ministry resources, recognized the value of this project, encouraged me from its inception, and helped me hone the title and subtitle. Editorial Assistant Bethany Dickerson's careful thematic editing, theological questions, and suggestions for clarification strengthened this work as she guided me through the process.

Elvis Ramirez facilitated the copyediting process and worked with me through the final deadlines to bring it to completion. The artist who designed the cover, Laurie Ingram, created just the right image to complement the title and spirit of this book.

I am indebted to all the theologians, authors, activists, and other individuals mentioned in these pages. Without their insights, commitments, and actions, this book would have been impossible.

I now know that long before I ever imagined writing a book, the Holy Spirit "spoke" to me through the first two chapters of 1 Corinthians, calling me to ministry and awakening me to the reality of Christ crucified and yet alive in me and at the heart of creation. These passages of Scripture, which foreshadowed and perhaps triggered my experience of call to ministry, became a touchstone for my life and continue as such to this day. They also provide the scriptural foundation for this book.

The meaning of "Jesus Christ, and him crucified" (1 Cor 2:2) has been debated by theologians through the ages. The cross has meant different things to different people. My aim in sharing my personal experience here in this preface is twofold: (1) I want you to know where I am coming from when I write about the cross, and (2) my story is one example of the insights, visions, and revelations countless people have had through the ages related to the life, death, and resurrection of Jesus.

This book is my fallible, limited, human attempt to preach Jesus Christ, and him crucified, in a way that is relevant to today's challenges and in a way that brings life and hope to this hurting world.

INTRODUCTION

THE CROSS IN THE MIDST OF CREATION

> To carry the cross as Jesus carried it, then, means taking
> up a solidarity with the crucified of this world—with
> those who suffer violence, who are impoverished, who
> are dehumanized, who are offended in their rights.
>
> **—LEONARDO BOFF, *PASSION OF CHRIST, PASSION OF THE WORLD***

ON GOOD FRIDAY in spring 2021, the reality of the cross in the midst of creation was brought home to me in a tangible way. I traveled with two teenaged grandchildren to Santa Cruz, California, to attend an event called "Walking Today's Way of the Cross." Publicity for the event had featured a quote by Howard Thurman, who wrote, "We too, must experience Jesus' walk to Calvary, the weight of the cross, the people encountered, the suffering endured."[1] By the time we arrived at the Santa Cruz County Courthouse, a small group had gathered beside a homemade cross. A few friends I had known when I lived there greeted us. Then Beverly Brook, a clergy friend of mine, initiated the walk by reading from the program:

> Good Friday is the day Christian communities remember
> and reflect on the crucifixion of Jesus. Jesus did not come
> into this world to die, rather he came into this world to offer

---

1. Missio Dei Community and Peace United Church of Christ, "Walking Today's Stations of the Cross," Stay Happening, April 2, 2021, https://stayhappening.com/e/walking-todays-stations-of-the-cross-E2ISTJFN5UG.

us ways to live in love and with justice. For centuries, the stations of the cross have helped Christian people reflect on the mystery of the suffering and death of Jesus in an intimate way. Sometimes communities and groups have taken to the streets, pausing at hospitals, jails, courthouses, war memorials, and shelters to reflect on the ways in which Jesus continues to suffer in the midst of us.

We all walked silently, socially distanced and wearing masks, to each of fourteen stations where we paused to reflect and pray. At the courthouse, we considered Jesus condemned to death and related his suffering to that of people caught up in a system that brings us the death penalty, the criminalization of the poor, and the inequities of our criminal justice system. We stopped and prayed at the county jail and at a bail bonds business, calling to mind the sufferings of people in jails and prisons, detention centers, and juvenile halls. We prayed at places that represent both suffering and relief: a medical clinic that welcomes everyone, a women's center, the Veterans Memorial Building, a chapter of the National Alliance on Mental Illness. Our prayers at a Jewish renewal center and an Asian-run business represented our solidarity with people who are vulnerable to racism and anti-Semitism. We stopped at a closed local storefront, praying for people suffering economic harm. Another station was the *Collateral Damage* statue, near the town clock, which shows a family huddled together, looking up at the sky. We reflected there on Jesus, who, according to the program, was "a person of active nonviolence, yet he comes to know violence against his person, the same violence that is seen in our wars, in the gun violence on our streets, and in our homes." As we crossed the San Lorenzo River Bridge, we stopped to remember environmental degradation, including hurricanes, floods, and fires caused by climate change, and the suffering such damage brings to vulnerable human beings as well as to other species.

One poignant station was the encampment of unhoused people in San Lorenzo Park, near the banks of the river, where dozens of tents had been set up, forming a community. There were children's tricycles and toys, folding chairs arranged as in any campground, even a small garden plot. We prayed, "Humbly, O God, we come before you as we witness the broken hearts of mothers, fathers, sons, and daughters who are forced to live with meager shelter. May we hear the cries and taste the tears of those who have been assaulted by our fears, neglect, and indifference. Bless us with the gift of tears that we may reach out in love and compassion to those who are wounded and broken . . . Amen." That prayer was answered for me—I was blessed with tears. This symbolic remembrance of Good Friday was a great blessing, as Christ's sufferings were related in visible and heartfelt ways to suffering that is taking place today.

The cross not only symbolizes the crucifixion and resurrection of Jesus that took place so long ago but also represents the same dynamic taking place here and now, throughout history and up to this present time. *The Cross in the Midst of Creation* asserts that it is God who suffers the cruel and heartless assaults that are being inflicted on creation, that God's heart breaks as war is waged, as children are abused, as people in poor circumstances are deprived of their basic needs, as people of color are treated as if their lives don't matter, as immigrants are mistreated, as people are imprisoned and forgotten, as the land is polluted, as species die, as the planet warms, as our young lose hope. The crucifixion of Christ is ongoing as human life is diminished and creation is destroyed. The cross stands in the midst of creation.

At the same time, the resurrection is ongoing as people rise from despair and take courageous actions for the sake of the world. The spirit of the risen Christ lives in us as we come alive as fully human beings, living in resistance to the powers that would diminish us, creating life-giving alternatives, and persisting in the work of bringing peace, justice, and healing to the world. Following Jesus opens a way toward both personal and social transformation.

Yet not everyone understands Christianity in this way. Divisions in Christianity are apparent throughout the global church, along with a resurgence of Christian nationalism under far-right leaders like Brazil's Jair Bolsinaro[2] and Hungary's Viktor Orban.[3] In this book, I primarily focus on US Christianity, since that is my context and what I know best. Still, the insights in this book are relevant for people facing similar situations in other contexts. Furthermore, humanity faces unprecedented challenges that will require global cooperation to resolve. In these pages, I propose an understanding of the gospel of Jesus Christ that fosters cooperation with people of all faiths and philosophies who seek a more hopeful world.

I turn now to a pivotal moment in the United States. On January 6, 2021, while Congress was certifying the 2020 presidential election, hundreds of people surrounded and then broke into the US Capitol under the slogan "Stop the Steal" in response to a call to action by then president Donald Trump, who claimed that the 2020 presidential election had been stolen. During the attack, 140 law enforcement officials were injured and five people died. This violent insurrection at the US Capitol, which took place just three months before the Good Friday Way of the Cross event, was suffused with Christian symbols.

2. Raimundo Barreto and João B. Chaves, "Christian Nationalism Is Thriving in Bolsonaro's Brazil: Understanding the Political Situation in the US's Mirror-Image Nation," *Christian Century*, November 18, 2021, https://www.christiancentury.org/article/critical-essay/christian-nationalism-thriving-bolsonaro-s-brazil.

3. Shaun Walker, "Orbán Deploys Christianity with a Twist to Tighten Grip in Hungary," *Guardian*, July 14, 2019, https://www.theguardian.com/world/2019/jul/14/viktor-orban-budapest-hungary-christianity-with-a-twist.

Several groups carried large wooden crosses, leading the way for people with red Make America Great Again (MAGA) hats, clothing and signs with racist and anti-Semitic slogans, Trump paraphernalia, insignia of white supremacist groups and right-wing militias, guns, spears, and even a gallows with a noose. A huge portrait showed Jesus wearing a MAGA hat. People flew "Jesus 2020" and Christian flags alongside US, Confederate, and Trump flags. Banners and T-shirts read "In God We Trust," "Make America Godly Again," and "Jesus is my Savior / Trump is my President." Some blew shofars they had brought from the previous day's Jericho March, during which they had reenacted the biblical story of God assisting the Israelites as they besieged the enemy city of Jericho: when Joshua blew his trumpet, the city's walls collapsed and the attackers slaughtered every man, woman, child, and animal (Joshua 6:1-21).[4] After the rioters breached the Capitol and gathered in the Senate chambers, a man yelled, "Jesus Christ, we invoke your name!" Then Jacob Chansley, the "QAnon Shaman," prayed through a bullhorn as others solemnly bowed their heads.[5] This illustration of far-right political extremism merged with far-right Christianity is an example of Christian symbols being used as religious justification for violent actions in support of antidemocratic nationalism and white supremacy.

How is it that the cross and other Christian symbols can represent actions so opposed to one another in meaning? How has Christianity become so divided? I am convinced that the answer lies in how those of us who identify as Christians understand the central

4. Robert P. Jones, "Taking the White Christian Nationalist Symbols at the Capitol Riot Seriously," *Religion News*, January 7, 2021, https://religionnews.com/2021/01/07/taking-the-white-christian-nationalist-symbols-at-the-capitol-riot-seriously/.

5. Jack Jenkins, "The Insurrectionists' Senate Floor Prayer Highlights a Curious Trumpian Ecumenism," *Religion News*, February 25, 2021, https://religionnews.com/2021/02/25/the-insurrectionists-senate-floor-prayer-highlights-a-curious-trumpian-ecumenism/.

story of Christian faith, symbolized by the cross. The meaning that we ascribe to the story of the life, death, and resurrection of Jesus influences how we understand God. In turn, how we understand God has everything to do with our priorities, choices, and actions in the world, including how we respond to the suffering of humanity and the degradation of the earth. The story of Jesus carries both personal and social implications, depending on how it is told.

In this book, we will explore varied ways that Christians understand the story of Jesus, the meaning of the cross, and the content of Christian faith. We will weigh the value of different views by considering how consistent they are with Jesus's ministry and message, how true they are to the "word of the cross" as preached by Paul (1 Cor 1:18 RSV), and how well they express the good news of God's transformational love in our contemporary context. Our goal throughout will be to search for how to understand the gospel and follow Jesus in a way that is relevant for today.

THE WORD OF THE CROSS: GOOD NEWS?

> We can avoid much suffering and the bitterness of suffering,
> but only for a price that is too high—ceasing to love. . . .
> But then we forsake others and ourselves; we have sold
> our souls. Then we affirm only a little slice of reality, not
> the whole of reality in whose midst stands the cross.

—DOROTHEE SOELLE, *SUFFERING*

The Cross in the Midst of Creation is divided into four parts. Part 1, "The Power of the Cross: The Mystery of God," includes the book's first two chapters, which present the cross as a powerful symbol that has been interpreted in different ways. Chapter 1 explores the book's primary biblical text, 1 Corinthians 1:17–2:16, in which Paul

claims that the gospel revolves around the "word of the cross"—
that is, the story of "Christ crucified," which opens us to "God's
wisdom, secret and hidden" and to an awareness of "the mind of
Christ." Chapter 2 critiques popular Christian teachings based on
ancient atonement theories that portray the crucifixion of Jesus as
God's design to save individual sinners from the fires of a literal
hell and sets the stage for considering alternative ways to view the
cross and experience the gospel in life-giving ways.

Theologians through the ages have interpreted and debated
the message of the cross and the meaning of *salvation*. They have
come up with varied and often competing understandings of the
atonement—that is, how the life, death, and resurrection of Jesus
bring *at-one-ment* with God. No single, uniform theology of atonement has emerged. The story and symbol of the cross are still infused
with mystery that no doctrine or theory can explain.

I recently attended a worship service where we sang "How Great
Thou Art," a well-loved traditional hymn that expresses a theology
of the cross that many Christians embrace but that confuses some
people and offends others. The third verse includes these lines:

> *And when I think that God, his son not sparing, sent him to*
> *die, I scarce can take it in;*
> *that on the cross, my burden gladly bearing, he bled and died*
> *to take away my sin.*[6]

I later asked people how they felt and what they thought about
this verse in an online Christian group, leading to a lively discussion
and more responses than I can share here. The responses fell into
the following five categories: (1) this verse expresses "a deep mystery

---

6. Stuart K. Hine, "How Great Thou Art," in *The United Methodist Hymnal*, no. 77 (Nashville:
United Methodist Publishing House, 1989), 77.

of the absolute love of God" and "the absolute meaning of the atonement"; (2) all theories of the atonement, including this one, "carry some truth"; (3) this understanding of the atonement "can't be understood or explained but must be accepted by faith"; (4) the theology this verse expresses is "consistently troubling" because "it was humanity's choice to crucify Jesus" and "Jesus was executed unjustly while God chooses love"; and (5) this view is "deeply offensive," "primitive," "pagan," and "bordering on the repugnant" because "it characterizes God as an angry, abusive father who cannot be satisfied without blood sacrifice." Several respondents offered alternative views of the atonement and the nature of God, some of which I incorporate into later chapters.

This hymn and many others express a popular and perhaps today's dominant Christian understanding of the atonement, yet people respond to this interpretation in different ways. The range of responses to my informal survey illustrates that among Christians, there is confusion, disagreement, and lack of a shared understanding about the "the word of the cross" that Paul claims is the core of the gospel.

The dictionary definition of *gospel* is "the message concerning Christ, the kingdom of God, and salvation,"[7] but in Greek the word for gospel is *evangelion*, which means *good news*.[8] Clearly, the "word of the cross" was central to Paul's understanding and preaching of the good news of Jesus, and the symbol of the cross has been central to Christianity to this day. How has the cross, an instrument of torture and execution, become for many people a symbol of good news? To some people, this seems foolish (1 Cor 1:18), and to others, impossible.

---

7. *Merriam-Webster's Collegiate Dictionary*, 11th ed. (Springfield, MA: Merriam-Webster, 2003), s.v. "gospel," 541.

8. Clifton Black, "The Good News of the Gospel," Ligonier Ministries, accessed December 15, 2021, https://www.ligonier.org/learn/devotionals/good-news-gospel/.

Some people reject Christianity because they cannot conceive of God being identified with or represented by a poor, humiliated, suffering, crucified human being. For others, the symbol of the cross is anathema because they are appalled by "primitive" teachings about a judgmental God who has been so angered by human sin that he sent Jesus to be executed so that people who believe in him will be spared humanity's common fate of burning in hell for eternity. Many are put off by the Christian Right, which promotes Christian hegemony and supports policies that are the antithesis of the teachings and example of Jesus. People's rejection of the Christian religion as bad news has been furthered by its historical alignment with empire and its religious justification of patriarchal domination, crusades, colonization, genocide, slavery, racism, anti-Semitism, sexism, heterosexism, and anthropocentrism, with similar patterns continuing today. No wonder so many people who care about the common good reject such a seemingly heartless and cruel religion. Distortions and misuse of the gospel have, in some people's minds, fatally damaged the message and reputation of Christianity. In the words of Paul, quoting Psalm 69, "The name of God is blasphemed among the gentiles because of you" (Rom 2:24).

Still, many who love Jesus struggle to reconcile Christianity's violent historical and contemporary expressions and teachings about God's wrath with their belief in a God of mercy and love. They suspend disbelief, acknowledge or deny their discomfort, accept it as mystery, and make the best of it, because in Jesus they recognize the God of love. I confess that some hymns with themes like those of "How Great Thou Art" at times still move me deeply, pointing to a mystery of divine providence that goes beyond rational thought. Still, this does not mean that I take literally the belief that God sent Jesus to die a grisly death in order for God to forgive me.

Fortunately, the story of Jesus is not only being told by people who celebrate his death as a predetermined form of divine punishment that he endured in place of sinners. This book presents other ways to understand the story of Jesus's death and living presence, ways that are consistent with his life and teachings and true to the overall biblical message of the gracious, forgiving, liberating, nonviolent, unconditional love of God that Jesus both revealed and proclaimed.

New Testament writers used various metaphors to express the meaning of salvation and the message of the cross: metaphors related to law (justification), economics (ransom and redemption), oppression and enslavement (liberation), medicine (healing), personal relationships (reconciliation), cultic practices (sacrifice), and so on. Some of these metaphors complement one another while some conflict because of the varied ways early Christians experienced, and found meaning in, God's saving actions. We will explore some of these metaphors in later chapters. Taking any one of them literally may enable us to think we have the absolute right answer, but doing so also closes our minds and hearts to other spiritual truths. If we want to develop a mature faith, we must employ our human faculties and gifts of discernment to find spiritual understanding, clarity of faith, and guidance for following Jesus today.

FOLLOWING JESUS TODAY

Whoever does not carry the cross and
follow me cannot be my disciple.

—LUKE 14:27

Part 2, "God Weeps: Following Jesus in a Suffering World," includes two chapters that portray atonement as reconciliation (2 Cor 5:17–20) and explore what it means to follow Jesus in today's context of profound suffering and existential threats. It begins with chapter 3, which describes Christ as bearing both the sins and sorrows of the world, points to a God who offers reconciliation and the mutual liberation of both oppressor and oppressed, and calls on readers to recognize and alleviate the sufferings of Christ in our neighbors. Chapter 4 describes what is at stake as creation itself is being "crucified," explores the concepts *of deep incarnation* and *new creation*, and struggles with the meaning of reconciliation in this context. Because creation theology and a theology of the cross belong together, this chapter calls on followers of Jesus to go beyond creation care and to support movements for transformational change.

What does it mean to pick up our cross and follow Jesus today, in this time of danger, destruction, and death? The answer to this question must be consistent with Jesus's proclamation and demonstration of God's loving intentions for the world and his passion for the reign of God.

My ongoing connections with young people help sensitize me to the impacts of the multiple crises we are facing today. One spring day, while walking with several teenagers along a canal in the woods near my home, our conversation turned from lighthearted banter to their concerns about climate change. Sixteen-year-old Darren said, "When I think of the future, it's hard to be optimistic." It makes sense that many young people place the danger of climate change and ecological degradation near the top of their lists of concerns while relating it to other challenges they face, for they realize that their lives and futures are at stake.

As used in this book, *creation* does not mean the natural world set apart from humanity but includes human beings. We are interrelated and interdependent with all other parts of creation, yet many of us have failed to live as responsible members of the community of life. Now our children and youth are inheriting a world that has been gravely diminished.

Scientists warn of extreme and irreversible consequences to all life on earth, including humankind, if we do not change course. A headline screams, "'Completely Terrifying': Study Warns Carbon-Saturated Oceans Headed toward Tipping Point That Could Unleash Mass Extinction Event."[9] Another asks, "Are We Heading toward Extinction? The Earth's Species—Plants, Animals and Humans, Alike—Are Facing Imminent Demise."[10] The United Nations sounds yet another alarm: "UN Chief Warns World on 'Verge of the Abyss' as WMO Releases Climate Report."[11] This litany of disasters is ongoing day by day in an onslaught of bad news about the global environment, particularly advancing climate change.[12] In young Darren's words, "The media feeds you a lot of negativity."

Beyond accelerating ecological concerns, the lives of people around the world have been changed dramatically by the tragic physical, social, and economic impacts of Covid-19. The pandemic has exposed and magnified preexisting inequities and has exacerbated social and political divisions. Systemic racism and white supremacy—which have plagued the United States since its

---

9. Julia Conley, "'Completely Terrifying': Study Warns Carbon-Saturated Oceans Headed toward Tipping Point That Could Unleash Mass Extinction Event," Common Dreams, July 9, 2019, https://www.commondreams.org/news/2019/07/09/completely-terrifying -study-warns-carbon-saturated-oceans-headed-toward-tipping.

10. Catherine Ingram, "Are We Heading toward Extinction? The Earth's Species—Plants, Animals and Humans, Alike—Are Facing Imminent Demise," HuffPost, July 20, 2019, https://www.huffpost.com/entry/facing-extinction-humans-animals-plants-species_n _5d2ddc04e4b0a873f6420bd3.

11. Andrea Germanos, "UN Chief Warns World on 'Verge of the Abyss' as WMO Releases Climate Report," Common Dreams, April 19, 2021, https://www.commondreams.org/ news/2021/04/19/un-chief-warns-world-verge-abyss-wmo-releases-climate-report.

12. Brian Pascus, "Human Civilization Faces 'Existential Risk' by 2050 According to New Australian Climate Change Report," CBS News, June 4, 2019, https://www.cbsnews.com/ news/new-climate-change-report-human-civilization-at-risk-extinction-by-2050-new -australian-climate/.

beginning—are being manifest today here and in other countries as reenergized white nationalist groups and right-wing militias and are threatening people of color, their allies, and democracy itself. Internet echo chambers, right-wing media, and some politicians fuel bizarre and dangerous conspiracy theories based not on facts but on repetition. Economic inequity has increased as the rich continue to grow richer. Meanwhile, the everyday struggles of people to keep a roof over their families' heads and food on the table have become harder for many, and impossible for some, both in the United States and around the world.

How can we face the reality of this much destruction and death without turning away? How can we face the significance of this loss and find courage to take positive action for change when current conditions and institutional realities seem so intractable? What does this reality mean for anyone who sees the divine reflected in and through creation and who loves Jesus and weeps as he wept for the world? What does it mean for people of any faith tradition who trust that God continues to act to bring light out of darkness and life out of death?

Our proclamation of the gospel and how we understand the meaning of the cross must inform our response to today's challenges, because our understanding either inspires or limits our participation in solutions. Most people, including many who view the cross as a symbol of their faith, seem to be in denial or paralyzed by the growing violence, the social chaos, and the "death of nature"[13] in our time. Some forms of Christianity focus solely on individual conversion, personal morality, and the afterlife while ignoring or actively opposing initiatives that promote peace, social justice, and environmental healing. Others may support such causes but still

---

13. Carolyn Merchant, *The Death of Nature: Women, Ecology, and the Scientific Revolution* (New York: HarperCollins, 1980).

have no idea how to stop the ongoing diminishment of human life and the hemorrhaging of earth's life force. Yet this crucial time is not the time to give up. Rather, it is time to allow the story of Jesus's life, death, and resurrection to inform our understanding of the gospel, to inspire us by his passion for the reign of God, to renew our faith, and to reignite our commitment to following him in the direction of personal transformation and the transformation of the world.

ENGAGING THE POWERS

> Good Friday is the collision between the passion of Jesus and the domination system of his time. What killed Jesus was nothing unusual . . . this is simply the way domination systems behave. So common is this dynamic that . . . it can be called the normalcy of civilization.

—MARCUS J. BORG, "EXECUTED BY ROME, VINDICATED BY GOD"

Part 3, "Engaging the Powers: A Clash of Kingdoms," explores the social and political forces at work in Jesus's day and how we, as followers of Jesus, can respond to similar forces today. It begins with chapter 5, which describes Jesus's life and teachings, death and resurrection in the context of his ongoing conflict with the ruling powers. Chapter 6 explores today's version of a "wisdom of this age" (1 Cor 2:6), which reflects the dominant worldview based on the pursuit of status, wealth, and worldly power, the very values that Jesus rejected in his day. This *conventional wisdom* (also referred to in this book as the *prevailing wisdom*) is embodied in the institutions and systems that dominate the world today. Chapter 7 explores the "rulers of this age" (1Cor 2:6), that is, the global network of social, political, economic, and military institutions that make up today's domination system. It examines the inner and outer dimensions of these powers and calls on followers of Jesus to engage the powers and call them back to their rightful role as servants, not dominators, of life.

The Cross in the Midst of Creation breaks new ground by linking Christian understandings of *creation*, the *atonement*, and the biblical *principalities and powers* (Eph 3:10 RSV). It highlights the struggle between humanity and "the rulers of this age" in Jesus's time and in ours. It shows that there are forces at work today that are similar to those responsible for putting Jesus to death, forces that were revealed as false and futile by his resurrection.

In *An Ethic for Christians and Other Aliens in a Strange Land*, twentieth-century theologian William Stringfellow demythologized the principalities and powers, which had in modern times been largely ignored or interpreted in archaic ways. Walter Wink's trilogy on "The Powers"[14] advanced and clarified ideas represented by such terms, as do the works of contemporary author/activist Bill Wylie-Kellermann and others who continue to develop these themes. Such theologians have made the case that the powers and principalities are not disembodied spirits floating around in the air, as people may have believed in ancient times, but the inner dimensions and outer manifestations of "authorities, corporations, institutions, traditions, processes, structures, bureaucracies, ideologies, systems, sciences, and the like."[15] Stringfellow said, "According to the Bible, the principalities are legion in species, number, variety,

---

14. Walter Wink, *Naming the Powers: The Language of Power in the New Testament* (Minneapolis: Fortress, 1984); *Unmasking the Powers: The Invisible Forces that Determine Human Existence* (Minneapolis: Fortress, 1986); *Engaging the Powers: Discernment and Resistance in a World of Domination* (Minneapolis: Fortress, 1992).

15. William Stringfellow, *An Ethic for Christians and Other Aliens in a Strange Land* (Waco, TX: Word, 1973), 77.

and name."[16] In this book, I focus primarily on the major ideologies, representative human beings, institutions, and systems that dominate the world today, expressed in contemporary terms as the *powers that be* or simply as the *powers.*

Walter Wink also spoke of the *domination system:*[17] the interlocking network of political, social, economic, military, and ideological powers that dominates the world in different historical eras. The domination system is ever-changing, but even as it manifests differently in different ages, it demonstrates similar values, characteristics, and actions as it changes form.

In biblical times, the empires of Babylon and Rome embodied the domination system. Today the world's primary system of domination is the US-based globalized system of unrestrained free-market capitalism, also called *corporate globalization.* This system is based on an economic model that prioritizes market transactions and economic growth and is supported by an ideology that values hierarchy, materialism, and dominating power. We are enmeshed in this system, so it seems to reflect the "normalcy of civilization." Because we have been indoctrinated in these ideologies, many of us are either blind to the onslaught or paralyzed and unable to step out of the current paradigm.

How does this biblical language of the powers and principalities relate to the primary theme of this book—that is, how people understand the meaning of the cross? The crucifixion of Jesus, which happened long ago at a particular juncture of time and space, is also an ongoing story about our struggle "not against enemies of blood

---

16. Stringfellow, 77–78. To support this statement, Stringfellow refers to Luke 8:29–33; Gal 4:3; Eph 1:21; 6:10–13; Col 1:15–16; 2:10–23. He goes on: "They are designated by such multifarious titles as powers, virtues, thrones, authorities, dominions, demons, princes, strongholds, lords, angels, gods, elements, spirits. Sometimes the names of other creatures are appropriated for them, such as the serpent, dragon, lion, beast."
17. Wink, *Engaging the Powers,* 46.

and flesh, but against the rulers, against the authorities, against the cosmic powers of this present darkness, against the spiritual forces of evil in the heavenly places" (Eph 6:12). Christ continues to be crucified as the powers enlist human beings in their service, subject the most vulnerable to abuse and oppression, wreak violence around the world, and plunder the earth for their own gain.

Still, only God is absolute—the powers are "doomed to perish" (1 Cor 2:6). The crucifixion of Jesus reveals their godlessness, and the resurrection of Jesus demonstrates their futility.

TRANSFORMING THE WORLD: HOPE IN ACTION

The salvation of all creation, the reconciliation of humanity
with one another and with God, the participation in
the reign of God—that is what God ultimately draws
us toward. It is the task of the faithful to be active
participants. . . . The keyword here is *active*.

—CHET PRICHARD, "THE MEANING OF FAITH"

Part 4, "Transforming the World: Practicing Resurrection," points to the gospel as a source for personal and social transformation. It begins with chapter 8, which explores several biblical metaphors that portray the saving power of the gospel in ways that are true to the gracious love of God that Jesus proclaimed and demonstrated. Chapter 9 addresses prayer, which fosters ongoing communion with God and offers clarity, guidance, comfort, and strength for action in the outer world. Chapter 10 returns to the idea of following Jesus in today's world by joining with others to embody the values he demonstrated and taught, to create inclusive community, to resist the current unjust order, and to follow him into the heart of the struggle for a transformed world.

Two months after the conversation I had about climate change with the young people along the canal near my home, when Darren expressed how hard it was for young people to be optimistic about the future, they all attended a Climate Change Agents Camp organized by Full-Circle Learning,[18] a locally based international nonprofit that has worked in thirty countries to equip children and youth to become agents of change. At the camp, they learned about mitigating climate change by reducing their carbon footprints, adapting to climate change by helping build a resilient community, educating others, advocating for sound climate policies, and acting in solidarity with vulnerable people who are suffering the immediate impacts of climate change.

As part of the camp program, I gave a presentation on movements being led by young activists working for climate justice, including the nationwide Sunrise Movement,[19] Indigenous youth and other young activists from frontline communities,[20] and the teenage plaintiffs in Our Children's Trust climate lawsuit.[21] I also told them about Greta Thunberg, the Swedish teenager who started the Global Climate Strike.[22] At a speech she gave on the climate crisis at the 2019 World Economic Forum, she said, "Adults keep saying we owe it to the young people to give them hope. But I don't want your hope, I don't want you to be hopeful. I want you to panic, I want you to feel the fear I feel every day. And then I want you to act, I want you to act as you would in a crisis. I want you to act as if the house was on fire, because it is."[23]

18. Full-Circle Learning, accessed December 15, 2021, https://www.fullcirclelearning.org/.
19. Sunrise Movement, accessed February 2, 2022, https://www.sunrisemovement.org/.
20. Mike Givens, "'Let Us Be Heard': Indigenous Youth Speak on Climate Justice," *Cultural Survival Quarterly Magazine*, June 2021, https://www.culturalsurvival.org/publications/cultural-survival-quarterly/let-us-be-heard-indigenous-youth-speak-climate-justice.
21. Our Children's Trust, accessed February 2, 2022, https://www.ourchildrenstrust.org/.
22. Global Climate Strike, accessed December 15, 2021, https://globalclimatestrike.net/.
23. Greta Thunberg, "World Economic Forum 2019 Special Address," World Economic Forum, January 24, 2019, http://opentranscripts.org/transcript/greta-thunberg-world-economic-forum-2019/.

In a TED Talk, Ms. Thunberg later clarified, "Yes, we do need hope—of course, we do. But the one thing we need more than hope is action. Once we start to act, hope is everywhere. So instead of looking for hope, look for action. Then, and only then, hope will come."[24]

I later asked Darren how the camp had impacted him. He said it had helped him in several ways. He acknowledged that the media does show some positive stories of people working to bring about change, but that "it's more believable to be among people who are actually working for change." He also spoke of hope: "It helped to be with people living, eating, and sleeping together while working toward the common goal of conserving the world. Sharing the same passion gives me a sense of hope and obligation to act upon that hope." He added, "It gives me a sense of security to know we have the support of our prior generations. It helps to know we have someone older than us backing us up."

Less than a year later, these same teenagers formed a local hub of the Sunrise Movement, a diverse youth-led national movement that is calling for a Green New Deal that includes green jobs, climate policies based on science, a speedy transition away from fossil fuels, and a just transition to a regenerative future. Young people claim moral high ground by stressing their right to a livable future.

This is just one example of the many grassroots organizations working for change in varied locations around the world. Whether such groups are faith based or secular, they set a high bar for those of us who seek to follow Jesus, for many who are involved live out the values of the gospel by working tirelessly for a world of participatory democracy, peace, justice, climate stability, and ecological

---

24. Greta Thunberg, "The Disarming Case to Act Right Now on Climate Change," TEDxStockholm, November 2018, https://www.ted.com/talks/greta_thunberg_the _disarming_case_to_act_right_now_on_climate?language=en.

healing. Together, such groups make up an interlocking global network of grassroots organizations working for systemic change, a movement for global justice that has been called a "movement of movements," a "people's globalization," a form of "globalization from below." The slogan of this global justice movement is "Another world is possible."

This is a time of global turmoil and great challenge. Our action or our inaction will impact not only today's most vulnerable people, including children and youth, but also generations into the distant future. Where is the church in this struggle? How well are we backing up our youth and offering them a hopeful future through our actions? The church's teachings and example must relate directly to today's global challenges and inspire action for positive change. Otherwise, the gospel will be left behind as irrelevant or, even worse, as a hindrance to such change.

Does this focus on action mean that we are to trust in ourselves rather than in God? Not at all. We look to Jesus; we trust in God. Yet we are not bystanders to God's action in the world, for "it is the task of the faithful to be active participants in the reign of God."

Christian teachings have long held that the reign of God has both a present and future aspect, that God's reign is already present among us but not yet fully revealed. This understanding implies that we are called not only to pray, "Your kingdom come. Your will be done, on earth as it is in heaven" (Matt 6:10), but also to work to manifest the compassionate and inclusive community that Jesus proclaimed and made visible when he walked on earth. Because Jesus revealed not only what God is like but also what human life can be when lived in the presence of God, I understand the kingdom of God that he proclaimed to mean the world as God intends it to be. This book holds up this vision of God's intended world as a contrast to the status quo. It points to the gospel as a force not only for personal transformation but also for social transformation.

This view of the gospel requires our participation. One way to understand this is to consider Galatians 2:20, which can be translated in either of two ways: "It is no longer I who live, but it is Christ who lives in me. And the life I now live in the flesh I live by faith in [or by the faith of] the Son of God, who loved me and gave himself for me." Using the word *faith* as active (by the faith of) rather than as passive (by faith in) changes the meaning of this and related passages, implying not simply that we believe in Jesus but that we live with the faith (faithfulness) that motivated Jesus. Richard B. Hayes explains, "Thus, as the result of Jesus' faithfulness, the life that we now live in Christ we live 'by the faith of the Son of God' (Gal 2:20). We are taken up into his life, including his faithfulness, and that faithfulness therefore imparts to us the shape of our own existence."[25] This is the favored translation in this book, for the gospel is not a doctrine to be believed but an invitation to participate in the story of God's transforming action through Jesus Christ at work in the world.

By our own strength alone we are not able to transform ourselves at a deep level or bring about the structural changes that are needed, but the Spirit empowers us to follow Jesus, to engage the powers, and to pray and work to create transformational communities that demonstrate the reign of God in our midst. In these ways, we bring hope to seemingly hopeless situations and begin to see signs of resurrection all around. In Greta Thunberg's words, "Once we start to act, hope is everywhere."

The Cross in the Midst of Creation proposes a view of the gospel that requires our participation and is based on the story and vision

---

25. Richard B. Hayes, *The Faith of Jesus: The Narrative Substructure of Galatians 3:1–4:11* (Grand Rapids, MI: William B. Eerdmans, 2002), xxxii.

of Jesus, relevant to today's challenges, and true to the Spirit of the crucified and risen Christ. Still, each of us must discern for ourselves what the gospel means for us today. This does not require uniformity in either belief or action, for there are many life-affirming ways to interpret Scripture and follow the way of Jesus. In this book, we explore and then set aside preconceived notions, doctrines, and conventional teachings about the cross. We consider alternative views that support personal transformation and empower faithful action for a transformed world. By doing so, we approach the mystery of the cross and what it represents from varied perspectives, as people of faith seeking understanding and empowerment to act faithfully in this time of global crisis.

The purpose of this book is to encourage readers to embark on a path of awakening and ongoing transformation. It challenges those of us who seek to follow Jesus to throw off despair and complacency, exposes disempowering and hate-filled teachings that claim to be Christian, and reclaims the gospel as a force for healing, empowerment, and transformation. By participating in the ongoing story of the life, death, and resurrection of Jesus, we discover the creative power at the heart of this and every universe: the all-encompassing, infinite, eternal love of God.

PART I

THE POWER OF THE CROSS
THE MYSTERY OF GOD

CHAPTER 1
THE WORD OF THE CROSS

For Christ did not send me to baptize but to proclaim
the gospel, and not with eloquent wisdom, so that the
cross of Christ might not be emptied of its power.

—1 CORINTHIANS 1:17

WE BEGIN HERE with part 1, "The Power of the Cross: The Mystery of God," which presents the cross as a powerful symbol that can be used for good or for harm. This first chapter presents the scriptural foundation for the book and describes how early Christians understood and preached the gospel, which Paul describes in 1 Corinthians 1:18 as "the word of the cross" (RSV). Chapter 2 exposes some of today's distortions of the gospel and their historical precedents while pointing toward life-giving ways to understand the good news of God's love.

If we are to discern the meaning of the gospel for today's world, we must be grounded in Scripture. This chapter focuses on 1 Corinthians 1:17–2:16, the primary scriptural source for developing the following arguments of this book: The cross symbolizes the life, death, and resurrection of Jesus that took place two thousand years ago, but it also represents an ongoing dynamic that exists at the heart of reality. The contemporary wisdom and worldly power of the domination system are at odds with the true wisdom and spiritual power of God. God is intimately present in the suffering of creation and in solidarity with all who suffer abuse by the powers, which crucified Jesus and continue to perpetuate harm. At the same time, God is at work in creation's redemption as people awaken to the Spirit's transformative power.

These early passages from 1 Corinthians offer a glimpse into some key features of Paul's Gospel, which he calls the "word of the cross." For Paul, this means the proclamation of the whole gospel—that is, the good news of the power of God working through the life, death, and resurrection of Jesus and the power of the Holy Spirit working in and through our lives to bring about transformation. A true understanding of the gospel cannot separate the death and resurrection of Jesus from the way he lived his life and the content of the message he proclaimed.

The Hebrew Scriptures and the traditions of Judaism informed Jesus's message and way of life. This is demonstrated in the story of Jesus introducing his mission in the synagogue of his home-town of Nazareth (Luke 4:16–30). He did so by reading from the scroll of the prophet Isaiah: "The Spirit of the Lord is upon me, because [God] has anointed me to bring good news to the poor. [God] has sent me to proclaim release to the captives and recovery of sight to the blind, to let the oppressed go free, to proclaim the year of the Lord's favor" (Luke 4:18–19). After reading this passage, Jesus rolled up the scroll, gave it back to the attendant, sat down, and said, "Today this Scripture has been fulfilled in your hearing" (Luke 4:21).

Following in the prophetic tradition, with these words Jesus identified the people toward whom his message was especially directed: those who were poor, captive, blind, oppressed, and without hope. In proclaiming "the year of the Lord's favor," many scholars believe that Jesus was referring to Leviticus 25, which calls for a Jubilee for the Israelites every fifty years, during which debts were to be canceled, enslaved people released, and land returned to its original owners (Lev 25:8–17). This announcement by Jesus initiated his ministry and ongoing preaching about the coming of the kingdom of God.

Throughout his ministry, Jesus consistently showed concern for those who were poor, weak, sick, hurting, and oppressed, and he challenged the leaders, laws, and social structures that led to such conditions. He called people to live according to a new and inclusive vision of the compassionate reign of God, and he created a community based on that vision. In these ways, he revealed what God is like and what human life can be when lived in the presence of God.

Not everyone appreciated Jesus's message or the vision of the reign of God that he proclaimed and demonstrated. His mission statement was a direct affront to people of high status, the wealthy, and those who had worldly power. Good news to the poor may sound like bad news to some who are rich. Those who keep people captive may not want captives to be released. Those who are invested in systems of oppression may not want those who are oppressed to be set free. People who benefit from the structures of society as they are may not be happy with the social redress and economic redistribution indicated by a call for Jubilee. Jesus's message about the imminent coming of the kingdom of God is especially important to understand in the context of the word of the cross because it was his passion for the kingdom of God and his actions to support its coming, including his resistance to the religious and political authorities, that led them to oppose him fiercely and conspire to have him crucified.

In the first chapter of 1 Corinthians, after a brief introduction, Paul challenges the divided congregation to find unity in Christ: "Now I appeal to you, brothers and sisters, by the name of our Lord Jesus Christ, that all of you be in agreement and that there be no divisions among you, but that you be united in the same mind and the same purpose" (1 Cor 1:10). In calling for unity, Paul is referring to life in the Spirit and "the mind of Christ," themes to which he returns in the second chapter.

Paul then describes his calling: "For Christ did not send me to baptize but to proclaim the gospel, and not with eloquent wisdom, so that the cross of Christ might not be emptied of its power" (1 Cor 1:17). The term *gospel* (Greek: euangélion) that Paul uses here is the same term Jesus uses to describe the *good news* that he has come to bring in the passage above from Luke 4. In both cases, the Greek word *euaggeliz* means "to announce good news," "to declare glad tidings," or "to preach the gospel."[1] Paul's Gospel is also grounded in the Scriptures and traditions of Judaism and is based on the good news that Jesus proclaimed. Paul affirms, expands, and highlights its universal significance by incorporating the story of God working through Jesus's life, death, and resurrection and by emphasizing the power of the Holy Spirit to transform lives.

A GOSPEL THAT IS HARD TO HEAR

For the message about the cross is foolishness to those who are perishing, but to us who are being saved it is the power of God.

—1 CORINTHIANS 1:18

Paul makes clear that the gospel is a message that saves but can be hard to hear, especially for people whose ideas are shaped and lives are built upon social constructs, superficial values, and prevailing

---

1. James Strong, *A Concise Dictionary of the Words in The Greek Testament; With Their Renderings in the Authorized English Version, in The Hebrew-Greek Key Word Study Bible, King James Version*, rev. ed. (Chattanooga, TN: AMG, 1984, 1991), 33.

assumptions. The gospel sets up a stumbling block for those who depend on their own wisdom, intellectual ability, cleverness, or expertise and frustrates those who seek to attain success based on the values of the dominant culture, such as status, wealth, and worldly power. They cannot comprehend how the values Jesus taught, his passion for the reign of God, or the story of his life, death, and resurrection could enhance their goals. Paul continues:

> Where is the one who is wise? Where is the scribe? Where is the debater of this age? Has not God made foolish the wisdom of the world? For since, in the wisdom of God, the world did not know God through wisdom, God decided, through the foolishness of our proclamation, to save those who believe. For Jews demand signs and Greeks desire wisdom, but we proclaim Christ crucified, a stumbling block to Jews and foolishness to gentiles, but to those who are the called, both Jews and Greeks, Christ the power of God and the wisdom of God. For God's foolishness is wiser than human wisdom, and God's weakness is stronger than human strength. (1 Cor 1:20–25)

The Greek word translated here as "wisdom" is *Sophia*,[2] which Paul uses to indicate the vast difference between the so-called wisdom of the world and the true wisdom that comes from God. Paul discounts professional debaters and orators who use logic and rhetoric to convince their hearers through philosophical persuasion. He insists that they are all foolish and that they miss the true wisdom of the gospel of "Christ crucified."

---

2. Richard Horsley, *Abingdon New Testament Commentaries: 1 Corinthians* (Nashville: Abingdon, 1998), 58.

Paul makes clear that his critique of intellectual and religious argument points to a deeper power at work, the power of the Spirit, which validates the truth of the gospel regardless of the intellectual prowess of the preacher. He even claims that using eloquent rhetorical devices to explain the gospel through logical argument empties the cross of its power (1:17). Ironically, at the same time, Paul uses all the tools of rhetoric and persuasion in which he was trained as a Pharisee to reveal the truth of the gospel. Paul is using language creatively here to make the case that it is only by the Spirit that people recognize the truth of the gospel, regardless of the eloquence of the preacher. For those who are immersed in the conventional wisdom, Paul's creative use of language, including his play on words such as *wisdom, foolishness, weakness*, and *strength*, will fall on deaf ears.

There are two paradigms at play here—the paradigm of "civilization's normalcy"[3] and the paradigm of the Spirit. What is important in the eyes of the dominant culture is not the same as what is important to God. The reality of the Spirit is often hidden from those who build their lives on attaining worldly success. But, says Paul, for those who are "being saved" and are "called," God's power and wisdom are revealed in Jesus Christ.

THE WEAKNESS AND FOOLISHNESS OF GOD

Jesus's message provided the first Christians with the background, the key, and the field of vision they needed in order to understand his passion, his cross, and his post resurrection appearances.

—RICHARD HORSLEY, *NEW TESTAMENT COMMENTARIES*

---

3. Marcus J. Borg and John Dominic Crossan, *The Last Week: What the Gospels Really Teach about Jesus's Final Days in Jerusalem* (New York: HarperSanFrancisco, 2006), 8.

Here we return to the story of Jesus, whose life and teachings, death and resurrection provide the content of the gospel message. His story exemplifies what Paul means when he speaks of the weakness and foolishness of God. Jesus of Nazareth was a lowly Jewish preacher, teacher, prophet, and healer from Galilee who was despised by most of the religious elite and executed as a subversive by the Roman Empire. No one, according to the world's standards, can say that Jesus died a noble death. He died a shameful death, beaten, tortured, degraded, cursed, and crucified.

Although the cross is a common symbol today and rarely, if ever, shocks anyone who is familiar with Christianity, those who initially heard the gospel were familiar with the Roman cross and the horrors of crucifixion. The Roman Empire used crucifixion frequently, especially against rebellious slaves and subversives. The cross was not even supposed to be mentioned in polite Roman society. For the Jews, being crucified was synonymous with being cursed by God: "Cursed is everyone who hangs on a tree" (Gal 3:13; see also Deut 21:23). Paul calls this message a "stumbling block," which can also be translated as "scandal," "offense," "occasion for stumbling," and "the thing that offends." The idea of a crucified messiah was offensive, scandalous, pure folly. No wonder this message was one that most people in first-century Rome could not hear.

In 1 Corinthians 15:3–4, Paul summarizes the gospel: "That Christ died for our sins in accordance with the Scriptures, and that he was buried, and that he was raised on the third day in accordance with the Scriptures." The idea that Jesus, a carpenter and lowly prophet from Nazareth who had undergone crucifixion, had risen from the dead was unthinkable. A crucified messiah was an extreme contrast to the Jewish hope for a messiah along the lines of David and other earthly rulers. After his crucifixion, his disciples expressed deep disappointment because they had believed Jesus to be "the one to redeem Israel" from Roman rule (Luke 24:21). Even after they realized that he had risen and was still present with them, they asked, "Lord, is this the time when you will restore the kingdom to Israel?" (Acts 1:6).

Yet they came to understand that Jesus's vision was of a different kind of kingdom, an "upside-down kingdom"[4] that upended the values of the dominant culture and revealed the reality of life in the Spirit. People who experienced the Spirit's transforming power in their lives and communities became convinced that Jesus was, indeed, the long-awaited Messiah. The deep humiliation undergone by one who embodied the very presence of God is what the early church proclaimed. The basis of the early Christian proclamation that "Jesus is Lord" was that the long-awaited Messiah, God's own son, had undergone suffering and death and had risen to new life "in accordance with the Scriptures" to save the people from sin, to overcome the powers, and to initiate a new creation. These ideas, which started circulating after Jesus appeared to his disciples, became the foundation for the Christian message.

If the story of Jesus had ended with his death, it would have simply been a tragic story about a godly man. It was only after his post-death appearances that his Jewish followers remembered his words and actions in this new context and discovered that their Scriptures provided a rich source of metaphor, poetry, history, and prophecy that pointed to a different kind of messiah, one who would "suffer these things and enter into his glory" (Luke 24:26). It was from the perspective of the resurrection that early Christians understood the crucifixion as not just "a horrible accident, a tragic mistake, but

---

4. Donald J. Kraybill, *The Upside-Down Kingdom*, anniversary ed. (Harrisonburg, VA: Herald, 2018).

the strange fulfillment of the long narrative of Israel's Scriptures."[5] In this sense, it is clear to see what the early Christians meant when they said that Christ died and rose "in accordance with the Scriptures." The resurrection appearances revealed to them a whole new reality, a new paradigm of life in the Spirit.

It is more difficult to understand exactly what they meant when they claimed that "Christ died for our sins." This concept developed from references and metaphors in the Hebrew Scriptures and has been interpreted in varied ways since the time of Jesus to develop varied theories of the atonement—that is, the reconciliation (at-one-ment) of God and humankind through Jesus Christ. For example, biblical statements that "Christ died for our sins" (1 Cor 15:3) or "died for us" (Rom 5:8; 2 Cor 5:14) have been interpreted in many ways, including the following: (1) that Jesus's crucifixion was the price God required to settle heavenly accounts with human sinners; (2) that in God's timeless reality, as sinners we are all guilty and share in the responsibility for the crucifixion of Jesus but are forgiven and saved by believing in him; (3) that as people who are enmeshed in and complicit with sinful social structures, we are not all that different from the people who killed Jesus long ago, so we share in the blame but can take heart because he was raised and offers forgiveness and eternal life; and (4) that the self-giving love demonstrated in the death of Jesus touches our hearts and leads to repentance, forgiveness, and transformation.

The meaning of Jesus's death, however, can only be truly understood and appreciated in the context of his teachings, his way of life, and his risen presence among us. Jesus preached his healing, saving message not solely for his early disciples but for all. He rejected the

---

5. N. T. Wright, *The Day the Revolution Began: Reconsidering the Meaning of Jesus's Crucifixion* (New York: HarperCollins, 2016), 206.

world's superficial values; manifested his vision of a compassionate, inclusive community; forgave sinners; challenged the governing authorities; stood firm when facing death; and rose to new life not for his early followers alone but for those who would come after. He lived and died faithfully "for us."

The beliefs that early Christians developed were integrally related not only to the Hebrew Scriptures but to Jesus's teachings and way of life. They believed and preached the forgiveness of sin, God's undying love, new life in the Spirit, the coming of God's reign, and "eternal fellowship with God."[6] These teachings became the heart of the gospel.

The word of the cross that Paul proclaimed was not just about Jesus dying "for us" but also about the resurrection of the crucified one: a lowly carpenter, an itinerant healer and teacher, crucified and cursed by the powers, whose message and mission were vindicated by the resurrecting power of God. For many, this was a deeply counterintuitive message, but others, both Jews and Greeks, heard and were moved by the stories of Jesus and experienced for themselves the power of the Spirit and the presence of the risen Christ. They came to understand that the lowly Jesus, who was "despised and rejected by others; a man of suffering and acquainted with infirmity; and as one from whom others hide their faces" (Isa 53:3), the one who had been crucified and risen, was the long-awaited Messiah. Paul preached that as foolish as this sounded, Jesus was the very embodiment of the power and wisdom of God, "for God's foolishness is wiser than human wisdom, and God's weakness is stronger than human strength" (1 Cor 1:25).

---

6. Wright, 26.

GOD'S POWER MADE PERFECT IN WEAKNESS

God chose what is low and despised in the world, things
that are not, to reduce to nothing things that are, so
that no one might boast in the presence of God.

—1 CORINTHIANS 1:28

Throughout his letters, Paul insists that the lowliness of Jesus is to be reflected in his disciples, and he applies this to himself. In his second letter to the Corinthians, he makes this case in striking terms by boasting of his trials, sufferings, and tribulations, for, he says, "whenever I am weak, then I am strong" (2 Cor 12:10). God's power is not necessarily revealed in our lives when everything is going well for us, but perhaps at times when we feel most taxed and tested. When appealing to God to remove a "thorn in the flesh," perhaps some pain or disability that was causing him grief, God's answer was not to remove the thorn but to tell Paul, "My grace is sufficient for you, for my power is made perfect in weakness" (2 Cor 12:9). Again, God's work in and through us does not just take place when we are healthy and successful, for God's power is revealed in unlikely and unexpected ways.

In 1 Corinthians 4:8–13, Paul speaks bluntly to those members of the church who were boasting, taking sides with different leaders, and being "puffed up in favor of one against another" (1 Cor 4:6). Using irony, he writes, "We are fools for the sake of Christ, but you are wise in Christ. We are weak, but you are strong. You are held in honor, but we in disrepute. To the present hour we are hungry and thirsty, we are poorly clothed and beaten and homeless, and we grow weary from the work of our own hands" (1 Cor 4:10–12). Here again, Paul reiterates that what appears weak and foolish when measured by worldly standards is revealed by the Spirit to be the power and wisdom of God.

In 1 Corinthians 1:26–31, Paul makes clear to the congregation that none of them has a basis for boasting in themselves or their leaders, and he challenges those who were creating factions in the church by reminding the Corinthians of their state of being when they were called:

> Consider your own call, brothers and sisters: not many of you were wise by human standards, not many were powerful, not many were of noble birth. But God chose what is foolish in the world to shame the wise; God chose what is weak in the world to shame the strong; God chose what is low and despised in the world, things that are not, to reduce to nothing things that are, so that no one might boast in the presence of God. [God] is the source of your life in Christ Jesus, who became for us wisdom from God, and righteousness and sanctification and redemption, in order that, as it is written, "Let the one who boasts, boast in the Lord." (1 Cor 1:26–31)

Not many of the people Paul was addressing had been regarded as wise or influential when they were called, nor had they been rich or born of nobility, perhaps because those who are lowly according to the world's standards are more likely to hear and respond to God's call. This parallels the point Paul makes earlier about the foolishness of God according to worldly wisdom. In God's wisdom, it is "you" (who were not wise, influential, or of noble birth) who are not just called but also "chosen." Why? "So that no one might boast in the presence of God," so that all the glory may go to God.

Ironically, this is a message of empowerment. It calls people to arise and stand firm by the power of the Holy Spirit regardless of their origins, status, or life circumstances. Paul makes the case that even if we are low and despised according to worldly standards, even if we are nothing in the world's eyes or even in our own eyes—no matter. In our very lowliness we are blessed.

This was indeed good news for early Christians and continues to be good news for us today. In whatever condition we find ourselves, rich or poor, strong or weak, wise or foolish, God comes to us in Jesus. Any grounds for boasting in ourselves is extinguished in gratitude for what we have received: wisdom from God, the power of the Holy Spirit, righteousness and redemption and sanctification through Jesus Christ. These gifts include forgiveness from sin and freedom from enthrallment to the ruling powers. Acknowledging all these gifts, Paul exclaims, "Let the one who boasts, boast in the Lord." This attitude contrasts with the boastful apostasy of the Roman Empire and all worldly powers and brings them to nothing.

At the beginning of chapter 2, Paul continues his message about the difference between worldly and spiritual understanding. Here he contrasts "lofty words" with the mystery of God and the power of the Spirit:

When I came to you, brothers and sisters, I did not come proclaiming the mystery of God to you in lofty words or wisdom. For I decided to know nothing among you except Jesus Christ, and him crucified. And I came to you in weakness and in fear and in much trembling. My speech and my proclamation were not with plausible words of wisdom, but with a demonstration of the Spirit and of power, so that your faith

might rest not on human wisdom but on the power of God.
(1 Cor 2:1–5)

When Paul speaks of deciding "to know nothing among you but Jesus Christ and him crucified," he indicates an awareness of divine participation in the sufferings of Jesus and in the sorrows of the world. We are invited to reflect on the story of Christ crucified by the powers and to recognize the ongoing dynamic of Christ crucified today. Because God is deeply present in creation's suffering, Christ is crucified wherever people are persecuted or suffer unjustly, and as species are extinguished and ecosystems degraded, the earth itself is being crucified. At the same time, Christ is risen and the Spirit is alive wherever compassion and justice reign—in peoples' hearts, in social movements, in transformed people and societies. Knowing "Jesus Christ and him crucified" means staying in communion with Christ crucified and risen, living by the faith of Jesus, following his teachings and example, and acting with compassion and in solidarity with those who suffer today.

Spiritual awakening involves waking up to that which is ultimate and to what it means to be human—not in a vacuum but in community with people who are suffering, poor, and oppressed, and in relationship with the whole interconnected community of life. This realization enables us to look at life from the perspective of the lowly Jesus, to face the reality of the depth of the world's pain, and to identify with those who are not at the top of the world's hierarchy but at the bottom.

Simply put, the word of the cross is a direct challenge to false gods, especially to the idolatrous principalities and powers that seem to rule the world. The gospel of Jesus Christ is a message not of gain of those things that the dominant culture values but of loss. In Paul's words, "I regard everything as loss because of the surpassing value of knowing Christ Jesus my Lord" (Phil 3:8). Following Jesus requires hard choices and may include a sense of loss, which for Paul is far surpassed by his relationship with Jesus Christ. The challenge for us is to consider what we are willing to lose in order to live by the faith of Jesus in the context of our suffering world today.

Paul's word of the cross, like the good news of Jesus, is both countercultural and anti-imperial. Its effect is to subvert the prevailing wisdom and to challenge, indict, and predict the "doom" of the dominating powers (1 Cor 2:6). Tragically, the words of both Jesus and Paul have been distorted through the centuries to support hierarchical systems, the accumulation of wealth (as in the prosperity gospel), and dominating power backed by violence. This distortion can only be sustained if people understand God in a way that is completely different from the God whom both Jesus and Paul proclaimed—that is, the God of peace, compassion, forgiveness, justice, and love.

THE DOOM OF THE RULING POWERS

Properly understood, [the cross] is the heart of Christianity, and it is fitting that it is Christianity's central symbol. But not because it was the way by which Jesus died to pay for our sins. . . . No longer is it an image of personal and political transformation. But that's what it was in the beginning.

—MARCUS J. BORG, *CONVICTIONS*

The symbol of the cross originally held not only personal but also political meaning based on Jesus's life, the events that led to his death, and his subsequent resurrection. The early gospel did not primarily focus on the fate of individual souls after death but on recognizing God's presence in the story of Jesus, living by the Spirit, and participating in the coming reign of God that Jesus proclaimed. In 1 Corinthians 2:6–8, Paul writes,

> Yet among the mature we do speak wisdom, though it is not a wisdom of this age or of the rulers of this age, who are doomed to perish. But we speak God's wisdom, secret and hidden, which God decreed before the ages for our glory. None of the rulers of this age understood this; for if they had, they would not have crucified the Lord of glory.

According to New Testament scholar N. T. Wright, "When Paul speaks of the 'rulers and authorities,' he means both the visible rulers, the Herods, the Caesars, the governors, and the priests, and the 'invisible' rulers, the dark powers that stand behind them and operate through them."[7] Paul, along with other New Testament writers, was convinced that the crucifixion and subsequent resurrection of Jesus both brought about and signaled the triumph of God over the ruling powers and inaugurated the beginning of a new age. Here Paul alludes to the Jewish apocalyptic concept of two ages: the present age, ruled by the powers that are "doomed to perish," and the age to come, ruled by the crucified and risen Jesus. Wright says, "The first Christians saw the message and accomplishment of Jesus as the long-awaited arrival of God's kingdom, the final dealing-with-sin that would undo the powers of darkness and break through to the 'age to come.'"[8] This new age, inaugurated by the resurrection of Jesus, was characterized by forgiveness from sin, freedom from enslavement to the (doomed) ruling powers, life in the Spirit, and incorporation into the body of Christ as agents of reconciliation

---

7. Wright, 77.
8. Wright, 280.

entrusted with the mission of sharing this good news and carrying on Jesus's mission to the world. From the perspective of an expanded view, all people and all generations are included in those for whom Jesus died; all human history and creation itself are incorporated into the saving power of God in the life, death, and resurrection of Jesus, represented by the cross.

In the passage above, Paul contrasts what he calls a "wisdom of this age" (what we might call the contemporary or prevailing wisdom) with God's "secret and hidden" wisdom, which cannot be perceived by the powers that make up the domination system. He claims that (1) the ruling powers didn't understand the will of God or the significance of what they were doing when they crucified Jesus, (2) they wouldn't have crucified him if they had, and (3) although the powers didn't recognize it, Jesus is "the Lord of Glory." This assertion, that Jesus is "the Lord of Glory," is consistent with other core New Testament claims, including the following: "They shall name him Emmanuel," which means "God is with us" (Matt 1:23); "The Word became flesh and lived among us, and we have seen his glory, the glory as of a father's only son" (John 1:14); and "He is the reflection of God's glory and the exact imprint of God's very being" (Heb 1:3). Paul can claim that Christ is the "power of God and the wisdom of God" (1 Cor 1:24) and is our "righteousness and sanctification and redemption" (1 Cor 1:30) because God's very being is revealed in Jesus Christ.

GOD'S WISDOM IN A MYSTERY

But we speak God's wisdom, secret and hidden, which
God decreed before the ages for our glory.

—1 CORINTHIANS 2:7

All this points to a revolutionary new reality. Here Paul speaks about God's wisdom, which goes beyond sight, sound, and imagination:

> *But, as it is written,*
> *"What no eye has seen, nor ear heard,*
> *   nor the human heart conceived,*
> *what God has prepared for those who love him"—*

> these things God has revealed to us through the Spirit; for the Spirit searches everything, even the depths of God. For what human being knows what is truly human except the human spirit that is within? So also no one comprehends what is truly God's except the Spirit of God. Now we have received not the spirit of the world, but the Spirit that is from God, so that we may understand the gifts bestowed on us by God. (1 Cor 2:9–12)

One cannot know God or the gospel through worldly wisdom, for they can only be perceived through the enlightening spirit of God. Those who are immersed in this world's values, focused on appearances, and shaped by the domination system cannot discern "God's wisdom, secret and hidden," which is more accurately translated as "God's wisdom in a mystery" (1 Cor 2:7).[9] Yet discerning God's wisdom is possible through the Spirit that "searches everything, even the depths of God," and that enables us to recognize our spiritual gifts and discern God's call. Paul goes on:

> And we speak of these things in words not taught by human wisdom but taught by the Spirit, interpreting spiritual things

---

9. Horsley, *Abingdon New Testament Commentaries*, 58.

to those who are spiritual. Those who are unspiritual do not receive the gifts of God's Spirit, for they are foolishness to them, and they are unable to understand them because they are spiritually discerned. Those who are spiritual discern all things, and they are themselves subject to no one else's scrutiny. (1 Cor 2:9–15)

Here Paul is speaking not just about subjective experiences of isolated individuals but about a tangible spiritual reality that is revealed by the Spirit and that can be not only discerned but also shared, spoken about, and acted upon. The Spirit teaches us and enables us to "interpret spiritual things to those who are spiritual." Jesus's followers through the ages have come to know the reality of this wisdom of God in a mystery and have experienced the presence of the crucified and risen Christ.

Paul then asks rhetorically, "For who has known the mind of the Lord so as to instruct [God]?" Of course, the literal answer to this question is no one. But, says Paul, "we have the mind of Christ" (1 Cor 2:16). This phrase, "the mind of Christ," is a reminder of Paul's call to unity at the beginning of this letter to the Corinthians, where he exhorts them to "be united in the same mind and the same purpose" (1 Cor 1:10). This state of unity is illustrated in the ancient hymn found in Philippians:

Let the same mind be in you that was in Christ Jesus, who, though he was in the form of God, did not regard equality with God as something to be exploited, but emptied himself, taking the form of a slave, being born in human likeness. And being found in human form, he humbled himself and became obedient to the point of death—even death on a cross. Therefore God also highly exalted him. . . . (Phil 2:5–9)

The reality that is being expressed here is the experience of humility and spiritual connection in the mind of Christ, forever identified with Jesus of Nazareth, crucified by the powers and raised by God. We are to live by the faith of Jesus, follow his teachings and example, and stay in communion with God and in unity with one another. In this way we are empowered to live by the transforming power of the Holy Spirit, demonstrating the love we have been shown for the sake of the church, the human family, and the whole community of life.

Our study of 1 Corinthians 1:18–2:16 in this chapter sets the stage for future chapters, which point to the gospel of Jesus Christ, the word of the cross, in ways that are true to its original meaning and relevant to our time. However, as we have seen, the cross has become a symbol that represents widely divergent viewpoints about the meaning of the gospel and the nature of God. In fact, it is such a potent symbol that it can be used in ways that are divorced from the compassionate Spirit of Jesus and counter to his teachings and example. Spiritual truths have been distorted with falsehoods and even turned upside down, leading to great harm. According to William Stringfellow, such verbal distortion is one of the "stratagems of the demonic powers."[10]

The next chapter unmasks some of these distortions. It refutes popular models of the atonement that portray a wrathful God and a deterministic view of both cross and creation and shows how such belief systems foster apathy, resignation, cruelty, violence, chaos, and accommodation to the status quo. It also critiques several historical models of the atonement and lays the groundwork for chapters that follow, which offer alternative views of the atonement that inspire hope and empower courageous moral action.

---

10. Stringfellow, *Ethic for Christians*, 97.

Living by the faith of Jesus opens a way to both personal and social transformation, enabling us to recognize that the love that lived in Jesus lives in us. The wisdom of God becomes apparent in the outpouring of love and in the shared perception of the mind of Christ. Love is the foundation and the key.

CHAPTER 2
REJECTING THEOLOGICAL CRUELTY

The responsibility to reinterpret the character and
heart of God from that of violent to anti-violent,
looms before us as we work toward a theology of peace,
reconciliation, and restoration through Christ.

—SHARON BAKER, "THE REPETITION OF RECONCILIATION"

IN A 2020 book, *Christ and Coronavirus*, high-profile preacher and best-selling author John Piper described his views on the pandemic, purportedly to offer perspective and comfort to his readers. In it he argues that (1) God is sovereign and in control of everything, that nothing is outside of God's will; (2) God sent the virus as punishment for sinners, some of whom will be infected with the disease, and as a wake-up call to others to be ready for the return of Christ; (3) God's sovereignty is a mystery, so don't try to understand it; and (4) God is the rock under our feet that can never be shaken. He summarizes his views by saying, "The coronavirus was sent, therefore, by God. This is not a season for sentimental views of God. It is a bitter season. And God ordained it. God governs it. He will end it. No part of it is outside his sway. Life and death are in his hand."[1]

The book has over a thousand reviews on Amazon.com, which indicates the popularity of John Piper. It has an average star rating

---

1. John Piper, *Coronavirus and Christ* (Wheaton, IL: Crossway, 2020).

of 4.5. But the lower-ranking reviews include some biting critiques,[2] including the following, with which I agree:

> For Piper, the secret story of the Bible is that Jesus was wrong. God's will actually is being done always and everywhere— we just can't see how everything evil really is good in the end.

> If God sent the virus to the world as Piper here argues . . . , then it is hard, nay, impossible, to avoid the conclusion that Piper's "god" is evil.

> Piper ascribes to God such a hateful and vengeful nature as to send a virus as divine judgement. Of course if you accept Christ and ONLY if you accept Christ you're worthy of his tiny little god's love.

> Worshiping a God who has personally orchestrated every death in human history is vile and ridiculous. It is this rank absurdity that made me reject Christianity.

Note how different the tone and message of Piper's book are from the "word of the cross" that Paul proclaimed. When compared to the teachings of Jesus, its message is unrecognizable. Yet many forms of conservative Christianity promote similar ideas about the nature of God and God's relationship with human beings.

Throughout history, many have understood God to be a divine king or judge, a patriarchal authority figure at the top of the world's

---

2. Piper, *Coronavirus and Christ*, Customer Reviews, Amazon.com, https://www
.amazon.com/gp/product/1433573598?pf_rd_r=YD0RRGREXV2FDXYQ07PB&
pf_rd_p=5ae2c7f8-e0c6-4f35-9071-dc3240e894a8&pd_rd_r=e6f4997a-d148-4430
-9e57-4e367fe7ae40&pd_rd_w=GjLKE&pd_rd_wg=bBhGP&ref_=pd_gw_unk
#customerReviews.

power structures who keeps people in line by rewarding, granting privileges, and doling out punishment. Like the God in John Piper's book, this is a God who directly controls and deliberately causes everything, even great suffering. Sadly, it is not only privileged people who accept this view of God but also many who are sick, poor, or in unjust circumstances. This compounds their suffering and may lead them to blame themselves for their misfortunes or to accept them as the will of God.

At the core of such belief systems is a deterministic understanding of the atonement that perpetuates domination and violence while promoting acceptance of suffering as God's will. The foundation of such theories is the idea that God sent Jesus into this world for the purpose of dying on the cross to save individuals who believe in him from the eternal torment to which all others are doomed. In short, Jesus was born to die.

This chapter refutes *theological cruelty*—that is, teachings about God based on popular views of the atonement that tolerate and further suffering while explaining it away in religious terms. It summarizes several historical theories of the atonement and critiques popular Christian teachings that portray the crucifixion of Jesus as God's design to save individual sinners from the fires of a literal hell. This chapter sets the stage for exploring alternative understandings of the atonement that reveal the transforming power of the Spirit at work through Jesus Christ, who came not to die but to proclaim the reign of God and to show us what God is like and what human life can be when lived in the presence of God.

Jesus wasn't born to die—he was born to be a living
invitation. . . . An invitation to live differently, to live fully,
to be an imitator of God by being an imitator of Jesus—the
one who was the ultimate revelation of what God is like.

**—BENJAMIN L. COREY, "NO, JESUS WASN'T BORN TO DIE
(THE PART OF THE CHRISTMAS STORY WE SCREW UP)"**

The idea that Jesus was born to die, and that dying on the cross was his primary purpose, is central to the teachings of the Christian Right. John Piper, the pastor and author mentioned above, also wrote *Fifty Reasons Why Jesus Came to Die*. Among the reasons he lists are to absorb the wrath of God, to cancel the legal demands of the law against us, to provide the basis for our justification, and to rescue us from final judgment. The back cover introduces this book by stating, "The most important questions anyone can ask are: Why was·Jesus Christ crucified? Why did he suffer so much? What has this to do with me? Finally, who sent him to his death? The answer to the last question is that God did."[3]

Likewise, popular preacher John McArthur, author of over four hundred books and study guides, including the thirty-three volume McArthur New Testament Commentary, expounds on this theme in a Christmas message, describing God's violent intentions for the baby Jesus:

Here's a side to the Christmas story that isn't often told: Those soft little hands, fashioned by the Holy Spirit in Mary's womb, were made so that nails might be driven

---

3. John Piper, *Fifty Reasons Why Jesus Came to Die* (Wheaton, IL: Crossway, 2006), back cover.

through them. Those baby feet, pink and unable to walk, would one day stagger up a dusty hill to be nailed to a cross. That sweet infant's head with sparkling eyes and eager mouth was formed so that someday men might force a crown of thorns onto it. That tender body, warm and soft, wrapped in swaddling clothes, would one day be ripped open by a spear. . . . Jesus was born to die.[4]

Cruel teachings about the atonement—that Jesus was born to die and that God sent Jesus to the cross—reflect a deterministic understanding that points to his crucifixion as something that God intended from the beginning, planned, and orchestrated. Belief systems based on these ideas vary in details and emphases, but they all revolve around the idea that God required the death of Jesus to grant forgiveness to individuals who believe in him and to save them from eternal punishment. Theories of the atonement that seem most visible right now in conservative Christian circles are based on the idea that Jesus was, quite literally, born to die.

SATISFACTION AND SUBSTITUTION

For satisfaction atonement, it appears that . . . God is
ultimately the one who arranged for the death of Jesus
as the payment that would satisfy divine honor or as the
compensatory punishment required by divine law.

—J. DENNY WEAVER, *THE NONVIOLENT ATONEMENT*

---

4. John MacArthur, "Why Was Jesus Born?," *For the Love of His Truth: A Christian Blog about Fundamental Facts*, accessed February 8, 2022, https://fortheloveofhistruth.com/2011/12/02/heres-a-side-to-the-christmas-story-that-isnt-often-told/.

As mentioned in the introduction, there has never been a generally agreed-upon theory of the atonement. Varied theories were developed in the context of different cultures and historical periods. Anselm of Canterbury developed the *satisfaction theory* of the atonement in the eleventh century in the context of medieval feudalism; it reflects the worldview of the times. The system of feudalism was held together and enforced by a code of honor in which feudal lords were to be honored, feared, and obeyed. If a peasant dishonored or disobeyed his lord, it was seen not as an isolated offense but as a threat to the feudal system itself. In such cases, some form of satisfaction was required, either payment or punishment, to reestablish the lord's honor and to restore the feudal system to effective working order.

Because this was the context of his times, Anselm envisioned God in the image of a feudal lord who ruled the universe as a lord ruled his fiefdom, with the universe itself thrown out of order by human sin. Because sin of any kind creates disorder in God's harmonious universe, God cannot just flip a switch to bring about the needed reconciliation with humanity without interfering with the divine order—the legal demands of God's law must somehow be satisfied to restore order to the universe and correct sin's offense against the glory of God. But human sin dishonors God so egregiously and throws the universe out of order so completely that mere mortals cannot provide the required satisfaction. This dilemma leaves all humanity destined for eternal punishment. Yet God provides a way to save individuals from the fires of hell by giving his son over to crucifixion to provide satisfaction and to restore the universe to balance and harmony. Jesus, the sinless son of God, was able through his absolute obedience, voluntary suffering, and sacrificial death to provide satisfaction, restore the honor of God, reestablish balance to the universe, and bring those individuals who believe in him to at-one-ness with God.

The *substitution* theory, also called *penal substitution*, was developed along similar lines in the sixteenth century during the Protestant Reformation, but instead of focusing on restoring God's honor, it focuses on God's wrathful response to human sin. According to this theory, we each stand in a divine courtroom before God, the Judge. Because all humans have sinned against God, we all deserve eternal punishment and, without salvation, are condemned to hell forever. Someone must be punished, but human sin is so pervasive and egregious that there is no way for us to atone. To resolve this dilemma, God sent his son into the world to suffer our punishment by bearing our sins on the cross. Because Jesus was both human and divine, his sacrificial death was sufficient. Because he was without sin, he served as the perfect substitute who alone could set things right. He bore the vicarious punishment for the sin and guilt of all humanity on the cross. We are the ones who deserve death, but Jesus was sacrificed in our place. Despite deserving to be pronounced "guilty" and condemned, we are *justified*, pronounced "not guilty," and even declared "righteous" by the divine Judge because Jesus died in our place. Both the satisfaction and substitution models of the atonement portray Jesus's death on the cross as a payment for human sin.

The belief that human beings need to be reconciled through blood sacrifice to restore God's honor or appease a wrathful God is basic to many forms of Christianity and is reflected in popular culture. A scene from the movie *The Apostle* illustrates this view. At the high point of the movie, the main character, a charismatic preacher played by Robert Duvall, holds up a baby in front of the congregation and says, "Could I ever drive a nail through the hand of this precious baby? I couldn't, but God could. That's what God did for you and me."[5]

---

5. *The Apostle*, a US film made in 1997 that was written, directed, and produced by Robert Duvall.

Mel Gibson's *The Passion of the Christ*, criticized for its gratuitous violence, anti-Semitism, and lack of historical or political context, conveys a similar message through its portrayal of a passive and miserable Jesus whose ministry and teachings are submerged by unrelenting scenes of his sadistic torture. The point is clear—that Jesus went through all this horrendous suffering to save you and me. Yes, it was God's plan, but the grotesque caricatures of the Jews, the savagery of the Romans, and the ambiguously gendered devil in the movie make clear who the villains were whom God delegated to carry it out. In critiquing the film, feminist theologian Arnfríður Guðmundsdóttir says,

> Gibson sees the amount of Christ's suffering as a clear sign of Christ's love, namely, "more pain, more gain." This interpretation of Christ's passion can be seen as a classic example of a glorification of suffering, in which violence is not only justified as being the will of God but is also a necessary prerequisite for the good that is expected to come out of it.[6]

These contemporary illustrations of the atonement seem crass. The theologians who developed both the satisfaction and substitutionary theories were much more theologically sophisticated in their attempts to explain how these views express God's love for humanity through Jesus's death on the cross according to the worldview and context of their times. Yet soon after these atonement theories were developed, there was great persecution of those who did not accept them or who were not considered "saved."

---

6. Arnfríður Guðmundsdóttir, *Meeting God on the Cross: Christ, the Cross, and the Feminist Critique* (Oxford: Oxford University Press, 2010), 147.

Belief systems that understand Jesus's crucifixion as required by God to pay for human sin distort both the personal and political implications of the gospel. They substitute a dogma about a wrathful God who requires human sacrifice for the good news of the gospel, which includes the whole story of the life and teachings, death and resurrection of Jesus. Such belief systems seek to make the death of Jesus seem acceptable while trapping people in a deterministic religion devoid of the transforming power of the Spirit. They reduce the importance of Jesus to the last few hours of his life.

THE DANGERS OF DETERMINISM

To put forward the events of Holy Week as a kind of divinely predetermined . . . play whose author and director is none other than Almighty God is to have substituted for biblical faith a fatalism that may belong to Stoicism, but not to the tradition of Jerusalem. Afterwards—but only then—faith is allowed to see the hand of God in this human tragedy.

—DOUGLASS JOHN HALL, *THE CROSS IN OUR CONTEXT*

Was the crucifixion of Jesus really the price God demanded as atonement for human sin? Was Jesus "born to die" to save us? Did God send Jesus to suffer and die on our behalf to make it possible for God to forgive us? Was the crucifixion God's divine plan and action, and therefore good and right, or was it planned and carried out by the enemies of God and therefore evil? How we answer these questions reflects our view of God. If the execution of Jesus was God's direct intention, then John Piper's two-word answer to the question "Who sent Jesus to his death?" is correct—God did. In other words, God orchestrated, delegated, and carried out the killing.

Such deterministic belief systems have repercussions. As feminist theologians point out, the crucifixion of Jesus has often been interpreted in ways that glorify suffering and self-sacrifice as values in themselves, usually in service to the powers—that is, suffering and self-sacrifice that preserve the status quo. Such distorted interpretations of Jesus's death have been used to send women back to their abusive husbands, to keep poor and oppressed people from rebelling, to convince people that by submitting to their fate ("bearing their cross"), they will find a reward in heaven. People who profess beliefs such as these may be sincere in their love for Jesus and helpful to those around them, but they are participants in a system of beliefs that have real-life negative impacts on others. These views perpetuate human suffering and justify oppressive relationships in which Christ continues to be crucified today.

Jesus did not counsel people to accept their lot in life or accept injustice or stay in abusive situations, nor did he model such behavior. He stood up courageously against unjust laws, religious mores, and social structures, even though his actions led to his own suffering and death at the hands of the religious and political leaders of his day.

To believe that Jesus was born to die and that his death was God's purpose and intent can lead to religious justification of the suffering of oneself or others and apathy in the face of injustice. Such beliefs allow us to justify not only Jesus's execution but other injustices as well. For if all is well and it was God's intent for one man, Jesus, to be tortured and executed by the State, why not others? If things have been set right by the death of Jesus and everything is going according to God's plan, why try to change anything? Why not accept everything that happens, every injustice, every execution, as God's will? But religious justifications that support violence, abuse, exclusion, and hierarchical domination are based on the worst aspects of Christianity: a strict but selective biblical literalism that defies reason, a coldhearted rejection of the compassion that motivated Jesus, and a faulty understanding of who God is and why Jesus died.

This is theological cruelty. It is the antithesis of the spirituality of Jesus. It is an expression of religion that supports empire. It serves the powers. In the words of Walter Wink,

> The Gospel evidence is that Jesus was not executed by God, but by the Powers That Be, specifically, the religious authorities and the Romans. God may have been able to work out redemption despite the Powers, and even through the blind operation of the Powers, but God did not kill Jesus or have him killed or even allow him to be killed, and every view to the contrary depicts God as committing an unconscionable sin.[7]

Entrapment of the innocent, torture, and execution by the State are not now and have never been in accordance with the will of God. The death of Jesus was not God's intent. Rather, God's intent in sending Jesus was to show us what God is like and to enable us to glimpse what human life and community can be when lived in the transforming presence of the Spirit. Clearly, such a life was (and is) a threat to the powers that be. Jesus understood that being a beloved child of God put him at odds with the world's power structures. He was tempted in the wilderness to seek status, wealth, and worldly power, but instead he chose the foolishness and weakness of love. He chose "God's wisdom in a mystery," which the rulers of his

---

7. Walter Wink, *The Human Being: Jesus and the Enigma of the Son of Man* (Minneapolis: Augsburg Fortress, 2002), 293.

age did not understand: "If they had, they would not have crucified the Lord of glory" (1 Cor 2:8).

If I stand by, approving the execution of Jesus as a human sacrifice given in my place to a judgmental God, I stand with the High Priest Caiaphas, who argued to the council that it was "expedient that one man should die for the people" (John 18:14 RSV). If I applaud the crucifixion of Jesus as a good plan, even God's plan, I place myself (and God!) on the side of the Roman Empire, which crucified subversives, including Jesus, as a matter of course, just as governments execute dissidents and subversives today. If I collaborate with those who put Jesus to death by justifying his murder on religious grounds, with theories of why his blood needed to be shed, I put myself on the side of the religious collaborators and bloodthirsty mob who called for Jesus to be crucified. If I ignore the political context and accept the execution of Jesus as a predetermined event that happened just as God intended, the cross becomes a symbol of God's approval of the status quo rather than a symbol of hope for the transformation of the world.

Many people, Christian and non-Christian alike, reject the cruel depiction of a punishing and deterministic God who would condemn the masses to hell but save a few by sending his son to suffer and die. Still, for many, such belief systems are compelling. Fear of hell provides a huge incentive to doubters to believe ("What if it is true?") and creates an urgent need for believers to convert others, since the significance of our short lives and even the fate of the earth pales in comparison to what they believe is at stake: whether we will spend eternity in heaven or hell. But fear-based belief systems are dangerous, leading people to doubt their own insight, experience, and at times, even common sense.

Furthermore, if the primary task of Christianity is to convert individual sinners so that in the afterlife they will experience bliss instead of torture, there is no reason to work for a better world—only to convince individuals to accept these teachings and give themselves over to this version of salvation. There is no motivation here to pray or act for God's kingdom to come or God's will to be done on earth as it is in heaven (Matt 6:9–10). If God is completely in charge and everything that happens is God's will, then we can accept not only the death of Jesus but every death, even the death of nature, as God's will. Such resignation is one of the dangers of deterministic models of the atonement and of God's actions in the world.

OTHER HISTORIC MODELS OF THE ATONEMENT

Most of the traditional theories have been those that reduce the passion to an equation, "formulated by a divine mathematician" so that a special death is necessary in order to balance the cosmic accounts. That death was afforded by Jesus Christ.

—SHARON BAKER, "THE REPETITION OF RECONCILIATION"

Satisfaction and substitution models of the atonement are part of popular contemporary Christian culture and perhaps the dominant views, but they are not the only ways that Christians through the ages have understood salvation. I summarize and critique two other historic theories of the atonement here before moving on.

Abelard, a younger contemporary of Anselm, promoted the *moral influence* theory in the eleventh century and was persecuted for opposing Anselm's dominant satisfaction model. The moral influence theory is kinder because it is based on a view of God as loving rather than wrathful and because it focuses not only on Jesus's death but also on his life and teachings. According to this model of the atonement, because sin has separated us from God, we have lost sight of how to live. To deal with this dilemma, God does not condemn us or require a payment for our salvation but reaches out to us in Jesus and offers us forgiveness and unconditional love. Jesus's moral teachings, his exemplary life, and especially his sacrificial death bring about atonement by inspiring a subjective response of gratitude, which in turn inspires believers to follow Jesus's example of self-sacrificial love.[8]

In his groundbreaking book *Christus Victor*, published in 1931, theologian Gustaf Aulén articulated an earlier "classic" theory of the atonement, which he called *Christus Victor* (Christ the Victor). It points to Christ's victory in a cosmic drama that features a conflict (or "war") between God and the demonic powers of sin, death, and the devil, which hold human beings in bondage. It portrays Jesus's crucifixion as a decisive battle against the powers of darkness and his subsequent resurrection as breaking their dominion over humanity. (Note that the other theories omit or barely mention the resurrection.) Aulén claimed that this was the primary understanding of the early church and that it was revived by Martin Luther during the Reformation. Some early Christian illustrations of this model use the metaphor of ransom, with Jesus's death being the price paid for humanity's liberation from the demonic powers.[9] In this model of the atonement, the incarnation is central, as exemplified by early church teachings about God entering into human life and redeeming it. Rather than the dualistic image of God sending Jesus to restore God's honor or to placate God's wrath, the *Christus Victor* theory maintained that "God was in Christ" and that it was not God who killed Jesus but the powers.

---

8. It is important here to reiterate that self-sacrifice and suffering are not redemptive in themselves and that adopting self-sacrifice as a model for living may cause harm by perpetuating oppressive or unjust conditions.

9. Gustaf Aulén, *Christus Victor: An Historical Study of the Three Main Types of the Idea of the Atonement*, trans. A. G. Herbert (Eugene, OR: Wipf & Stock, 2003), first published 1931 by SPCK.

While most Christians are influenced by one or more of these traditional models of the atonement, Mark Galli explains why most evangelicals favor the substitutionary model, even those who allow for other biblically based atonement theories: "Like the ransom model: We are held in the power of the devil until Christ died and freed us from his grip. And *Christus Victor*: The malevolent principalities and rulers of this age have been defeated by Christ on the cross. And the moral model: Seeing the lengths to which Christ went to demonstrate his love by dying on the cross, we respond in love."[10] Galli acknowledges that the substitution model has been abused, but he points out that its message often evokes a deep, personal response of gratitude and relief: "Where *Christus Victor*, for example, is a wonderful model to describe *cosmic* redemption, substitutionary atonement is about *my* salvation: Christ died *for me*. It doesn't get any more personal than that. And evangelical religion is nothing if not personal."[11]

Galli makes a good point here. Perhaps that is why I still respond at a deep emotional level to some traditional hymns based on this model, for instance, "O Sacred Head Now Wounded" ("tis I deserve thy place"), "What Wondrous Love Is This" ("that caused the Lord of bliss to bear the dreadful curse for my soul"), Handel's Messiah ("and with his stripes we are healed"), and others. By critiquing ancient atonement theories, I do not intend to dismiss elements of tradition that people have found meaningful or weaken anyone's faith. Rather, I hope to open readers' minds to the myriad ways that God works in the human heart. If we are touched by a particular understanding of the atonement, we are not required to

10. Mark Galli, "It Doesn't Get Any More Personal: Why Evangelicals Give Pride of Place to Penal Substitutionary Understandings of the Cross," *Christianity Today*, January 11, 2018, https://www.christianitytoday.com/ct/2018/january-web-only/penal-substitutionary -atonement-it-doesnt-get-more-personal.html.
11. Galli.

adopt it as our sole understanding or take it literally. Rather, our faith can also be informed by other scriptural and theological views.

Biblical metaphors related to the theme of atonement are plentiful, but metaphors are not intended to be taken literally. Did God really require a human sacrifice before God could forgive? Was Jesus's execution a ransom paid (to God or the devil) to liberate people from the powers? Did Jesus have to suffer the torments of crucifixion to model compassion, empathy, and sacrificial love? Of course not. In *Executing God: Rethinking Everything You've Been Taught about Salvation and the Cross*, Sharon Baker warns, "But as we move forward let's keep in mind that we speak metaphorically. Jesus did this; Paul did this; the great theologians of the Christian tradition did this. We get in trouble when we take the metaphors literally. If we do, we end up with the rigid dogma of absolute certainty that eliminates the need for faith."[12] In the coming chapters, we will explore many biblical metaphors that describe how people experience and understand the meaning of the gospel. Taken together, they can open our eyes in new ways to the transforming power and love of God in Jesus Christ.

One problem with the historic theories of the atonement mentioned in this chapter is that they all require Jesus to be killed. The moral influence and *Christus Victor* theories are more nuanced than the satisfaction and substitutionary models, and they portray God not as wrathful but as loving, but Jesus's death is still deemed necessary for the salvation of human beings. In the case of the moral influence theory, God sends his beloved son to live in a self-sacrificial manner and to die on the cross in order to engender a grateful response and to effect the moral transformation of believers. In the case of *Christus Victor*, Jesus's death was necessary for

---

12. Sharon Baker, *Executing God: Rethinking Everything You've Been Taught about Salvation and the Cross* (Louisville: Westminster John Knox, 2013), 148.

Christ to achieve victory in the struggle with the powers and to free human beings from their grip. All of these theories ultimately bring us face-to-face with a violent view of God.

There are many alternatives. In his book *The Nonviolent Atonement*, J. Denny Weaver revives the ancient *Christus Victor* theory and modifies it to portray a nonviolent view of the atonement and a nonviolent view of God. While the premise of his "narrative Christus Victor" theory is based on the struggle between God and the powers, Denny asserts that the violent language about God's victory over the evil powers in the book of Revelation is figurative and that Revelation expresses an overall message that is consistent with narratives about the nonviolent Jesus that all four Gospels proclaim. In this model, God is not implicated in Jesus's death as in other atonement motifs, for God did not plan (much less need) the death of Jesus to forgive human sin. God sent Jesus not to die but to witness to the reign of God, and the powers that were opposed to the reign of God killed him. Jesus didn't return the violence of the powers with violence but responded with nonviolence, providing us with an example to follow. Jesus's death at the hands of the powers and his resurrection by "the nonviolent God" brought about God's triumph over the powers by vindicating Jesus's life and message, unmasking the powers, and demonstrating their futility. I find this theory thought provoking, and some aspects of narrative *Christus Victor* reflect my views. But no single theory of the atonement can fully encompass the scope and depth of the mysterious ways of God.

Richard Rohr puts forward a nonviolent understanding of atonement based on traditional Franciscan thought, which teaches that God did not need or demand the sacrifice of Jesus to love and forgive us because God has freely loved all creation from the beginning. God comes to us in Jesus not in reaction to human sin; rather,

God freely acts out of perfect love: "Love is the beginning, the way itself, and the final consummation."[13]

If God is punitive and violent, then we can feel justified in being punitive and violent as well, as has been demonstrated throughout the church's violent history. But if not, our excuses for violence are taken away. The nonviolent Jesus lived through rejection, failure, and abuse yet still forgave his enemies and called on his followers to do likewise. The death of Jesus was not necessary for God to love creation or to forgive human beings. Rather, "Jesus is pure gift and grace and glory."[14]

CHANGING OUR MINDS ABOUT GOD

Jesus did not come to change the mind of God about humanity (it did not need changing)! Jesus came to change the mind of humanity about God!

—RICHARD ROHR, "SALVATION AS AT-ONE-MENT"

Fortunately, there are many ways to view the cross without rigid dogma and to experience the gospel message of forgiveness, freedom from guilt, spiritual connection, transformation, empowerment, and the unconditional grace and love of God. In coming chapters, we will explore various ways of understanding the story of the life, death, and resurrection of Jesus and its meaning for us today. By following Jesus, living by his Spirit, and being true to

---

13. Richard Rohr, "Salvation as At-One-Ment—Incarnation Instead of Atonement," Center for Contemplation and Action, July 25, 2017, https://cac.org/incarnation-instead-atonement-2017-07-25/.

14. Richard Rohr, "The Franciscan Opinion," in *Stricken by God? Nonviolent Identification and the Victory of Christ*, ed. Brad Jersak and Michael Hardin (Grand Rapids, MI: William B. Eerdmans, 2007), 212.

his message and vision, we become familiar with the healing and transforming power of the God of love that Jesus both revealed and proclaimed.

In the meantime, I rest in the not-knowing, in not having all the answers. But I find comfort in these words from New Testament scholar Marcus J. Borg about the meaning of the Christian message: "What's the Christian life all about? It's about loving God and loving what God loves. It's about becoming passionate about God and participating in God's passion for a different kind of world, here and now. And the future, including what is beyond our lives? We leave that up to God."[15]

---

15. Marcus J. Borg, *Convictions: How I Learned What Matters Most* (New York: HarperOne, 2014), 231.

PART II

GOD WEEPS

FOLLOWING JESUS IN A SUFFERING WORLD

CHAPTER 3
THE SUFFERING AND RECONCILING GOD

Is God the transcendent and untouched stage manager
of the theater of this violent world, or is God in Christ
the central engaged figure of the world tragedy?

—JÜRGEN MOLTMANN, "THE CRUCIFIED GOD"

IN THIS AGE of pandemic, growing inequity, ecological devastation, grave injustices, and unspeakable violence, what does it mean to follow Jesus? In all this suffering, where is God? This is the theme of part 2, "God Weeps: Following Jesus in a Suffering World." Here in chapter 3, we consider God's presence within us, including in human suffering. In chapter 4 we extend our view to recognize God as deeply present in and through all creation.

The refrain of a popular song includes the words "God is watching us from a distance."[1] This image of God reflects a widespread understanding of Christianity that is focused on the transcendent aspect of God: God as a Supreme Being who watches from a distance, judges individuals and societies, hears and answers prayers, and occasionally intervenes in miraculous and providential ways. Yet in traditional church writings, God is said to be both *transcendent*, beyond and encompassing the world of matter, and also *immanent*, within our hearts and in and through all creation. By

---

1. "From a Distance: Bette Midler," lyrics.com, accessed December 15, 2021, https://www
.lyrics.com/lyric/25910894/Bette+Midler/From+A+Distance.

focusing on God's transcendence while ignoring God's immanence, people end up with a distorted view of God.

Biblical passages related to the atonement do not always focus on the justification of sinners, with the metaphor of a transcendent God as the divine Judge and human beings as the guilty accused. In Paul's second letter to the Corinthians, he speaks of the immanent God who is intimately involved with the world and who reconciles and restores broken relationships:

> So if anyone is in Christ, there is a new creation: everything old has passed away; see, everything has become new! All this is from God, who reconciled us to himself through Christ, and has given us the ministry of reconciliation; that is, in Christ God was reconciling the world to himself, not counting their trespasses against them, and entrusting the message of reconciliation to us. So we are ambassadors for Christ, since God is making his appeal through us; we entreat you on behalf of Christ, be reconciled to God. (2 Cor 5:17–20)

In this passage, the Greek word for "reconciliation" or "restoration to (the divine) favor" (*katallage*) can also be translated as "atonement." The metaphor of reconciliation points to a different way of looking at atonement, without images of courtrooms or laws or judgment. Instead, reconciliation calls to mind intimate or restored relationships, such as might take place between spouses or among family or friends. According to *Harper's Biblical Commentary*, "The word of 'reconciliation' is the gospel itself, God's saving power made present through the cross."[2] Several other New Testament passages

---

2. James L. Mays, gen. ed., *Harper's Biblical Commentary* (San Francisco: Harper & Row, 1988), 1196.

also refer to reconciliation as atonement, sometimes using explicit imagery of the cross (Eph 2:13–16; Col 1:19–20). Though people will hear and respond to this message differently, this is good news to all people regardless of beliefs, characteristics, history, or conditions, for all are invited into a reconciled relationship with God.

Further, those of us who have experienced the blessings of reconciliation with God in Christ are invited to engage as participants in God's atoning action, to embody and share God's reconciling love as God's appeal is made through us. We are entrusted with this message of reconciliation and sent out as ambassadors of Christ. Here we have a job description for those who would respond to Jesus's call to follow him.

As we begin to explore what it means to follow Jesus in today's context of profound suffering and existential threats, we acknowledge that God is not only transcendent but also immanent, incarnate in flesh and blood, and intimately involved in relationship, as we see in the revelation of Jesus Christ. Here we consider God in Christ as "the central engaged figure of the world tragedy" who bears both the sins and sorrows of the world.

A "RIGHTEOUSNESS" THAT STANDS BEHIND SUFFERING

That explanation of suffering that looks away from the
victim and identifies itself with a righteousness that
is supposed to stand behind the suffering has already
taken a step in the direction of theological sadism,
which wants to understand God as the torturer.

—DOROTHEE SOELLE, *SUFFERING*

In the spring and summer of 2018, tears flowed around the United States and the world for the immigrant children who had been separated from their parents and incarcerated by US Immigrations and Customs Enforcement (ICE). Undocumented immigrants crossing into the United States had previously had the right to claim asylum, but now were subject to arrest and criminal prosecution for illegally crossing the border. Border patrol agents removed children from their parents and detained them separately. Reports showed many of the children being held in crowded cages in squalid conditions. Even television news anchors and visiting public officials were visibly moved by their plight. During this relatively short period, over 2,500 children were taken from their parents, some under age five, including nursing infants. Many parents were deported while their children remained in custody. Although a number of these families have now been reunited, the trauma they have suffered will never be erased. Some children may never be reunited with their families and have essentially been orphaned.

The attorney general, Jeff Sessions, justified the Trump administration's recently changed immigration policies by referring to Scripture. He said, "I would cite you to the Apostle Paul and his clear and wise command in Romans 13, to obey the laws of the government because God has ordained them for the purpose of order. Orderly and lawful processes are good in themselves and protect the weak and lawful."[3] Soon afterward, more than six hundred United Methodists filed charges against Mr. Sessions (a United Methodist) for violating church principles on child abuse, immorality, racial discrimination, and dissemination of doctrines contrary to those of the United Methodist Church.[4] Mr. Sessions's use of Scripture

---

3. Julia Jacobs, "Sessions' Use of Bible Passage to Defend Immigration Policy Draws Fire," *New York Times*, June 15, 2018, https://www.nytimes.com/2018/06/15/us/sessions-bible-verse-romans.html.
4. Monica Corsaro and David Wright, "We're Ministers in Jeff Sessions' Church. His Immigration Stance Defies Our Values," *Washington Post*, June 20, 2018, https://www.washingtonpost.com/news/posteverything/wp/2018/06/20/were-ministers-in-jeff-sessionss-church-his-immigration-stance-defies-our-values/?utm_term=.d52b9b6b6130.

to justify harsh immigration policies is an example of religion that "looks away from the victim and identifies itself with a righteousness that is supposed to stand behind the suffering." It was an attempt to use religion to justify cruelty in order to further a political agenda.

As with other texts, Romans 13 cannot be understood in a vacuum. Scholars note that this text has been used to justify slavery, repress dissent, and demand obedience to brutal regimes. Session's out-of-context proof texting[5] ignored the fact that authorities do not always act as "the servant of God to execute wrath on the wrongdoer," as stated in Romans 13:4. People are not "wrongdoers" simply because they flee from poverty, oppression, or climate catastrophe to seek safe haven in the United States. US authorities who "execute wrath" by instituting or carrying out harsh policies against immigrants, including children, are not acting as God's servants.

Furthermore, most of the Trump administration's harsh immigration policies targeted immigrants from certain countries generally, not just those without legal documents. They were designed to strip various protections from legal immigrants, asylum seekers, refugees, and detainees and to deter people from migrating to the United States. Ironically, several of these policies violated US and international law.

Using Romans 13 to justify this strict law and order approach to immigration ignores the overall scope and tenor of Scripture, which, as Jesus shows us, prioritizes mercy for those who are vulnerable and calls us to love God and neighbor. Surely this includes offering hospitality to our immigrant neighbors (Lev 19:33–34; Deut 10:18–19; Zech 7:10; Heb 13:2). And in spite of its historical

---

5. "*Proof texting* is the method by which a person appeals to a biblical text to prove or justify a theological position without regard for the context of the passage they are citing." Theopedia, s.v. "proof texting," accessed December 15, 2021, https://www.theopedia.com/proof-texting.

misuse, Romans 13 itself is illuminated by its primary claim in verse 10 that "love is the fulfilling of the law."

When unjust policies cause extreme suffering, is God looking on from a distance, impassive and unmoved? Worse yet, are such things God's will, part of God's plan? Is God a Judge who exacts punitive justice on those who are not absolutely obedient, a tyrant at the top of worldly systems of power who shows no mercy to those who are most vulnerable? Is wealth a sign of God's favor, as preachers of the prosperity gospel profess? Does God inflict suffering on some because they are less deserving than others, perhaps because of their country of origin? Does God favor those who dominate the world?

Not at all. Dorothee Soelle says, "God is not in heaven; he is hanging on the cross. Love is not an otherworldly, intruding, self-asserting power—and to meditate on the cross can mean to take leave of that dream."[6] The symbol of the cross belies the common assumption that God is at the apex of the established order looking down on us from heaven and making sure that everyone gets what they deserve. Rather, the cross reveals the ongoing injustice and cruelty of the ruling powers, in Jesus's time and in ours. When we consider "Jesus Christ, and him crucified" (1 Cor 2:2), those who love him see God there.

Dietrich Bonhoeffer said, "Only the suffering God can help,"[7] yet the idea of a suffering God is counterintuitive for anyone raised in a society that values status, money, and worldly power. If we are aligned with such a culture, we prefer a God who will confirm our values and bless the status quo—until we hear and understand the implications of the good news that turns this point of view upside down.

---

6. Dorothee Soelle, *Suffering* (Philadelphia: Fortress, 1975), 148.
7. Dietrich Bonhoeffer, *Letters and Papers from Prison*, ed. E. Bethge, trans. R. H. Fuller, 4th ed. (London: SCM, 1971), 361.

IN SUFFERING: WHERE IS GOD?

Christ is the brother of the victims and the redeemer of the guilty. He "carries," on the one hand, "the sufferings of the world" and, on the other hand, "the sins of the world."

—JÜRGEN MOLTMANN, "THE CRUCIFIED GOD: YESTERDAY AND TODAY; 1972–2002"

In *Night*, the late Nobel Laureate Elie Wiesel described a scene he witnessed during his internment in Auschwitz where a child was executed by hanging. His body was so light that it took a long time for him to die. The other prisoners were forced to watch as the suffering went on and on. This hanging had a profound impact on Wiesel and on the other prisoners, many of whom wept, and even on the SS guards. Wiesel wrote, "Behind me, I heard [a man] asking: 'For God's sake, where is God?' And from within me, I heard a voice answer: 'Where is He? This is where—hanging here from this gallows.'"[8]

Where is God in suffering? In Jesus's violent death on the cross, God was fully present, experiencing the suffering firsthand. God is not removed from human experience but is immersed in it. It is God who suffers the torments of human injustice and experiences the extremities of human sufferings—the God who is Love.

Theologian Jürgen Moltmann, in *Experiences of God*, wrote about how he became aware of this suffering God as a nineteen-year-old German prisoner of war in an Allied prison camp. He endured not only physical suffering and deprivation but also loss of meaning and a sense of being abandoned by God because he had become aware of the great evils of the Nazi regime. Despairing and alone,

---

8. Elie Wiesel, *Night* (New York: Hill & Wang, 1972, 2006), 145.

he saw fellow prisoners who "collapsed inwardly, how they gave up all hope, sickening for the lack of it, some of them dying. The same thing almost happened to me." And yet, he wrote, "the experience of misery and forsakenness and daily humiliation gradually built up into an experience of God." An army chaplain gave him a copy of the New Testament and Psalms that, he said, "opened my eyes to the God that is with those 'that are of broken heart.'"[9] These early experiences molded him as he came to understand that the crucified Christ expresses and embodies not only God's forgiveness of sinners but also God's solidarity with all who suffer.

In the United States, the most obvious and recent parallel to the crucifixion of Jesus is the lynching of Black Americans, largely by white self-proclaimed Christians. Lynching reached a zenith in the early twentieth century with mass public spectacles that were attended by hundreds or thousands of men, women, and children. In *The Cross and the Lynching Tree*, Black theologian James Cone writes,

> The crowd's shout, "Crucify him!" (Mk 15:14) anticipated the white mob's shout "Lynch him!" Jesus' agonizing final cry of abandonment from the cross, "My God, my God, why have you forsaken me" (Mk 15:34), was similar to the lynched victim Sam Hose's awful scream as he drew his last breath, "Oh, my God! Oh, Jesus." In each case, it was a cruel, agonizing, and contemptible death.[10]

Ignored by white theologians (to our shame), Black Christians have long recognized the similarities between the cross of Christ

9. Jürgen Moltmann, *Experiences of God* (Philadelphia: Augsburg Fortress, 1980), 6–9.
10. James Cone, *The Cross and the Lynching Tree* (Maryknoll, NY: Orbis, 2011), 161.

and the lynching tree, ever since enslaved Blacks redeemed their masters' religion by identifying with Jesus and recognizing him as a kindred spirit and bearer of the transcendent power of God. Their spirituals point to the experience of the presence of Christ even in circumstances of grievous oppression, inhumane cruelty, and horrendous suffering and to faith in a God of love who can "make a way out of no way."[11]

White supremacy continues today as racial discrimination and racist abuse continue, including lynching in different forms. The killing of George Floyd and so many others by police led to the rise of the Movement for Black Lives and continues through racial justice organizing and advocacy even in the face of organized hate and extremism. The ongoing threat of white supremacy was demonstrated at the January 6 insurrection at the Capitol where, as mentioned earlier, several large crosses and other Christian symbols were on display, along with symbols of violent hate groups, including a noose. Those of us who live in the United States and seek to follow Jesus must confront the "original sin" of racism in this nation and its ongoing legacy among us. We are called to repent, resist, and advocate for reparations in solidarity with those who are being crucified on the cross of white supremacy today. In James Cone's words, "The real scandal of the gospel is this: humanity's salvation is revealed in the cross of the condemned criminal Jesus, and humanity's salvation is available only through our solidarity with the crucified people in our midst."[12]

The idea that "God was in Christ" (2 Cor. 19, NKJV) and suffers in and with "the crucified people in our midst" is incomprehensible

---

11. A popular phrase of Black Christians. See "Making a Way Out of No Way," an exhibit at the Smithsonian National Museum of African American History and Culture, accessed December 15, 2021, https://nmaahc.si.edu/explore/exhibitions/making-way-out-no-way.
12. Cone, *Cross and the Lynching Tree*, 160.

to those who think of God as at the top of the hierarchy of ruling powers, directly controlling everything that takes place. This vision of a self-emptying God who is intimately involved with us seems like foolishness to those who equate divinity with the values of the dominant culture and worldly systems of political, economic, or military power (1 Cor 1:18–25). However, themes about the suffering of the Messiah can be found in the Hebrew Scriptures, as in Lamentations 1:12, "Behold, and see if there is any sorrow like my sorrow" (NKJV) and in Isaiah 53:2–4, "He [was] despised and rejected by men; a Man of sorrows and acquainted with grief. . . . Surely He has borne our griefs and carried our sorrows" (NKJV). As we have seen, after Jesus's death and resurrection, early Christians looked back through Scripture and interpreted these events as the fulfillment of prophecy.

Jesus did not seek suffering for himself, nor was his crucifixion the plan of a wrathful God. Rather, in full integrity and freedom of choice, Jesus was true to his calling—to announce and demonstrate the good news of the coming of the reign of God. Despite the hostility and threats he received, Jesus refused to back down or betray his mission, the people he loved, or his God. By his preaching, teaching, healing, community building, and other actions that challenged the ruling powers, he incurred their wrath. As a result, the authorities had him executed. Jesus's death was the result of the way he lived his life.

Further, in the agony of Jesus, the suffering God endured the full impact of human sin and evil, and that same God continues to suffer as God's beloved children and creation itself are crucified today. The story of the crucifixion of Jesus brings about a great reversal of spiritual perspective. Instead of seeing God as king, judge, or director of human events, in the crucified Christ we see God as the object of scorn, shame, ridicule, and judgment, as abandoned and brokenhearted, as lover, as Love.

The idea that God could suffer is and always has been shocking and scandalous. Richard Bauckham points out, "For the Greeks, suffering implied deficiency of being, weakness, subjection, instability. But the cross shows us a God who suffers out of the fullness of his being because he is love."[13] For those who believe that God was in Christ, divine suffering is part of reality. God was in Christ, experiencing oppression, judgment, torture, and execution at the hands of the powers. God was in Christ, even when Jesus felt abandoned and forsaken by God. God was in Christ, loving and forgiving anyway, praying, "Father, forgive them, for they do not know what they are doing" (Luke 23:34). God was in Christ, even when Jesus cried out, "My God, my God, why have you forsaken me?" (Mark 15:34).

Did God hear Jesus's prayers from the cross? Of course, for God's presence with us is intimate, closer than we are to ourselves. At times, we may sense the Holy Spirit's presence within. Sometimes we may feel in our suffering that we are utterly forsaken and alone. But this sense of emptiness and absence does not mean that we have been abandoned by God, who always seeks intimate relationship and reconciliation. In his experience of abandonment, Moltmann discovered something deeper—a sense of communion and at-one-ment (reconciliation) with God. He wrote, "I am a Christian for Christ's sake. I found my desolation in him, and I found God in my desolation."[14]

---

13. Richard Bauckham, "Only the Suffering God Can Help: Divine Passability in Modern Theology," *themoleos* 9, no. 3 (April 1984), https://www.thegospelcoalition.org/themelios/article/only-the-suffering-god-can-help-divine-passibility-in-modern-theology/.
14. Moltmann, *Experiences of God*, 17–18.

CHRIST CRUCIFIED TODAY

Jesus continues to die before our eyes; his death has not
ended. He suffers wherever people are tormented. . . .
Insofar as we forget the continued dying of Jesus
in the present, we deny the passion itself.

—DOROTHEE SOELLE, *SUFFERING*

This is a time of pandemic and climate change, white supremacy
and conspiracy theories, police killings and insurrection, corporate
bailouts and mammon's domination of politics, the enrichment
of the wealthiest 1 percent of humanity and the impoverishment of
millions, mass incarceration and massive weapons buildup, the
militarization of police and drone warfare. Tens of thousands of
bereaved people have lost their loved ones to Covid-19 while people
invoke their freedom by refusing to socially distance or wear masks.
People are suffering in ways that call to mind the people living in
Jesus's day under the oppressive system of Roman power.

Christ continues to be crucified as today's ruling powers enlist
human beings in their service, subject the most vulnerable to abuse
and oppression, inflict violence around the world, and plunder the
earth for their own institutional gain. And in the same way that
the Jewish religious elite collaborated with Rome, many forms of
contemporary Christianity collaborate with today's domination
system through active participation, passive compliance, or theological justification.

Proclaiming the message of Christ crucified and present in
human suffering undercuts the authority of today's ruling powers
by exposing their cruel and unjust tactics, their desperate attempts
to dominate the world, and their violent opposition to the God
who is love. This message reveals the true scandal of the cross:

that it is through our "solidarity with the crucified people in our midst" that we are saved, reconciled, brought into communion with the God of Jesus Christ, the God of love. This is the good news of the gospel, God's power made perfect in weakness, the word of the cross.

The understanding of Christ (and thus, God) as the one who suffers is the foundation of Christian charity and service to the poor and oppressed. Jesus said, "'Truly I tell you, just as you did it to one of the least of these who are members of my family, you did it to me'" (Matt 25:40). He made clear that a person's moral stature is gauged by how they treat their brothers and sisters, members of the human family, those who are poor, hungry, thirsty, sick, weak, imprisoned, excluded, or maligned, all who are victims of violence or injustice. This point is made consistently throughout the New Testament: "The commandment we have from him is this: those who love God must love their brothers and sisters also" (1 John 4:20–21). We are called to serve all who are vulnerable, oppressed, and broken, to see Christ in them, to reach out to them in mercy, to stand in solidarity with them, and to take actions of compassion and justice on their behalf. Dietrich Bonhoeffer said, "Christians stand with God in God's suffering."[15] By doing so, we participate in God's reconciling work, making clear that all people are included within the circle of God's caring concern.

Such actions may have repercussions. We return here to the issue of immigration, with which we began this chapter. Since the inception of Christianity, countless Christians have risked and often endured legal penalties for their actions serving those who are in greatest need or at greatest risk, and for challenging

---

15. As quoted by Jürgen Moltmann, "Only the Suffering God Can Help," *The Cry* 7, no. 4, The World Made Flesh International, May 6, 2009, https://wordmadeflesh.org/only-the -suffering-god-can-help/.

unjust laws or systems. In our day, in response to immigration policies that are sometimes deadly, members of the interfaith group No More Deaths regularly hike for miles, each carrying several gallons of water to leave at stations for migrants crossing the deadly Sonora Desert from Mexico into Arizona, where over three thousand people have perished in the first two decades of the twenty-first century. Those who deliver water claim they are acting from their religious convictions. Many have been arrested. Some have been tried, convicted, and have served time in jail.[16]

This is only one example of actions that people have taken to protect migrants and to reform the US immigration system, which has caused so much suffering. Thousands of people have responded to inhumane immigration policies through mass protests at airports and detention centers, intervention through the courts, watchdog actions and investigative reporting, sanctuary actions, demonstrations and vigils, political advocacy, and humanitarian aid projects on both sides of the US-Mexico border. Such organizing has taken place around the country, and some changes have come about as the result of political pressure from the grassroots, including the Latinx community. Yet the human need is overwhelming as people flock to the border due to economic instability, climate disruptions, and violence in their home countries. The political and logistical challenges are great. People will need to continue advocating for the improved treatment of immigrants if such efforts are to succeed.

---

16. Scott Warren, "I Gave Water to Migrants Crossing the Arizona Desert. They Charged Me with a Felony," No More Deaths, May 28, 2019, https://nomoredeaths.org/i-gave-water-to-migrants-crossing-the-arizona-desert-they-charged-me-with-a-felony/.

HEALING, RECONCILIATION, AND MUTUAL LIBERATION

Good Friday is at the center of this world, but Easter morning
is the sunrise of the coming of God and the morning of the
new life and is the beginning of the future of this world.

While working to relieve suffering through acts of mercy, solidarity, and justice, we are not to have contempt for or take revenge on perpetrators of violence or injustice, for they, too, are our brothers and sisters. We are invited to both receive and share God's reconciling love, for "all have sinned and fall short of the glory of God" (Rom 3:23). The understanding of God as present in deep solidarity with all who suffer does not diminish the gospel message of the forgiveness and reconciliation of sinners but enhances it by revealing the extent of God's faithfulness and steadfast love. In Christ we are offered forgiveness, reconciliation, and the presence and love of "God with us" even in our pain.

How we understand these things has everything to do with how we understand God. If we understand God to be a ruler at the top of the world's hierarchy of powers, we may experience hardship and suffering as punishment that is deserved. If we understand God as a harsh judge who condemns people, we may consider those who have committed offenses, including ourselves, as being beyond redemption. But in Christ we are offered a different understanding and experience of God—as an intimate parent who loves her child and who freely forgives and restores as Jesus did, as one who enters the world's suffering and lives in "the least" of our brothers and sisters here on earth, as one whose light cannot be extinguished even by death, that final sanction of the powers.

The focus on reconciliation of sinners does not translate to "cheap grace" (Dietrich Bonhoeffer), where "not counting their trespasses against them" (2 Cor 5:19) means people can go on harming or ignoring the suffering of others. Reconciliation is costly. It originates with freely given unconditional love on God's part, but for it to be effective in one's life, it requires a radical shift in both attitudes and behaviors on the part of human beings. As we receive the message of reconciliation and carry it to others, we are sharing the gospel, the good news itself. In so doing, we become participants in the story of the work of Christ, the transforming power of the Holy Spirit, and the redeeming love of God at work in the world.

God in Christ bears both the sins and sorrows of the whole world. As those who seek to live by the faith of Jesus, we are called to love as he did and offer God's love to everyone we meet. In so doing, we help relieve the sufferings of Christ and bring reconciliation to a hurting and broken world. Furthermore, as we offer to others the gifts of forgiveness, acceptance, and unconditional love that we have received, we experience God's love in new ways—not just given *to* us but given *through* us. This enables us to live into Jesus's great commandments: to love God above all and our neighbors as ourselves. We are transformed.

In the story of Jesus, suffering, sin, and death are not the end. The ruling powers do not have the last word. The Spirit is present in the determination of people of every faith and philosophy who stand in solidarity with those who are oppressed and who nonviolently resist the powers on their behalf. Christ is alive; those of us who follow Jesus are called and empowered by the Holy Spirit to join with others to work for an inclusive and compassionate world. Our goal is to remember the path Jesus walked and accompany him, to fully surrender to God as he did, and to act in solidarity with those who are being crucified on the cross of empire today as he was so long ago. Christ is alive, offering healing, reconciliation, and the mutual liberation of both oppressor and oppressed. As Jürgen Moltmann said, "Every theology of the cross must end in a theology of resurrection."[17]

17. Moltmann, *Experiences of God*, 29.

CHAPTER 4
CREATION CRUCIFIED

THE PASSION OF THE EARTH

Are not two sparrows sold for a penny? Yet not one of
them will fall to the ground apart from your Father.

—MATTHEW 10:29

I AM A birdwatcher. I often sit out on our deck watching birds visit
our feeders, marveling at those that come year after year and looking up new species so I will recognize them next time they come.
When I hear the calls of migrating geese or cranes, I go outside
to honor them as they fly in formation overhead. When I am out
walking in the woods and spot a bird that I rarely see, I stand
watching and listening in awe. In recent years these have included
Kingfishers, Flickers, Pileated Woodpeckers, and Great Blue Her-
ons. To me, these birds are messengers from God. At the same
time, they have their own lives and agency and are motivated to
live "according to their kinds" (Gen 6:20): to fly, to search for food
and water, to multiply and care for their young, to ensure that life
goes on. If we ignore God's other-than-human messengers and are
blind to their intrinsic value and motivations as sentient beings,
we are likely to devalue creation in other ways as well.

Having considered what it means to follow Jesus in the midst
of human suffering, in this chapter we expand our perspective to
encompass other species and the living earth. In this age of ecological awareness, our understanding of what it means to be human in

relationship with the divine must be grounded in an awareness of our profound interdependence with the rest of the created world. Yet we human beings participate in the destruction of the very creation through which God nurtures us and our fellow creatures. As members of the human family and the wider community of life, we share creation's passion for life as well as creation's suffering. We share in the passion of the earth.

In the previous chapter, I cited a text on atonement as reconciliation that begins with the words, "So if anyone is in Christ, there is a new creation: everything old has passed away; see, everything has become new! All this is from God, who reconciled us to himself through Christ, and has given us the ministry of reconciliation" (2 Cor 5:17–18). The passage makes clear that the scope of reconciliation extends beyond God and the individual to all creation. Other passages that extend reconciliation to the whole creation include Ephesians 1:7–10, 4:17–24; Colossians 3:1–11, 1:19–20; and Galatians 6:12–16. We see this most clearly in Romans 8:18–26, where creation itself is groaning and laboring for liberation from bondage that is tied to the liberation (salvation) of human beings. These texts speak of God's action to bring about reconciliation (atonement) as we live into the reality of restored relationships with God, with our neighbors, and with creation itself.

This chapter explores the meaning of the gospel in this time of ecocide, as we face death on a global scale and experience losses that diminish prospects for a future of abundant life. Here we allow concepts such as *deep incarnation* and *new creation* to inform our understanding of the word of the cross in the context of the ongoing ruin of the natural world. As we discern the significance of the ecological harm being done and repent for our complicity in such harm, the Holy Spirit enables us to discern what hope in action looks like and to faithfully follow Jesus as we come to terms with the cross in the midst of creation.

DEEP INCARNATION

God's in us and we're in God, Halleluiah.

Western civilization, including Western Christianity, has been built upon an anthropocentric worldview that has enabled the plundering and despoiling of God's world. An example for today comes from John McArthur, the megachurch pastor mentioned in chapter 2. In a sermon refuting global warming and supporting the idea of stewardship in order to extract everything we can for the use of human beings, he said, "God intended us to use this planet, to fill this planet for the benefit of man. Never was it intended to be a permanent planet. It is a disposable planet. Christians ought to know that."[1]

If we see the natural world as intended simply for human use and consumption, we lose sight of the interrelationships with the rest of creation that make us human and deny the spirit of God within us and within all. By discarding our privileged and outdated anthropocentric perspective, we may recognize creation's intrinsic value and

---

1. Paul Braterman, "God Intended It as a Disposable Planet: Meet the US Pastor Preaching Climate Change Denial," The Conversation, October 12, 2020, https://theconversation .com/god-intended-it-as-a-disposable-planet-meet-the-us-pastor-preaching-climate-change -denial-147712.

the presence of God in all parts of creation. One way of expressing this is through the concept of *deep incarnation.*

Many Scripture passages point to the reality of an inner dimension of nature in which all creatures participate. Psalm 19:1 proclaims, "The heavens are telling the glory of God; and the firmament proclaims his handiwork." Job said, "But ask the animals, and they will teach you; the birds of the air, and they will tell you; ask the plants of the earth, and they will teach you; and the fish of the sea will declare to you. Who among all these does not know that the hand of the Lord has done this?" (Job 12:7–9). Jesus said, "Are not two sparrows sold for a penny? Yet not one of them will fall to the ground apart from your Father" (Matt 10:29). These passages point to a God who is intimately present throughout creation, not solely to human beings, but to other-than-human beings as well.

Understanding God as immanent is not the same as pantheism, for it also acknowledges the transcendent aspect of God. The spirit of God is deeply present throughout creation but is not confined within creation. In fact, it's just the opposite, for "in [God] we live and move and have our being" (Acts 17:28). This way of understanding the relationship between God and the physical universe has been called *panentheism,* which is differentiated from *pantheism* as follows: "In panentheism, the universal spirit is present everywhere, which at the same time 'transcends' all things created. While pantheism asserts that 'all is God,' panentheism claims that God is greater than the universe."[2] The Strathdee hymn quoted above that proclaims "God's in us and we're in God, Halleluiah" applies not only to us but to all parts of creation. This is a view of God as all in all, as Ground of Being, Ultimate Reality, Unfathomable Love, not

---

2. "We Believe in God," Portland Center for Living, accessed December 15, 2021, https://cslportland.org/lessons/we-believe-in-god/.

exclusive to any religion. John Wesley referred to this "omnipresent" God as "the Soul of the universe."[3]

The astounding claim of Christianity is that this God, who both transcends and is immanent within creation, was made known to us in a unique way in Jesus. "God was in Christ," living a Spirit-infused life, suffering and dying at the hands of the powers, raised to new life by God. The Gospel of John refers to the concept of *incarnation* when it announces, "The Word became flesh [*sarx* in Greek] and lived among us" (John 1:14). This emphasizes the coming of God to us in human form in a way that we humans can comprehend. The revelation of Jesus Christ created a paradigm shift in our understanding of divine-human relationships by revealing the all-encompassing love and eternal presence of *Emmanuel,* which means "God is with us" (Matt 1:23).

The concept of deep incarnation expands on this understanding to encompass all creation as the dwelling place of God. Elizabeth A. Johnson explains, "Deep incarnation understands John's gospel to be saying that the *sarx* [flesh] that the Word of God became not only weds Jesus Christ to other human beings in the human species; it also reaches beyond us to join the incarnate one to the whole evolving biological world of living creatures and the cosmic dust of which they are composed."[4] This idea corrects the misunderstanding that human beings are isolated individuals and reconnects us to the network of interrelationships that make us human. Not even Jesus was separate from the web of relationships that constitute human and all other life on planet earth, the very web that is being undone today.

---

3. Wesley, Sermon 23, "Upon Our Lord's Sermon," 1:516–17.

4. Elizabeth A. Johnson, *Creation and the Cross: The Mercy of God for a Planet in Peril* (Maryknoll, NY: Orbis, 2018), 186.

The Word became not only human flesh but all flesh and dwelt not only among human beings but among all parts of creation not just since the time of Jesus of Nazareth but eternally, throughout all time and space. This expanded view reveals the presence of the Spirit in the depths of matter, the love that exists at the heart of the universe, the divine presence in all creation, the mind of Christ that binds us all together, and the love of God that even death cannot conquer. This idea that God is made flesh in myriad forms affirms the intrinsic value of creation as a dwelling place for God.

THE EXISTENTIAL SIGNIFICANCE OF OUR TIME

Grasping the cross in a more biblical light will allow an ecological view to emerge that sees God accompanying creation through time with mercy, which in our day encompasses a planet in peril.

—ELIZABETH A. JOHNSON, *CREATION AND THE CROSS*

On the morning of my forty-fifth high school reunion, sitting on the bank of the Feather River, just three blocks from my childhood home, I realized more deeply than ever the significance of this time in which we live and the dangers we face. I had returned to my small Northern California hometown of Oroville not just to attend the reunion that evening but to say a final goodbye to my mother and sprinkle the last of her ashes. We had sprinkled most of them as a family some weeks before.

It was a sunny fall day with a cool breeze. As I sat on the shore in partial shade, the sunlight created diamond patterns reflected in the river. Salmon were jumping, traveling upstream. Sitting there on the river bank, I thanked God for my mother's life. She had also grown up in Oroville and had struggled through a difficult childhood during the Great Depression. She had returned to Oroville after my parents' divorce and had worked hard to raise my sister, brother, and me. As I reflected on her life, my thoughts expanded to my father and to my grandparents and great-grandparents on both sides, through generations of ancestors going back, generations passing, all of them working and sacrificing to keep life going forward despite so many hardships; then to my own children, grandchildren, and generations of the future.

As I sat there watching the salmon jumping, reflecting on the love that motivates us to do whatever it takes to ensure that life goes on, it occurred to me that salmon, too, work to keep their generations going forward. They fight their way upstream, ending up battered and bloodied in their attempts to go back to their spawning grounds. In fact, all animals struggle to survive, reproduce, thrive, and make sure life goes on, despite the incalculable suffering inherent in the ongoing cycle of life and death as we know it here on earth. Looking at the mixed forest around the river, I thought about how even plants have survived and multiplied through natural selection over eons of evolutionary time. So much energy and sacrifice and passion for life have gone into the process of evolution of the interconnected life-forms here on planet earth since it was formed along with the rest of the solar system about 4.5 billion years ago.

I was struck by the realization that God, who brought the universe into being and who exists even at the heart of matter, has invested so much love in bringing life here on earth to fruition and abundance. It was in this mindset that I sprinkled the last few pinches of my mom's ashes onto the riverbank. I sat and prayed and said the words of the Ash Wednesday liturgy acknowledging our mortality: "Remember, O mortal, that you are dust, and to dust you will return." There was a finality to this ritual of saying goodbye to my mother, although I continued to feel an unbroken connection with her, as I do even today.

Then I picked up a rock from the riverbank, a smooth oblong rock that fit perfectly in my hand. It was such a contrast to the ashes, so solid and enduring. I wondered how long the rock might have been in this very place. Maybe it had been traveling down the river and had just arrived this morning. Maybe it had been here on this bank since my childhood, or even since my mom's childhood. The rock in my hand got me thinking about geological time, the fifteen-billion-year process of the evolution of the universe.

What an amazing universe we live in! Scientific evidence continually reveals new aspects of the universe, showing us that it is complex, interconnected, and mysterious beyond imagining. The vast distance between stars revealed by contemporary astronomy corresponds to the spaciousness in the inner dimensions of matter as revealed by quantum physics. All these wonders and more were contained for me in that precious rock, which I still hold often when I pray. The universe is a wonder, and the fact that we are alive today is a wonder as well.

In previous generations, no matter how difficult things were, people at least trusted that the natural cycles of life would go on, that life on earth would continue, that generations would come and go. We cannot take that for granted anymore. Now the damage being done to creation is having generational effects, as rising global temperatures, weather-related disasters, extreme extraction of resources, and harmful industrial development are driving people in vulnerable areas from their homes and casting a shadow of foreboding over humanity's future. Destruction of ecosystems is having evolutionary effects, as many species try to adapt to the changing climate or are driven to extinction. Animals and plants are moving up to higher elevations as temperatures rise. Coral reefs are dying. Climate change is even impacting what goes on in geological time, as the hydrologic cycle is altered, the jet stream and polar vortex patterns are distorted, seasons change, sea levels rise, and glacial melt creates changes in the earth's axis.[5]

We are at an in-between time at this critical juncture in the history of life on earth, a time of danger and a time of choice. Many people are confused, despairing, and do not know which way to turn. Will we go along passively with the forces carrying us inexorably toward ecological and social catastrophe, or will we as a species find the courage to actively resist this momentum and take the actions necessary to bring systemic transformation? Will we preserve and pass on the wealth of nature and our varied cultures to future generations, or will they inherit a wasteland? This is the primary spiritual issue of our time.

God's presence extends in and through the vastness of all time and space, and here we are, born into this particular time and place. This is significant. The earth is our home—the only home we have. This is our time—the only time we have in which to act on behalf of life. In the words of Paul, "'At an acceptable time I have listened to you, and on a day of salvation I have helped you.' See, now is the acceptable time; see, now is the day of salvation!" (2 Cor 6:2).

We certainly need to be saved. But what does salvation look like in this context? It cannot mean simply saving individual people out of this world and leaving everyone else to live on a progressively degraded earth. Surely the God who created abundant life wants it to continue and flourish. Salvation must include release from the apathy, moral confusion, and hopelessness that characterize our

---

5. Damian Carrington, "Climate Crisis Has Shifted the Earth's Axis, Study Shows," *Guardian*, April 23, 2021, https://www.theguardian.com/environment/2021/apr/23/climate-crisis-has-shifted-the-earths-axis-study-shows.

time. It must mean personal transformation that gives us hope and equips us for loving action in the world, for God's intention is the liberation and reconciliation of all creation.

ECOCIDE: UNDOING CREATION

The work of the demonic powers in the
Fall is the undoing of Creation.

**—WILLIAM STRINGFELLOW, *AN ETHIC FOR CHRISTIANS
AND OTHER ALIENS IN A STRANGE LAND***

Because of my love for birds, it hit me hard when migratory birds in the southwestern United States were caught up in an "unprecedented" die-off in the fall of 2020. Hundreds of thousands of birds are estimated to have died in an area that includes five states. Wildlife biologists at universities and at state and federal agencies gathered carcasses of the varied species, "from warblers to woodpeckers, hummingbirds to loons," and discovered that the dead birds were emaciated due to long-term "severe starvation." They suffered an overall loss of body fat, severely shrunken muscles controlling their wings, blood in their intestinal tracts, and kidney failure.[6]

The cause of starvation was the scarcity of water and food (both seeds and insects) caused by a severe drought in the Southwest. The birds began their migration in poor health and were met by an "unseasonable cold snap," which led to many birds getting caught in the snow and ice storm and freezing to death. Some birds may have used up vital energy stores and increased their exhaustion by

---

6. Kevin Johnson, "Study: Starvation and Freak Snow Storm Caused the Southwest Mass Bird Die-Off," *Audubon Magazine*, December 16, 2020, https://www.audubon.org/news/study-starvation-and-freak-snow-storm-caused-southwests-mass-bird-die.

altering their migration paths to avoid smoke plumes from wild-fires. Jon Hayes, executive director of Audubon Southwest, said that birds in the Southwest survive "on the margins" and that the region's rising temperatures, larger and more frequent wildfires, and stronger storms add further stress. The drought-induced starvation that left the birds emaciated, the out-of-control wildfires that may have altered their migration patterns, and the "unseasonable" cold snap that ultimately killed them are all consistent with weather-related disasters caused or exacerbated by climate change.[7]

Jesus assures us that God's caring concern extends even to sparrows, yet this mass die-off of birds brings us face-to-face with the suffering of our other-than-human companions here on earth. Surely God not only celebrates and declares "good" the abundance and diversity of creation but grieves its loss when it is diminished and as human beings stand by unwilling or unable to act. Some have used the term *ecocide* to characterize the current depletion of wildlife, accelerating loss of species, destruction of ecosystems that sustain life, and advancing climate change. Since "in [God] we live and move and have our being" (Acts 17:28), this ecocide takes place within God, destroying relationship and tearing apart the fabric of life. Does not God experience this rending of relationship in God's very being? Surely God weeps for the extinction of species, the polluting of our waters, the warming of the planet that is taking place in our time. The cross stands in the midst of creation.

Today we face the scandal, the stumbling block, the horror not only of Jesus's crucifixion two thousand years ago but also of creation crucified in our day. The ecological balance we have enjoyed throughout human history, with its predictable natural processes and a relatively stable climate, is being disrupted. The interdependent

---

7. Johnson.

web of life that not only sustains but also constitutes human life is being unraveled, accompanied by simultaneous social breakdown. Indeed, scientists say that human encroachment on wild nature, climate change, and the destruction of ecosystems set the stage for Covid-19 and other viruses to mutate and spread from animals to humans, while global transportation systems allow such viruses to quickly spread around the world and become pandemics.

This does not bode well for humans or for other life-forms with whom we share the earth. Life is being diminished—signs of death are all around. Many people around the world are grieving for the profound loss that this represents.

In addition to facing the loss that comes with the diminishment of creation's ability to sustain life and to reflect God's glory, we must also face our complicity, because we know that the ecological devastation being visited upon the earth could be prevented if we humans had the communal will to do so. Although many of us try as individuals to treat creation with the respect it deserves, we participate in institutions and systems that plunder the earth, leaving it despoiled and desecrated. Those of us who live as beneficiaries of industrial civilization carry a moral burden that previous generations have not carried, and we are aware that our choices will impact generations far into the future. We are complicit with the institutional powers in what William Stringfellow called "undoing creation." For the sake of all we have ever loved and for the sake of our souls, we must come to terms with this dilemma.

This is not taking place in a vacuum, nor is it part of an inevitable natural process. Rather, it is the direct and predictable result of a human-constructed global system of institutional powers that has grown beyond human control and has taken on a life of its own. Its underlying assumptions, institutions, and operating systems function efficiently to enslave humans in their service and devour the gifts of the earth to bring profit, prestige, and power to the elite few. The air, water, land, and stable climate necessary for sustaining life are being destroyed by the institutional imperatives of today's corporate-dominated global empire. This cannot be the plan or design of the God of love, the God of creation. Creation itself is being crucified. In this dying of earth's life systems, her children, both human and other-than-human, suffer. Songs of praise become cries of pain and lament, "My God, my God, why have you forsaken me?" (Matt 27:46), cried Jesus. In our distress, our hearts might cry out: "God help us! Has God forsaken us? Where is God?"

But God has not forsaken us. God is right here: experiencing the desecration of the persecuted and tortured earth, suffering in and with earth's creatures, experiencing our forsakenness. God weeps for the harm done, because God experiences it all from the inside—the exhaustion of the weakened sparrow that flies into a snowstorm, the terror of the polar bear who discovers she cannot swim the distance to the next ice floe, the confusion of the monarch butterfly, whose migratory homes are being destroyed, the lone-liness of the last golden toad who croaks unceasingly for a mate. God experiences the alarm of people in island nations being sub-sumed by rising seas and the devastation of families whose crops fail and children die because of increasing drought. God experiences the desolation of young people who realize that beloved species are dying and who want a future of abundant life. And God is with us, too, as we experience the sorrow and the burden of complicity that characterize our time.

As we consider creation's plight, we may be stuck at the foot of the cross, witnessing the manifold crucifixions that are taking place in our time. There is not a path that we can take of our own volition to get from cross to resurrection, for that requires God's action. The only way out of this horror is through—that is, through facing the reality of the damage, the institutional forces that are driving it, our complicity with those forces, and our call to follow in the direction of a more hopeful future. To the degree that we are willing to face and mourn the extent of creation's suffering, in the presence of God who is with us in all suffering, we are saved from denial. To the degree that we are motivated and enlivened by the Spirit, we are open to truth and are saved from both fear and manipulation by the demonic powers.

Still, this is not the end of the story. For the God who creates is also the God who saves, and all creation is included in the saving grace of God.

THE GOD WHO CREATES IS THE GOD WHO SAVES

I lift up my eyes to the hills—from where will my help come?
My help comes from the Lord, who made heaven and earth.

—PSALM 121:1–2

As we look to God for help in the midst of the multiple crises facing our human family and the rest of creation, it is clear that we don't have the wisdom or power to bring about the profound changes that are required. Still, as followers of the crucified and risen Jesus, we are called to live by the Spirit and do our part to bring about creation's healing and transformation.

Theologians who seek to be faithful to this call have been working for decades to articulate a theology of creation that will motivate *creation care*. The biblical term *stewardship* is often used to express human responsibility to care for the natural world, based on the idea that all things belong to God and that we do not own land or any other part of creation but are merely exhibiting stewardship over it on behalf of God. Biblical passages that reinforce calls for *environmental stewardship* include the claim that "the earth is the Lord's and all that is in it" (Ps 24:1) and the statement that "the Lord God took the man and put him in the garden of Eden to till it and keep it" (Gen 2:15), thus portraying the human vocation as stewards of the land.

However, in this time of extreme ecological devastation, the concept of environmental stewardship has limited value. Although this well-meaning concept calls for responsibility and care for the earth, it reinforces the anthropocentric concept of human dominion over the natural world (Gen 1:26) and leaves intact the view that humans are somehow above and separate from the natural world. It portrays the idea of a universe created for and centered on human beings, which devalues the rest of creation and sanctifies hierarchical ideas that have led to widespread ecocide.

There are other scriptural themes that can help guide us as we seek to follow Jesus in this time of ecological destruction. Psalm 104 offers a vision of interrelated ecosystems in which God provides sustenance (food, water, and habitat) to all parts of creation, including human beings. Psalm 148 presents human beings, along with all other members of the community of life, praising God together. Laws in Leviticus 2 call for every seventh year to be a Sabbath for the land and animals, during which time the land is to be left fallow and the animals free to graze. The Hebrew prophets often linked the fruitfulness of the land to faithfulness to God and pointed to both human suffering and ecological destruction as caused by the nation's idolatry and injustice. Jeremiah does this repeatedly, as when he says, "How long will the land mourn, and the grass of every field wither? For the wickedness of those who live in it the animals and the birds are swept away, and because people said, '[God] is blind to our ways'" (Jer 12:4). Such passages point to a degree of understanding about the interrelatedness and interdependence of all living things, the inherent value and rights of animals and land (implying the value of water, air, and other gifts of creation), and the call to environmental justice for the sake of people and the earth.

Most people with whom Jesus interacted were Jews who lived close to the land, praying and working for a fruitful harvest and offering thanks and a portion back to God through their taxes and offerings to the temple. Jesus drew on metaphors from the natural world and agrarian life to impart teachings his followers could relate to about God's loving relationship with human beings and the rest of creation. He pointed to the God who feeds the birds of the air and clothes the grass with the lilies of the fields as the same God we can trust to care for us. Likewise, he used seeds to illustrate the mysteries of the reign of God (Matt 13:3–9, 25–30, 33) and the power of faith (Mark 4:30), and he used the images of vine and vineyard to demonstrate human connection with God in Christ (John 15:1–10). Jesus spent most of his time outdoors. He was "with the wild beasts" during his forty days in the wilderness (Mark 1:13). He often slept outside. He observed that "foxes have holes, and birds of the air have nests; but the Son of Man has nowhere to lay his head" (Luke 9:58). In that ancient culture, people's lives were embedded in the cycles of nature; they were aware of the natural world in ways those of us who live with modern conveniences have perhaps forgotten.

For Christians who have been working to incorporate concerns about creation into church ministries, the above themes are familiar. The hope is that by recognizing the intrinsic value of creation, we will be motivated to treat the natural world with the care that it deserves. By realizing that we human beings are part of the inter-related and interdependent community of life, we will be more likely to protect its integrity. By allowing science to inform our understanding and complement Scripture, we will awaken to the story of the origins and nature of the universe revealed by science, and awe will replace our utilitarian approach to the natural world. By seeing how vulnerable people suffer most from ecological devastation, compassion will move us to action. These are our hopes as we seek to craft a message that will motivate churches to practice creation care in a significant way.

This is important work. Awakening to both the glory and the destruction of creation is essential. However, simply knowing or caring about something does not always change human behavior, especially when it seems apparent that our actions will not make much difference in the overall outcome. No matter how faithful we are in making lifestyle changes or reducing our church's carbon footprint or hosting Earth Day celebrations or even forwarding emails calling for just and effective environmental policies, we know that such limited actions will not be sufficient to bring about the scale of change required to arrest and reverse the ecological devastation that is taking place.

Eco-theology and creation care are not enough. We cannot bypass the pain of the cross in the midst of creation with the soft message of creation care. Creation theology and a theology of the cross belong together. As we weather the storms of pandemic, ecological degradation, inequity and injustice, famine, displacement, violence, war, and the literal storms of a rapidly destabilizing climate, the word of the cross must proclaim the gospel in a way that is relevant for today, focusing on the story of Jesus, the ongoing suffering of Christ in creation, the powers responsible for Jesus's death and for creation's devastation today, and God's redemptive power to bring life out of death and to make a way where there is no way, sometimes through us. We will cover these themes in later chapters.

We who are followers of Jesus are called to participate in God's saving actions in our time. Jesus said, "Go into all the world and proclaim the good news to the whole creation" (Mark 16:15). For it to be relevant today, the gospel must offer hope in action that meets the existential challenges we face. We cannot settle for empty hope that keeps us on the current road toward annihilation, leaving us in the role of passive bystanders as Christ is crucified in creation. Real hope in our time must be embodied hope, where we are empowered to take concrete actions as participants in the ongoing process of God's reconciling work, which today must include resisting the harm being inflicted by the powers on creation and doing what we can to foster human well-being, regeneration of earth's natural systems, and a future of abundant life.

This requires us to face and repent of our participation in sinful institutions and systems that drive policies, perpetuate damage, and accelerate disaster. Such realizations can be difficult. They may move those of us who are privileged away from a somewhat romantic or even self-righteous view about our caring relationship with creation, or from our attempts to justify ourselves, by exposing the hypocrisy of how we benefit from social, ecological, and political structures that cause immeasurable harm to people and the earth. It would, perhaps, be easier to stay in denial or just focus on our personal lives. But if we refuse to explore the harm caused by today's institutionalized powers, we collaborate with them. On the other hand, by naming and challenging the many ways they crucify Christ today, we help bring to light their moral illegitimacy and point in the direction of a transformed world.

One way that churches are engaged in this work today is through their participation in the struggles for environmental and climate justice. Since the early 1980s, several US denominations have taken on the cause of environmental justice, thus merging concerns for creation with a commitment to racial and economic justice. Such efforts were initiated by Black churches and communities that were directly impacted by the disproportionate number of toxic waste dumps and polluting industries placed in their communities.

Today a number of churches and other faith communities have extended these efforts by emphasizing climate justice, which links alleviating climate change with justice for people disproportionately harmed by its impacts, justice for people in communities polluted by the extraction and processing of fossil fuels (usually Indigenous people and people of color), and justice for young people whose long-term prospects are bleak without a change of course. A primary challenge for churches is to join with the movement for climate justice in solidarity with people on the front lines of these struggles and to take a stand in opposition to the powers that perpetuate the harm.

According to the most recent report of the Intergovernmental Panel on Climate Change (IPCC), average global temperatures have risen 1.1 degrees Celsius, or 2 degrees Fahrenheit, since the dawn of the Industrial Revolution, largely caused by the burning of fossil fuels. The report says we must limit this warming to under 1.5 degrees Celsius to prevent the most catastrophic impacts, which means cutting greenhouse gas emissions *in half* globally by 2030 and to *net-zero* by 2050, which will require rapid and far-reaching changes in all aspects of society. Or in a slogan from the climate justice movement, "System change not climate change."

Climate justice advocates demand policies based on the science that will help bring about systemic change. Such policies include ending fossil fuels subsidies that the International Monetary Fund says amount globally to $10 million per minute, providing "loss and damage" payments to poor countries that have been impacted most and have contributed least to climate change, immediately transitioning to justly and sustainably sourced renewable power, and banning permits for long-lasting fossil fuel infrastructure projects like pipelines and offshore oil drilling rigs that will cause pollution and keep the fossil fuel party going for decades. The bottom line is to keep fossil fuels in the ground.

The problem is that there are powerful interests working to keep the dominant system intact. They propose complex carbon-trading schemes and postpone action based on the hope of untested carbon-capture and geoengineering technologies. They promise to move to net-zero domestically sometime in the future while continuing to increase fossil fuel exports. Many government and industry leaders see the magnitude of the dangers but won't go against the conventional wisdom of today's system of corporate-dominated globalization, which is built around profit, powered by fossil fuels, and backed by police and military power.

Meanwhile, the movement for climate justice is strong and growing. These struggles are often led by people who are marginalized in official decision-making processes—people from island and low-lying nations experiencing a sea-level rise, drought-stricken nations facing famine, frontline communities being turned into sacrifice zones by fossil fuel extraction and processing, Indigenous people whose lands are being polluted by pipelines or confiscated to plant tree farms to supply polluting corporations with carbon credits, and young people whose lives and futures are at stake—and they are supported by environmental groups, labor unions, and other civil society groups, including churches. Together, these groups make up the global movement for climate justice. They call for climate change to be treated as the emergency that it is and for governments to take immediate action. Participants are saying not just no to fossil fuels but yes to a transformed world, and they have plans to get us there.

These are two completely different approaches to the climate crisis: an approach that leaves our market-based global system intact and an approach that calls for a widespread social and economic transformation. They represent two conflicting paradigms and opposing worldviews.

Perhaps the answers to our search for climate solutions will come in ways that we least expect them. Leaders in struggles for climate justice are not high-status official representatives of the domination system, nor are they wealthy or powerful according to the wisdom of this world. But it may be that these will be the very people who will save us from climate catastrophe by opening our eyes to another worldview, by pressing for systemic change, and by demanding commonsense solutions that will keep fossil fuels in the ground. They may be considered "weak and foolish" by the world's standards, but they are organizing and networking together to build grassroots movements that have the power necessary to bring about the widespread social, political, and ecological changes that are necessary to transition to a more just, compassionate, peaceful, and ecologically regenerative world. Churches could amplify these movements by joining such campaigns and coalitions as respectful allies. In the words of climate justice organizer Bill McKibben, "The main way to counter the malign power of vested interests is to meet organized money with organized people."[8]

The word of the cross, as weak and foolish as it may seem, allows us to glimpse a new order, an alternative to the dominant culture and its values based instead on the compassion, justice, inclusivity, and nonviolence that characterized Jesus's life and (as we now know it must be) on care and concern for all creation. Martin Khor of the Third World Network speaks of something similar when he says that there are two paradigms at work in our world

---

8. Bill McKibben, "The Answer to Climate Change Is Organizing," *New Yorker,*
September 1, 2020, https://www.newyorker.com/news/annals-of-a-warming-planet/the
-answer-to-climate-change-is-organizing.

today: the top-down system of corporate globalization, backed by violence, and an emerging alternative system that is community based, people friendly, earth centered, and nonviolent. He points out that as we work within the dominant system to make it fairer, more just, and less ecologically destructive, we must also nurture seeds of hope to bring alive the second paradigm and "infuse it into the first paradigm as a kind of transition."[9] This worldview offers an alternative to the domination system that is consistent with traditional and contemporary Indigenous views and is supported by the understanding of God as immanent within creation. It recalls Jesus's proclamation of the reign of God and its contemporary secular counterpart that proclaims that "another world is possible."

The compassion and passion for the reign of God that motivated Jesus may yet save us, as his risen Spirit lives and loves through us and empowers all who give themselves to this crucial work. As we become willing, God breathes new life into us, inspiring us to speak truth to power and empowering us to participate in God's reconciling work to all creation and in the ongoing story of the universe.

NEW CREATION: RECONCILING THE WORLD IN CHRIST

In the midst of suffering and death—be it individual, social,
or ecological—the promise given to the Earth community
is that life in God will reign. So speaks the resurrection.

—CYNTHIA MOE-LOBEDA, "A THEOLOGY OF THE CROSS FOR THE UNCREATORS"

What is the good news for us today, in the midst of the passion of the earth and the suffering of Christ in creation? We return here to

---

9. Martin Khor, as quoted in John Cavanagh and Jerry Mander, eds., *Alternatives to Economic Globalization: A Better World Is Possible, a Report of the International Forum on Globalization*, 2nd ed. (San Francisco: Berrett Koehler, 2004), 31.

the first words of the text with which we began this chapter: "So if anyone is in Christ, there is a new creation" (2 Cor 5:17). This hopeful text speaks of atonement as reconciliation that extends to all creation. What does the concept of *new creation* mean in light of our suffering and dying earth?

The concept of new creation has been used to illustrate a hopeful vision of a renewed earth that may motivate people to take seriously our call to care for creation. One way that Christians have interpreted this concept is to relate it to the afterlife, as an assurance that no matter how bad it gets here on earth, no matter how many ecosystems are destroyed or how many species go extinct, God will ultimately reconstitute creation in a renewed and even better way. But such ideas bring little comfort to those of us who love life here on earth as we witness the escalating speed and efficiency of the institutional engines of death that are destroying it.

Of course, there are biblical texts that support the idea of all things ultimately being summed up in God at the end of time. For instance, Ephesians 1:10 refers to God's plan for reconciliation in "the fullness of time," to gather up all things in heaven and on earth in Christ. Acts 3:21 speaks of a time of "universal restoration." These are reassuring passages about the promise of resurrection and the renewal of creation at the end of time. Such passages offer us freedom from the fear of death and courage to face life's challenges.

But the biblical concept of new creation does not just symbolize hope that at the end of the world, God will reconstitute it in a new form. Rather, it symbolizes hope for the future of this world. Jürgen Moltmann said, "The new creation is not a different creation. It is the new creation of this deranged world. Eternal life is not a different life. It is the resurrection of this life into the life of God. . . . So the kingdom of God means that this world will be different and will be born anew out of violence and injustice to justice, righteousness and peace."[10] These ideas of reconciliation and new creation reflect Jesus's vision of the reign of God.

As extinctions become more numerous, climate change accelerates, and the powers assert themselves in ever more ecologically destructive ways, the biblical concept of new creation illustrates a spiritual reality that can be experienced and lived into. As followers of Jesus, we are already part of the new creation here and now, as is made clear in the text above. We are already part of a new creation because we are in Christ.

As reconciled people who are empowered as participants in God's saving work in our time, we are called to reach out with the message of reconciliation not only for individuals but for creation as well. This path is costly. Carrying the message of reconciliation must include challenging dehumanizing institutional idols that are undoing creation, and working for systemic change in ways that enable people to flourish. In this process, we are given a new orientation toward life and courage to rise even when faced with seemingly insurmountable odds.

Following Jesus enables us to recognize the glory of God in creation, to live in reconciled relationships, to comfort those who suffer, to stand in solidarity against oppressive powers, to allow the love that we have received to flow through us, to acknowledge that all creation exists within the circle of God's care, and to take actions that embody hope for the future and are proportional to the challenges we face. This is atonement. This is salvation: to live into the reality of the new creation.

---

10. Jürgen Moltmann, *Jesus Christ for Today's World* (Minneapolis: Fortress, 1994), 22–23.

PART III

ENGAGING THE POWERS

A CLASH OF KINGDOMS

CHAPTER 5
JESUS AND THE POWERS

The vision of the cross in all four gospels does not allow us to rest content with a detached, ahistorical understanding of either the kingdom or atonement.

—N. T. WRIGHT, *THE DAY THE REVOLUTION BEGAN*

AS WE HAVE seen in previous chapters, this book contends that the crucifixion of Christ is ongoing as the ruling powers continue their domination and violence and that the resurrection is ongoing as human beings rise in courage to live into the reality of a world transformed by God's love. We have explored different historical and contemporary ways of understanding the atonement, including atonement as reconciliation that acknowledges God as transcending and encompassing creation as well as deeply present within and throughout all time and space.

We now begin part 3, "Engaging the Powers: A Clash of Kingdoms." Here we continue our search for how to understand the word of the cross as relevant for today by exploring the social and political dynamics that led to Jesus's death and similar forces that are at work today. We begin to flesh out a theology of the powers based on the story of Jesus and the violent opposition he faced from the religious and political authorities of his day. This dynamic is integral to Paul's proclamation of the word of the cross: he speaks of a "wisdom of this age or of the rulers of this age, who are doomed to perish" (1 Cor 2:6) and declares that it was the rulers of this age who "crucified the Lord of glory" (1 Cor 2:8). Here in chapter 5, we focus on the story of Jesus and his engagement with the powers and principalities, while chapters 6 and 7 reveal the conventional wisdom and the institutionalized rulers that characterize the domination system today.

For Christians, the story of Jesus's life, death, and resurrection, symbolized by the cross, both inspires and empowers us to follow him by faith in our day. Here we will consider the saving power of God revealed in the story of Jesus not as a theory but as a series of events, a narrative based on scriptural accounts of Jesus's life and teachings, the opposition he faced from the religious and political authorities who plotted his death, and his postdeath appearances that revealed a new spiritual paradigm and way of seeing and living in the world. Sadly, popular versions of the story of Jesus begin with doctrines about God's plan for him to die on the cross for our sins. Such belief systems are based on taking certain metaphors and phrases from the Bible literally and extrapolating on them. But we cannot substitute a dogma about the crucifixion of Jesus for the story itself. We cannot turn Jesus's death into an abstract formula, removed from his life and teachings, his passion for the reign of God, the social and political dynamics that led to his execution, and God's victory over the powers in his resurrection, without losing sight of him.

Biblical scholars have helped shed light on the story of Jesus, based on scriptural accounts, language studies, and historical research. I find scholarship and evidence-based speculation about the biblical record fascinating, but we will not engage in lengthy discussions on these topics in this book. They are unnecessary to its central purpose: to offer the word of the cross in a way that is relevant in our time and to reflect on what it means to follow Jesus today. For this reason, we will primarily stay with stories about Jesus as told in the Bible, the foundational authority for Christian faith.

As we become familiar with these stories and make them our own, our lives are transformed. We become participants in the ongoing story of God's love at work in the world. In Paul's words, "And all of us, with unveiled faces, seeing the glory of the Lord as though reflected in a mirror, are being transformed into the same image from one degree of glory to another; for this comes from the Lord, the Spirit" (2 Cor 3:18).

THE TEMPTATION OF JESUS: RESISTING CULTURAL POSSESSION

> Still, the Temptation narrative helps to clarify what the voices that work against God are saying within us and around us and how we may be prepared for both their bullying and their seduction. We need to be prepared for just how subtle and seductive they can really be.
>
> **—ALYCE MCKENZIE, "THE GREATEST TEMPTATION"**

There is a call in life to come to terms with who we are in relation to the universe, to give ourselves to something ultimate, to live in right relationship with the Ground of Being,[1] to fulfill our destiny, to enter into the Great Mystery. But we hear other voices as well, voices that we have internalized from our families and cultures, which we hear as our own. These voices tempt us. They present us with a choice: to be true to God and to ourselves and to live fully as free human beings or to be ensnared by idolatrous motives and end up being possessed by them.

---

1. Paul Tillich, *The Ground of Being: Neglected Essays of Paul Tillich*, ed. Robert M. Price (Wikimedia Commons: Mindvendor, 2015).

Jesus, too, experienced this conflict. At the time of his baptism by John in the Jordan River, he saw a vision in which the Holy Spirit descended upon him as a dove, and he heard a voice from heaven saying, "This is my Son, the Beloved, with whom I am well pleased" (Matt 3:16–17). This revelation led him to a time of fasting and testing in the wilderness, during which a spiritually strong but very human Jesus was tempted as he strove to find clarity about his identity and calling (Mark 1:12–13; Matt 4:1–11; Luke 4:1–13). He evidently struggled with what it meant to be "Son of God," a well-known designation in the ancient world that was usually applied to the Roman Emperor, who possessed status, wealth, and worldly power. Jews who awaited the Messiah were hoping for the coming of a king like David who would possess such signs of privilege to an even greater degree. Unsurprisingly, these were the very things that tempted Jesus. Luke presents this conflict with the tempter as Jesus's struggle "to be a servant-messiah or to interpret messiahship in the traditional terms of power, strength, and conquest."[2]

"If you are the Son of God," says the voice of temptation (the "devil") to Jesus, putting him to the test by presenting him with attractive opportunities to demonstrate his unique role. Jesus is not tempted here by greed or lust or other common "sins" but by things that the culture, supported by Scripture and tradition, considers good, including special abilities expected of a messiah. When the devil tempts Jesus to turn stones into bread, he is appealing to his physical hunger and weakness due to fasting, but he is also calling on Jesus to demonstrate his divine power to provide food for the people, like God providing manna in the wilderness. Likewise, if Jesus were to be rescued by angels after throwing himself off the pinnacle of the temple, people would flock to him because of his

---

2. Paul J. Achtemeier, *Harper's Bible Dictionary* (San Francisco: Harper & Row, 1985), 1032.

supernatural abilities. In both cases, Jesus refuses. Even when the devil promises to give Jesus the splendor, wealth, and power of all the world's kingdoms, Jesus rejects the idolatrous goal of situating himself at the top of the world's hierarchical system and professes loyalty to God alone. Each time the devil tempts him, Jesus steadfastly refuses to use whatever powers he might have to go beyond natural human limitations. Instead, he responds with words that emphasize his full humanity and that affirm his trust in the loving care of God.

If you are the Son of God," says the tempter, then prove it by refusing to be bound by human limitations, by putting your own needs and desires above all else, by capitalizing on your extraordinary abilities, by ignoring the laws of nature, by choosing an ego-driven path that leads to fame, fortune, and power over others. But each time Jesus hears the voice of temptation, he rejects it, choosing instead to be faithful, to respond with scriptural guidance, to follow the Spirit's direction, and to entrust himself to the will of God. We are called and empowered by grace to do the same.

The temptation stories make clear that Jesus rejected the domination system's values of status, wealth, and worldly power while embracing self-denial, humility, and radical faithfulness to God. These forty days in the wilderness were clarifying for Jesus. They set the stage for his ministry, his confrontation with the ruling powers, and the events that precipitated his death. By choosing a path of deep integrity instead of adopting the assumptions of the dominant culture, Jesus set himself against the religious, political, economic, and military rulers of his day. What would that look like for us, if we were to make such a choice, and how disruptive and dangerous for us might that be? How would we be received by our churches? In the case of Jesus, the religious elite, who collaborated with the Roman authorities and benefited from the Roman occupation, used religious doctrines against him, charged him with blasphemy and treason, targeted him, plotted against him, and turned him over to the Romans to be crucified.

THE DOMINATION SYSTEM IN JESUS'S DAY

> Jerusalem's elites lived in luxury. One would expect this, and recent archaeology in Jerusalem has confirmed it by unearthing one of their villas. The remains point to the opulence of the upper class. Their wealth attests to their position at the top of a domination system under which the economic condition of the peasant class was declining.
>
> **—MARCUS J. BORG AND JOHN DOMINIC CROSSAN, *THE LAST WEEK***

The domination system in Jesus's day was embodied by the Roman Empire. Religious, economic, political, and military institutions and those individuals who represented them all played a role in keeping the overall system going, as did the assumptions, values, and norms that made up the dominant worldview. These were the primary institutional and ideological powers and principalities of Jesus's time.

The Jewish society into which Jesus was born was highly stratified, built upon a hierarchy with several levels of strict social divisions. Class conflict contributed to this stratification, as did complex power arrangements. Judea was a monarchy but had been conquered by the Roman Empire; Jerusalem was under occupation by the Roman army. The Roman Empire maintained the Pax Romana (Roman Peace), a system of order that depended upon exerting social, economic, political, and military control over subjugated peoples. The emperor was above all others in status, wealth, and power. Caesar Augustus, who ruled at the time Jesus was born, referred to himself as "son of a God."[3] He was followed by his stepson Tiberius Caesar, who ruled at the time of Jesus's death.

Below the emperor in status was the Roman governor of Jerusalem, Pontius Pilate, who appears in the trial of Jesus in the Gospel stories. Below Pilate was the Herod the Great, king of Judea, who ruled during Jesus's childhood, and Herod Antipas, tetrarch of Galilee and Perea, who collaborated with Pilate in condemning Jesus to death. Ever since the time of the judges, when the people of Israel had prayed to God to "appoint for us . . . a king to govern us, like other nations" (1 Sam 8:5), the king had been at the top of the Jewish hierarchy. By the time of Jesus, however, this system had lost legitimacy in the eyes of many Jews because kings were appointed by Rome and collaborated with the occupation. Likewise, the high priests were not members of the hereditary priesthood but were appointed by the Romans.[4]

The Jewish religious leaders, who included landowners and other members of the wealthy elite, were members of the Sanhedrin, the council that interpreted, set, and enforced the Law. Rome allowed these religious authorities to administer home rule as long as they could maintain order and deliver tribute to Rome. Crucifixion was the ultimate penalty for those who challenged Roman rule, reserved for rebellious slaves, incorrigible robbers, revolutionaries, and anti-imperialist subversives. In case of revolt, Rome's backup plan was to crush disorder and opposition with overwhelming force as they did to restore order to other colonized nations under their control and as they ultimately did in Jerusalem in response to the Jewish rebellion that began in 66 CE.

---

3. "Augustus Caesar," 5 Minutes in Church History, Ligonier Ministries, May 23, 2018, https://www.5minutesinchurchhistory.com/augustus-caesar/.

4. Borg and Crossan, *Last Week*, 39.

The temple in Jerusalem was the administrative center of Jewish religious, economic, and political life. Sacrifices were made, taxes and tithes were collected, and tribute was paid through the temple, which also functioned as a bank. It was through the temple that lands had been foreclosed due to debt incurred by small farmers during years of poor harvest, leading to land being consolidated in fewer and fewer hands. This led to great hardship, for most people lived an agrarian lifestyle, dependent upon the fruitfulness of the land. Some scholars believe that Jesus's following was made up largely of peasants, many of whom may have been dispossessed by the unjust debt and foreclosure laws. This may have been the basis of Jesus's critique of the religious leaders when he accused them of "devour[ing] widows' houses" (Luke 20:47). Part of the attraction of Jesus's growing popularity may be apparent in the focus in the Lord's prayer on forgiveness of debt, which had a concrete meaning to peasants in that day, as did the request among hungry people for daily bread.

Many Jews resented the religious leaders' collaboration with the Roman occupation, considered their authority to be illegitimate, and awaited a messiah who would overthrow Rome and restore the kingdom to the house of David. These resentments fueled peasant uprisings. Some who had promoted violent revolution may have been among Jesus's followers, including Simon the Zealot, one of the original disciples.

JESUS AND THE CLASH OF KINGDOMS

What killed Jesus was not irreligion, but religion itself;
not lawlessness, but precisely the law; not anarchy, but the
upholders of order. . . . And because he was not only innocent,

but the very embodiment of true religion, true law, and true
order, this victim exposed their violence for what it was:
not the defense of society, but an attack against God.

Into this stratified ancient society came Jesus, speaking truth to
power and teaching another way to live. Jesus drew from the prophets in announcing his mission (Luke 4:16–21), in challenging the
people and the authorities (Matt 16:6–9; Luke 10:13–13), and in
characterizing his actions (Matt 21:12–27; Luke 19:46). The role of
the prophets in ancient Israel was to call God's people, especially
those with institutional power, away from idolatry and injustice
and back to a relationship of faithfulness to God. By his prophetic
witness, Jesus modeled a prophetic role that is still relevant for the
church in relation to the powers today.

As mentioned earlier, Jesus introduced his mission in his
hometown of Nazareth by quoting the prophetic words of Isaiah
to announce that he had come to preach good news to the poor, to
proclaim release to the captives and recovery of sight to the blind,
to set at liberty those who were oppressed, and to bring hope to
those without hope (Luke 4:16–21). Not everyone saw this message
as good news. At first the people in Nazareth "spoke well of him
and were amazed at the gracious words that came from his mouth,"
but they quickly turned against him when he challenged their prejudice by describing God's favor to foreigners and made it clear that
they would not receive privileged treatment. In a foreshadowing
of the opposition and conflicts that would arise during his ministry
and would lead to his death, people became enraged, rose against
him, and tried to throw him off a cliff. In a foreshadowing of the
saving action of God in the resurrection, "he passed through the midst
of them and went on his way" (Luke 4:30).

According to Mark, Jesus began his ministry by proclaiming, "The time is fulfilled, and the kingdom of God has come near; repent and believe in the good news" (Mark 1:15). While all four Gospel writers make clear that the coming of the "kingdom of God" was central to Jesus's teaching, Matthew usually uses the phrase "kingdom of heaven." Both phrases have the same meaning, as is apparent by their interchangeable use.

The Greek word *basileia*, often translated in the Bible as "kingdom," can also be translated as "reign," "dominion," or "empire."[5] Any of these translations make clear that Jesus's message was not just spiritual but also political in that it sets the kingdom or empire of God apart from and against the kingdom of Herod or the empire of Caesar. The authorities would probably have been fine with Jesus using the phrase "family of God" or "community of God," but "kingdom of God" was clearly a political statement and a direct challenge to the domination system. This phrase highlights the ongoing struggle between God's reign on earth and the kingdoms of this world. According to *The New Interpreter's Bible*, this "clash of kingdoms" is "the plot of the whole gospel of Matthew,"[6] which frequently portrays the religious elite testing Jesus. The conflicting loyalties implied by Jesus's use of the term *kingdom* become more explicit as his ministry progresses. Tensions increase and the powers respond predictably, with escalating challenges, threats, and plots, culminating in his arrest and crucifixion. Marcus J. Borg explains,

> [If] Jesus had been only a mystic, healer, and wisdom teacher, I doubt that he would have been executed. But he

---

5. *New World Encyclopedia*, s.v. "Kingdom of God," accessed December 15, 2021, https://www.newworldencyclopedia.org/entry/Kingdom_of_God.

6. Neil M. Alexander, ed., *The New Interpreter's Bible: A Commentary in Twelve Volumes*, vol. 8 (Nashville: Abingdon, 1995), 162.

was also a God-intoxicated voice of religious and social protest who had attracted a following. . . . In Jesus' world, this was enough to get arrested and executed by authorities who did not care for criticism and who feared popular unrest.[7]

The teachings of Jesus, which have inspired people from his time until ours, were seen by most of the religious leaders as a challenge to their authority and as interference in their responsibility to keep order in the nation. Take, for example, the Beatitudes, a series of blessings that Jesus delivered early in his ministry. I memorized these verses as a child and have seen both youth and adults baffled and amazed when looking closely at them in Bible study. The content of the teachings presents a challenge to the existing order and offers a new paradigm through which to see the world based on Jesus's vision of the reign of God.

Matthew and Luke offer different versions of the Beatitudes (Matt 5:1–11; Luke 6:20–26). In Matthew, which focuses on "spiritual" attitudes and rewards, Jesus says, "Blessed are the poor in spirit, for theirs is the kingdom of heaven. Blessed are those who mourn, for they will be comforted. Blessed are the meek, for they will inherit the earth" (Matt 5:3–12), then continues with other blessings along these lines. In Luke's Gospel, Jesus is more concrete, saying, "Blessed are you who are poor, for yours is the kingdom of God. Blessed are you who are hungry now, for you will be filled. Blessed are you who weep now, for you will laugh" (Luke 6:20–21). After continuing in this way with other similar blessings, Luke adds the woes: "Woe to you who are rich, for you have received your consolation. Woe to you who are full now, for you will be hungry"

---

7. Marcus J. Borg, "Why Was Jesus Killed?," in *The Meaning of Jesus: Two Visions*, by Marcus J. Borg and N. T. Wright (New York: HarperCollins, 1999), 91.

(Luke 6:24–25), and so on. Both versions make clear that the values of God's reign turn the values of this world upside down.

All of Jesus's parables are consistent with his message about the reign of God. The story of the good Samaritan critically portrays representatives of the religious elite as uncaring and elevates an outcast Samaritan as the compassionate hero (Luke 10:25–37). The prodigal son highlights the compassionate father who welcomes and celebrates the return home of the son who squandered everything but who also shows compassion to his other son, who was jealous and upset because he had stayed home and followed all the rules (Luke 15:11–32). These and other parables convey the message of a merciful God who forgives sinners and celebrates the return of all who are lost.

These teachings offered a striking contrast to the system developed by the elite religious hierarchy, which outlined official standards, including an elaborate system of purity codes based on the call of God's people to holiness: "You shall be holy, for I the Lord your God am holy" (Lev 19:2). Some of these codes included separating those who were considered "unclean" from the rest of the community. People could be considered unclean for many reasons, including disease, disability, menstruation, childbirth, certain forms of work, being "possessed by demons," touching a dead body, or being unable to perform certain temple rituals. By the time of Jesus, abiding by the purity codes required elaborate rituals that prevented many from gaining access to the official blessings that the leaders themselves enjoyed.

Throughout his ministry, Jesus taught and demonstrated that compassion is more important than abiding by standards of purity. He offered forgiveness and healing and taught his followers to do the same, but he offended the religious establishment by doing so outside the laws and rituals of the temple. Jesus restored people who were considered unclean to physical or emotional health but also to full community. He did this, however, without going through elaborate temple rituals or soliciting the approval of the religious authorities, who frequently accused Jesus of flaunting their Law and their authority by healing people on the Sabbath. They were angered when Jesus declared to a paralyzed man, "Your sins are forgiven," and then, to show that "the Son of Man has authority on earth to forgive sins," he healed him (Mark 2:5–12). When the religious leaders accused Jesus of allowing his disciples to pick grain on the Sabbath, he responded, "The sabbath was made for humankind, not humankind for the sabbath" (Mark 2:23–38). This indicates a God of compassion rather than a God who is preoccupied with whether people are following or breaking the rules. When Jesus entered a synagogue and healed a man with a withered hand on the Sabbath, "the Pharisees went out and began to conspire against him, how to destroy him" (Matt 12:9–14).

This conflict with the religious authorities became ever more apparent as Jesus created an inclusive community based on the values of the reign of God that he proclaimed. Judea was a patriarchal society in which women were not only subordinate to and dependent upon men; they were considered property. There were strict rules prohibiting women from talking with men they did not know. People from certain regions, including Samaria, were reviled. Yet to the amazement of his disciples and to the dismay of his opponents, Jesus crossed social barriers of every kind. He spoke to the woman of Samaria, who shared the good news of Jesus with her community (John 4:7–30). Likewise, children had no rights in that ancient society, yet when his disciples tried to dismiss children who had gathered around Jesus, he called the children to him. When the disciples argued about who was the greatest, he held up a child as an example to be followed, "for it is to such as these that the kingdom of God belongs" (Mark 10:14).

Central to Jesus's ministry was the practice of open table fellowship, symbolized today in the sacrament of Holy Communion. Jesus told stories about throwing a banquet to which the people invited did not come, so the host told his servants, "Go out at once into the streets and lanes of the town and bring in the poor, the crippled, the blind, and the lame" (Luke 14:15–23). At one dinner, a woman bathed Jesus's feet with her tears, dried them with her hair, and anointed them, although people judged her as a sinner (Luke 7:36–50). At another meal, people complained that a woman who had anointed him with costly nard was too extravagant (Mark 14:3–9). In both instances, Jesus held these women up as models of faithfulness and love. When Jesus was eating in the home of a tax collector named Levi, the scribes and Pharisees asked why he ate with tax collectors and sinners. Although tax collectors worked for the temple establishment, collecting temple taxes and tribute for Rome, not only were they resented by the people, but evidently the religious leaders who employed them also treated them with contempt. Jesus responded to their challenge by saying, "I have come to call not the righteous but sinners" (Mark 2:15–17).

Similar stories of the religious leaders criticizing Jesus's actions and putting him to the test continue throughout all four Gospels. They not only took Jesus's actions as a personal affront to their privilege but also believed that they were in the right and were carrying out God's Law. Not all members of the religious establishment were against Jesus, but as a ruling council, they opposed him because they felt responsible to keep the peace during the occupation.

These conflicts between Jesus and the authorities illustrate the direct challenge he posed to the domination system by revealing the compassionate nature of God and by creating a popular alternative community that was inclusive, equitable, and noncoercive. By doing so, Jesus challenged the religious hierarchy, the reign of

Herod, and the overarching rule of Caesar. These conflicts continued and intensified throughout his ministry, leading to the final confrontation between Jesus and the powers. As the story progresses, the tension builds and the plot thickens as Jesus heads for Jerusalem, deliberately planning his time there to coincide with the observation of Passover.

When considering what to do about Jesus, the chief priests and Pharisees held a meeting of the ruling council. They said, "If we let him go on like this, everyone will believe in him, and the Romans will come and take away both our holy place and our nation." Then Caiaphas, the high priest, said, "You do not understand that it is better for you to have one man die for the people than to have the whole nation destroyed" (John 11:50). They used their religious power and privilege to justify turning Jesus over to be crucified for the sake of national security.

Although the religious leaders were already looking for a way to kill Jesus, they were enraged when Jesus carried out two back-to-back demonstrations in the days leading up to Passover. The first has been called the "triumphal entry into Jerusalem." He entered the city on a donkey's colt, where crowds of people joyfully welcomed him, shouting "Hosanna," waving palm branches, calling him the "son of David," and throwing their cloaks on the ground in front of him. While this humble procession demonstrated the form of "kingship" that Jesus embraced, it can also be understood as a parody of the annual Roman procession that would soon be entering Jerusalem to keep the peace during Passover, with its elaborate display of chariots, banners, and other symbols of empire. Jesus's Palm Sunday procession was a highly symbolic demonstration that highlighted the contrast between these two conflicting kingdoms: the kingdom (or empire) of Caesar and the kingdom of God.

Then, in Jerusalem, Jesus overturned the tables of the money-changers in the temple and drove out those who were conducting business there. This action by Jesus has been called the "cleansing of the temple," but it was actually a symbolic action directed against the idolatrous and unjust economic system through which the religious establishment upheld the Roman occupation. This action challenged the legitimacy of the religious establishment's collaboration with Roman rule and further solidified the plans of the religious leaders to have Jesus killed. Some have called this temple action an exorcism. According to Walter Wink,

> The paradigmatic collective exorcism in the New Testament is Jesus' cleansing of the temple. . . . This act is depicted by the Synoptic Gospels as the climax of his ministry, the central focus of his journey to Jerusalem, and the final provocation of his arrest and execution. . . . Each account, even John's, uses the formulaic term for exorcism, *ekballo*, to describe his act of "driving out" those who did commerce in the temple.[8]

This act of "exorcism" at the temple does not contradict the claim that Jesus practiced active nonviolence. In fact, it is an example of what today might be called *nonviolent direct action*. This contemporary term refers to a symbolic or strategic action undertaken directly by individuals or groups to bring about social change through nonviolent means. Both Mohandas Gandhi and Martin Luther King Jr. pointed to Jesus as the inspiration for their campaigns of nonviolent action.

---

8. Wink, *Unmasking the Powers*, 65.

In his action at the temple, Jesus drove out both people and animals and created disarray, but he did not harm or intend to harm anyone. In fact, according to John, after the confrontation, Jesus stayed and cured people who came to him there in the temple, including some who had been blind or unable to walk. According to Matthew, what seems to have enraged the religious leaders most was that children in the temple area continued calling out, "Hosanna to the Son of David" (Matt 21:14–16). Because large and enthusiastic crowds responded to Jesus's message, the authorities believed that the growing popularity of this movement presented a dire threat to the stability of the whole interlocking network of institutional powers. The authorities clearly felt increasingly threatened as the movement grew, and they became more determined than ever to do away with Jesus, just as oppressive governments do today by targeting movement leaders when "people power" threatens the stability of the status quo.

Following this pivotal nonviolent direct action,[9] Jesus and his disciples occupied the temple area each day, like activists today who "occupy" a center of power. "Every day he was teaching in the temple" (Luke 19:47), to the dismay of the chief priests and scribes, who did not want to arrest him during Passover because they feared that "there may be a riot among the people" (Mark 14:1–2). Every night Jesus would go out to the Mount of Olives, but "all the people would get up early in the morning to listen to him in the temple" (Luke 21:37–38). By then, the power of the people had become evident. The authorities were looking for a way to put Jesus to death, "but they feared the people" (Luke 20:19; 22:2); they could not get near Jesus to arrest him, "because the whole crowd was spellbound by his teaching" (Mark 11:18).

---

9. *Nonviolent direct action* is a contemporary term that refers to actions taken by individuals or groups to bring about social change through nonviolent means.

THE GARDEN OF GETHSEMANE AND THE WILL OF GOD

The terrible silence of God in response to Christ's prayer in
Gethsemane was more than a deathly stillness. Mystics have
felt it too, in the dark night of the soul in which everything
that makes life worth living dries up, and hope disappears
from life. Martin Buber called it "the eclipse of God."

—JÜRGEN MOLTMANN, *JESUS CHRIST FOR TODAY'S WORLD*

Jesus went on publicly teaching, healing, and denouncing the chief priests, scribes, and Pharisees in the temple for several more days, in the presence of the crowds who supported him. On the evening of Passover, he gathered privately with his disciples in a small room. The Synoptic Gospels vary in reporting the words of Jesus as he shares "the last supper" with his disciples. According to Matthew, Jesus blessed a loaf of bread and gave it to them, saying, "Take, eat; this is my body." Then he offered thanks over a cup of wine, and offered it to them, saying, "Drink from it, all of you; for this is my blood of the new covenant, which is poured out for many for the forgiveness of sins" (Matt 26:26–28). Jesus's words are repeated by Christians around the world and resound through the ages as the words of institution of the sacrament of Holy Communion.

John's Gospel does not indicate that it was a Passover meal or mention Jesus offering bread or wine to his disciples but speaks of Jesus using this private occasion to explain to them what it means to follow him: to recognize that God is love and that God is present among them, to love one another as he has loved them, and to follow his example by being servants of one another. To demonstrate this form of servant ministry, Jesus washed their feet (John 13:1–17). Foot-washing rituals are still carried out during Holy Week in Maundy Thursday services that commemorate this symbolic act.

After the meal, Jesus went out with his disciples to the Mount of Olives and the garden of Gethsemane, where he prayed about how events in Jerusalem would unfold. He told his disciples to stay and keep watch with him, but they kept falling asleep. Jesus prayed, "My Father, if it is possible, may this cup be taken from me. Yet not as I will, but as you will" (Matt 26:39 NIV), and again, "My Father, if this cannot pass unless I drink it, your will be done" (Matt 26:42).

This story of Jesus praying in Gethsemane, "Your will be done," is sometimes used to back up the claim that Jesus's sacrificial death was God's will, perhaps even God's primary purpose for Jesus. In other words, God's preordained plan was for Jesus to die by crucifixion, and Jesus's designated role of self-sacrifice and obedience to this plan was already set. This view supports satisfaction or substitutionary "payment" theories of the atonement, which do not make sense if the whole story of Jesus is considered. Such theories assign to Jesus only a passive role, ignore his freedom of choice and self-determination, and dismiss his passion for the coming of the kingdom of God "on earth as it is in heaven," which was so central to his message.

A friend told me that one of her most striking experiences when visiting the Holy Land was at the Mount of Olives. As she stood there looking out over Jerusalem, she thought about Jesus on that final night before his crucifixion, praying through his decision to stay the course, which would take him into the city and to the certain death that awaited him there. Then she looked out in the other direction, realizing how easy it would have been for Jesus to take off in that direction, away from Jerusalem, to anonymity and freedom. His choice was real, just as our choices are real for us.

Jesus prayed there in agony, knowing he had a choice. According to Luke, "In his anguish he prayed more earnestly, and his sweat became like great drops of blood falling down on the ground" (Luke 22:44). He could foresee the likelihood of his death, considering the ways he had challenged the ruling authorities. He wanted the cup of suffering and violent death to pass from him. Still, he chose to be true to himself, to his followers, and to God by facing what awaited him in Jerusalem. Jesus must have understood faithfulness to God's will in this set of circumstances to mean facing likely arrest and execution by the authorities, but this does not imply that this was God's ultimate will or primary purpose for his life. Rather, Jesus had too much integrity to back down; he cared too much about others to run away. He trusted that God would be glorified, whether in his life or in his death. He stayed faithful to his calling, despite the personal cost, and entrusted the outcome to God.

Jesus waited and prayed in the garden until he was arrested and taken into the city and ultimately to his death. Judas betrayed him, Peter denied him, and his disciples, except for the women who "stood at a distance, watching" (Luke 23:49), abandoned him. Herod questioned him and turned him over to Pilate, who in turn questioned him and then, as the crowd that had gathered to demand the release of Barabbas called for Jesus to be crucified, sentenced him to death. The Roman soldiers stripped him, whipped him, and put a crown of thorns on his head. Passersby ridiculed him with the same words the devil had used to tempt him in the wilderness: *"If you are the Son of God*, come down from the cross" (Matt 27:40). Pilate had an inscription put on the cross that mocked him and the entire Jewish nation: "Jesus of Nazareth, the King of the Jews" (John 19:19). Near the end, Jesus cried out, "My God, my God, why have you forsaken me?" Then he "gave a loud cry and breathed his last" (Mark 15:34–37).

None of the Gospel accounts claim that Jesus was crucified because God required a human sacrifice to save sinners. None of them portray God planning or directing the execution of Jesus to punish him in place of sinful humanity or to uphold God's honor. God sent Jesus (as God in turn sends us) to heal, teach, proclaim, and demonstrate the good news of God's all-inclusive love. Clearly, such a life was (and is) a threat to the powers. Jesus's proclamation of the coming reign of God threatened the domination system of his age, as it threatens all systems of domination. The powers that rule the world must set conditions on love to enforce obedience. They pretend that God is at the top of systems of domination, but this lie is exposed in the crucifixion of Jesus as a subversive. God is not at the top of such systems but at the bottom, in solidarity with those who suffer the systems' harmful effects.

Jesus had settled for himself long before that being a beloved child of God meant being at odds with the world's power structures. He had been tempted early on to seek status, wealth, and worldly power. Instead, he chose the foolishness and weakness of Love. He chose "the wisdom of God in a mystery," which the rulers of his age did not understand. "If they had, they would not have crucified the Lord of glory." That is why Jesus died—because the ruling Powers killed him. They could see no other way.

THE REVERSAL OF GOOD FRIDAY

But Easter as the reversal of Good Friday means God's
vindication of Jesus's passion for the kingdom of God,
for God's justice, and God's "no" to the powers who
killed him, powers still very much alive in our world.

—MARCUS J. BORG AND JOHN DOMINIC CROSSAN, *THE LAST WEEK*

The crucifixion of Jesus was a travesty—an affront by the powers to the love and justice of God. The surprise is what came afterward. His execution did not put an end to the movement of people who responded to his message. He appeared to many, leading them to claim that "the Lord has risen" and to identify Jesus as the Messiah who had fulfilled Jewish prophecies in ways no one had expected. This brought about a spiritual breakthrough and paradigm shift in the understanding of the divine-human relationship, based not solely on Jesus's death but on how he lived his life. His message, values, and way of being were vindicated in the resurrection. Easter signifies "the reversal of Good Friday" and "God's no to the powers that killed him." The next two chapters will explore how "these powers are still very much alive in our world."

"At the beginning of Christianity there were two crosses," wrote Jürgen Moltmann, "one was a real cross, the other was a symbol."[10] For the first three centuries after Jesus's death and resurrection, Christianity was widely understood as being anti-imperial. His followers remembered the "real cross" upon which Jesus and so many others had been executed by the Roman Empire. Following his example, many Christians were martyred for refusing to pledge allegiance to the Roman emperor or serve in the Roman army. When Emperor Constantine converted to Christianity and made it the state religion in the fourth century, Rome began not only spreading but also enforcing this official religion under the icon of the cross. A theology that rationalized *just war* followed. Now soldiers were required to be baptized and to fight under the banner of a glorified cross to promote the spread of Christianity. The cross had become a symbol of the Holy Roman Empire.

---

10. Jürgen Moltmann, "The Cross as Military Symbol for Sacrifice," in *Cross Examinations: Readings on the Meaning of the Cross Today*, ed. Marit Trelstad (Minneapolis: Augsburg Fortress, 2006), 259.

During the past two thousand years, Christian understandings about the meaning of the cross have diverged. Dominant forms of Christianity have often been aligned with the State, as in the time of Constantine. This dynamic is at work today in US civil religion, which promotes American exceptionalism and celebrates the United States as a nation uniquely blessed by God. Christian nationalist groups have also used the glorified cross of domination to symbolize racist, sexist, and antidemocratic movements that merge patriotic and religious symbols, as at the insurrection at the US Capitol.

Yet those who are called to follow Jesus are invited to remember the "real cross" upon which Jesus suffered and died, as we sought to do at the Way of the Cross event in downtown Santa Cruz that I wrote about in the introduction. This means keeping alive the story of the nonviolent Jesus, his passion for the reign of God and his crucifixion at the hands of the powers, God's vindication of his life and ministry in the resurrection, his ongoing presence among us, and life in the Spirit that enables us to follow him.

The risen Jesus comes to us today in the power of the Spirit, offering us God's unconditional love and forgiveness, along with the invitation that he offered his first disciples so long ago. We are invited into at-one-ment with the God of love, without hoops to jump through, without ideologies, without conditions. We do not have to be enthralled by the powers or driven by desires or fears to conform and excel in their service at the expense of other people and the earth. There is a deeper way to live, which can be experienced by living in the presence of God and by following in the footsteps of the crucified and risen Jesus in the direction of his vision of the reign of God. Though it involves risk, this way of life offers immeasurable rewards. We are empowered by the Spirit to rise in courage, to resist cultural possession, and to live as fully human beings and as beloved children of God.

CHAPTER 6
THE PREVAILING WISDOM

THE WISDOM OF THIS AGE

Our involvement in evil goes far beyond our conscious,
volitional participation in evil. To a much greater extent than
we are aware, we are possessed by the values and powers of
an unjust order. It is not enough then simply to repent of
the ways we have consciously chosen to collude with evil; we
must be freed from our unconscious enthrallment as well.

—WALTER WINK, *UNMASKING THE POWERS*

ON JUNE 1, 2020, then president Donald Trump walked from the
White House through nearby Lafayette Park to Saint John's Church,
accompanied by senior administration officials, including the attorney general, William Barr, and the chairman of the Joint Chiefs of
Staff, General Mark Milley. Just minutes before, federal police had
used tear gas to clear peaceful Black Lives Matter protestors from
the park and churchyard, along with clergy and laity from other
churches who had come out to bring them water and snacks. After
the police drove them out, the president posed on the church steps
for a photograph of him holding up the Bible, surrounded by his
entourage. "We have a great country," he said. "Greatest country in
the world."[1]

---

1. Brian Bennett, "President Trump's Big Moment in Front of a Church Shows He Has Missed
   the Point of the Protests," *Time*, June 2, 2020, https://time.com/5846449/trump-church
   -protests/.

The photo op apparently backfired. The media scrutinized this use of the Bible "as a prop" designed to gain religious sanction for Trump's policies. Many Christians denounced it, including the Right Reverend Mariann Budde, Episcopal bishop of the Washington, DC, diocese, which includes Saint John's Church. Some called it fascist. But among his base, which includes over half of white US Christians,[2] many approved of this display as a symbol of God and country. Several influential conservative Christians affirmed his actions, including Franklin Graham, son of the late Billy Graham; Dallas megachurch pastor Robert Jeffress; David Brody of the Christian Broadcasting Network; president of the Congress of Christian Leaders Johnnie Moore; and Ralph Reed, chairman of the Faith and Freedom Coalition.[3]

These divergent views about this incident at Saint John's Church highlight the theological and political divisions among US Christians that parallel the extreme social divisions in US society. The demonstrators, with support from churchgoers, were passionately but peacefully taking a stand for racial justice in the face of white supremacy and systemic racism. The authorities were asserting their dominant role through violence, then using the Bible, a sacred symbol, to indicate divine approval for their actions.

This staged event was done crudely, but such linking of God and country has been part of US civil religion[4] since the beginning of the colonization of the Americas and throughout our nation's history

---

2. Gregory A. Smith, "White Christians Continue to Favor Trump over Biden, but Support Has Slipped," Pew Research Center, October 13, 2020, https://www.pewresearch.org/fact-tank/2020/10/13/white-christians-continue-to-favor-trump-over-biden-but-support-has-slipped/.

3. McKay Coppins, "The Christians Who Loved Trump's Stunt," *Atlantic*, June 2, 2020, https://www.theatlantic.com/politics/archive/2020/06/trumps-biblical-spectacle-outside-st-johns-church/612529/.

4. US civil religion elevates the nation's founding documents, ideals, and symbols to the status of religion and ascribes sacred purpose and "chosen" status to the nation.

up to this present time. Religious language and symbols, including the Bible and the cross, were used to enact the Doctrine of Discovery, which proclaimed God's blessing on colonization, to initiate and support the slave trade, to sanctify Manifest Destiny while clearing Western lands of most native inhabitants, to justify long-standing persecution of Jews and Muslims, to authorize the Chinese Exclusion Act and Japanese internment camps during World War II, to call for a crusade after the 9/11 bombing of the World Trade Center, to fuel anti-immigrant sentiment and justify separating immigrant children from their parents, and even to storm the Capitol on January 6, 2021. Using religious symbols or language in these ways misleads people, misrepresents God, and fosters moral confusion.

Worldview, ideology, and religion play an important role in upholding or resisting dominating systems of power, as well as being principalities in their own right. Religion is a powerful force; it can be used for good or for evil. It can inspire people to speak truth to power or it can distort truth, as when the devil quoted Scripture to try to convince Jesus that being "Son of God" meant being at the top of the world's hierarchy and that Jesus should assume the role of Messiah that the Jewish people were waiting for: a "Son of David" who would demonstrate kingly supremacy, provide the people with material abundance (at least all the bread they could eat), and command an army to expel the Romans and reestablish the former glory of the kingdom of Israel.

The values and goals represented by these temptations (status, wealth, and worldly power), woven together into a cohesive ideology and strengthened by religion, undergird the dominant social, economic, political, and military institutions of this and every age. They offer a key to the prevailing wisdom not only of Jesus's time but also of our own time. They influence our inner attitudes, assumptions, and beliefs and motivate our allegiances and actions in the outer world. People take these motivations to heart, shape their lives around them, and participate in organizations and institutions that perpetuate these goals, which to most people seem good, right, and normal. Even if we are not aware of it, we are to some degree "possessed by the values and powers of an unjust order."

Paul wrote, "Yet among the mature we do speak wisdom, though it is not a wisdom of this age or of the rulers of this age, who are doomed to perish" (1 Cor 2:6). This chapter describes the "wisdom of this age"—sometimes called the *prevailing wisdom* or *contemporary wisdom*—the corporate mindset of our now global culture that supports and animates the institutions and systems that dominate the world in our day. The very values that Jesus rejected are represented in the values, beliefs, and ideologies that are embodied and expressed by today's global domination system.

The prevailing wisdom of our time assumes (1) social hierarchy among human beings and the right of humans to dominate and exploit the natural world, (2) the market as the key organizing principle for society, and (3) the efficacy of domination and violence in ordering society and conquering evil. Most people take these assumptions for granted as simply the way things are. This keeps us "realistic" within the dominant milieu and prevents us from thinking outside the box of what seems possible. When these assumptions are unconscious or unexamined, they keep us in bondage to the powers, enthralled as collaborators, unconsciously giving our best energies to a system that is "doomed to perish" because it is opposing God and harming God's beloved world.

Religious collaboration is crucial to today's domination system, for it provides moral support and sacralizes these underlying assumptions, which are so pervasive that they are rarely noticed or questioned by most people, who are unknowing participants in an overarching global system that devours life to expand its reach.

By exploring these assumptions and how they manifest in our personal lives, relationships, institutions, and systems, we create space around them and make possible a change of perspective leading to both personal and systemic transformation. For as Walter Wink points out, we must go further than repenting of our conscious collaboration with the powers. We must "be freed from our unconscious enthrallment as well."

SUPREMACY, HIERARCHY, AND DOMINATION

> It cannot be denied that too often the weight of the Christian movement has been on the side of the strong and the powerful and against the weak and oppressed—this, despite the gospel.

> **—HOWARD THURMAN, *SERMONS ON THE PARABLES***

The belief in an authoritarian God lends validity to hierarchical worldviews, with God at the apex of power. Such belief systems may assume Christian superiority, justify religious discrimination, and support Christian hegemony as good, right, and normal.
Seeing God as a father who demands absolute obedience may be used to justify domination, violence, and abuse. Envisioning God as a king at the top of the world's power structures may support views and policies that promote unquestioning obedience. Seeing God as a judge who declares everyone "guilty" of eternal punishment, saved only if they accept Jesus, may lay a foundation for cruelty or scapegoating. Believing that God has granted absolute dominion to human beings over creation justifies destructive exploitation of the earth. But the teachings and actions of Jesus point in a completely different direction: toward a God of mercy, inclusion, justice, and love.

Just as the prevailing wisdom of Jesus's day supported the interconnected, mutually reinforcing network of political, economic, social, and religious institutions that made up the domination system of his time, so it is in our day. Commonly held assumptions support institutionalized systems of hierarchy, materialism, and dominating power and maintain the course of the current globalized system, which is propelling humankind and the natural systems of the earth toward a disastrous future.

The wisdom of this age takes for granted that there are hierarchies among human beings and that we are a superior species and should therefore dominate the natural world for our own gain. It implicitly supports systems of white supremacy, nationalism, settler colonialism, patriarchy, and other forms of bias and institutionalized discrimination, such as discrimination based on age, class, ability, religion, sexual preference, gender identity, immigration status, or other characteristics. Such hierarchies foster the exploitation of vulnerable people and establish the conditions for ecological destruction.

Varied forms of hierarchy intersect, compounding their effects. In the United States, white supremacy and institutionalized racism intersect with income and wealth disparity and with class stratification. Overall, people of color have lower levels of wealth and more difficulty accessing credit than people who are white and are more likely to be consigned to neighborhoods with lower-functioning schools, inadequate health care, poor-quality food (as in food deserts), and toxic pollution (environmental racism). All these factors, along with constant exposure to racist attitudes and policies, qualify as negative stressors that impact health. With the onset of the Covid-19 pandemic, these inequities became even more stark, as people of color died at a much higher rate than did those who were white.

This hierarchical, racialized social/economic system intersects with the realities of a criminal justice system that is biased against poor people and people of color, resulting in a "school to prison pipeline" and leading to disproportionate arrests and imprisonment and to longer sentences. The ongoing Movement for Black Lives began with outrage over police killings of Black people, while diverse racial justice movements continue to highlight the multiple injustices that people of color suffer due to institutionalized racism.

Religious views and institutions can either exacerbate or help alleviate such damaging values and systems. An example today of harm caused by religion is the Christian nationalism that links patriotism, white supremacy, and domination backed by violence with claims of God's blessing upon the United States as a chosen (Christian) nation. After the Capitol insurrection, the Right Reverend Mariann Budde, mentioned earlier, said that Christian nationalism demonstrated "the most heretical, blasphemous forms of Christianity." She then linked it to our nation's history, adding, "This has been part of our nativist, racist Christian past from the beginning. What has been different in the Trump presidency has been the legitimization of it."[5]

When considering examples of religious views and institutions that can help alleviate harm, the most obvious here in the United States is the Black church, which celebrates deep, personal faithfulness while also being true to the prophetic tradition that developed in the crucible of slavery. In "The Black Church: A Gift for All," Black Catholic scholar Daryl Grigsby speaks of the invisibility of the Black church, which "remains unseen, unheard, and unheeded by white Christians."[6] He argues that this invisibility has serious

---

5. Harry Farley, "Trump's Christian Supporters and the March on the Capitol," BBC News, January 15, 2021, https://www.bbc.com/news/world-us-canada-55578096.
6. Daryl Grigsby, "The Black Church: A Gift for All," *New Horizons* 5, no. 1 (2021), https://scholarcommons.scu.edu/newhorizons/vol5/iss1/7/.

consequences, for "it robs white Christians of wisdom derived from centuries of experience where believers depended not on political power, economic security, or racial privilege, but instead on God alone." While the Black church has engaged in the struggle for justice for centuries, its wisdom has not been incorporated to the point of it being considered part of our shared Christian legacy.

In terms of religious hierarchy, the white church in the United States is at the top, while the Black church is at the bottom. Grigsby points out, "White churches have the privilege of uncritically flying American flags near the pulpit or altar, celebrating Memorial Day like a religious ceremony, and seldom speaking with force or power to the demons of racism or nationalism. While white churches sit comfortably within the American paradigm, Black churches, especially in the South, were and are subject to hate crimes and burnings." Furthermore, as other Black liberation theologians have also made clear, by ignoring the Black church, white churches (and white theologians) are complicit in the racism of US culture. In fact, says Grigsby, "By ignoring the Black church, it is really the white church which is invisible and absent in many ways from God's struggle for human justice and dignity." Instead, he argues, "The Christian religion would do well to stop viewing the Black church as a marginal part of its tradition, but rather as a co-creator of its faith."

These relationships, largely unconscious on the part of whites, represent a mindset of superiority and entitlement among the powerful and privileged, which groups people into categories of higher and lower status. It is a manifestation of hubris, the sin of pride. According to many faith traditions, pride is a hindrance to spiritual growth, while humility is a virtue. Yet throughout the ages, people have established hierarchical systems. By identifying with such systems, people who find themselves on a scale above others may enjoy the benefits of privilege and avoid the sense of limitation, vulnerability, and exposure to the risks of social exclusion, economic insecurity, and related violence. People of lesser status may also adopt the values of the dominant system in hope of rising to a higher rung on the social and economic ladder.

Although the conventional wisdom in this age of economic globalization promotes the individualistic goal of pursuing the "American Dream," for many this dream has been a nightmare. By elevating some people who are already privileged over others who are not, this system further harms people who are already being treated unjustly, including people of color, people with disabilities, LGBTQ+ community members, unhoused people, people without medical insurance or other essential services, and many others. The system itself needs to be transformed, and many people are working to make that happen.

Human disregard for nature is another form of hierarchy, based on anthropocentric assumptions that claim human superiority and entitlement over all other parts of creation. Economic and political policies based on this worldview make possible the exploitation of the earth, resulting in grave damage to its living systems, including the climate system, which sustain and nurture human and all other life.

Today's ruling powers are working to establish supreme dominance over human beings and over the natural world. In many cases, we human beings have forgotten who we are: children of one God and members of one human family and of the one interrelated community of life, created from the dust of the earth together with all other life-forms. We are mortal, created to walk humbly with our Creator, in communion with our fellow human beings, and in responsible relationship with all other parts of creation.

> An ecological-feminist theology of nature must
> rethink the whole Western theological tradition of the
> hierarchical chain of being and chain of command.
>
> **—ROSEMARY RADFORD RUETHER, *SEXISM AND GOD-TALK***

Various liberation theologians have explored how concepts that support institutionalized social hierarchies intersect with anthropocentric and utilitarian worldviews that justify ecological destruction. I have surveyed such writings elsewhere and will not repeat them here.[7] I will, however, bring up some distinctive insights of ecofeminists, who have taken the connections between injustice and ecological destruction further by challenging a foundational ideology that has undergirded Western thought for millennia. They claim that the problem of human destruction of the natural world is the result of a worldview warped not just by *anthropocentrism* but also by *androcentrism*, a male-centered view that furthers domination and violence against both women and the earth. Systems of patriarchy present a distorted view of human society and of the human relationship to the natural world.

Further, ecofeminists claim that "all oppressions, such as those based on class, race, religion, gender, sexual preference, ableism, and the natural world, are interconnected within a logic of domination."[8] They link ecological destruction to the ancient Greek hierarchical view of the universe, in which God was seen as

---

7. Sharon Delgado, *Love in a Time of Climate Change: Honoring Creation, Establishing Justice* (Minneapolis: Fortress, 2017), 129–36. These pages include a survey of various feminist, womanist, Indigenous, Black, and other liberation theologians who have linked calls for human justice to ecological concerns.

8. "Ecofeminism," encyclopedia.com, updated August 4, 2020, https://www.encyclopedia .com/places/spain-portugal-italy-greece-and-balkans/malta-political-geography/ ecofeminism. Discrimination based on age should also be included in this list.

transcendent, impersonal, unchanging, and *impassible* (incapable of feeling or suffering).[9] As pure spirit, this "God" was seen as existing at the top of a hierarchical Great Chain of Being, with those nearest the top of the divine order as having the most spirit, and those nearest the bottom having the least. Angels, as purely spiritual, were closest to God, followed in descending value by human beings, animals, plants, and minerals, which were considered mere matter. Each link in the chain had its own hierarchy as well. For humans, kings were at the top, followed by free men of wealth and status, followed by the working classes, lower classes, and enslaved people. Women were near the bottom of the hierarchy, closest to nature, identified with the earth. This worldview supported the established social structure and enabled those in control to stay in power and to oppress people below them on the scale.

Such ideas influenced Western thought, including early Christianity, and were developed more fully in the Middle Ages. They continue to influence contemporary assumptions in conscious or in unconscious ways. As Rosemary Radford Ruether points out,

> An ecological-feminist theology of nature must rethink the whole Western theological tradition of the hierarchical chain of being and chain of command. This theology must question the hierarchy of human over non-human nature as a relation of ontological and moral value. It must challenge the right of the human to treat the nonhuman as private property and material wealth to be exploited. It must unmask the structures of social domination, male over female, owner over worker that mediate this domination over nonhuman nature. Finally, it must question the model

---

9. *Merriam-Webster's Collegiate Dictionary*, 11th ed., 621.

of hierarchy that starts with non-material spirit (God) as the source of the chain of being and continues down to nonspiritual "matter" as the bottom of the chain of being and the most inferior, valueless, and dominated point in the chain of command.[10]

In chapter 4 I included a necessary critique of Christian attitudes that emphasize dominion over nature and presented humans as dependent on God and as interdependent with all other parts of creation, for "In [God] we live and move and have our being" (Acts 17:28). Such teachings enrich a nonhierarchical understanding of a God whose presence pervades, sustains, and encompasses the whole universe and whose caring concern extends to all parts of creation. They complement and add biblical support to the worldviews of many Indigenous peoples about a Creator who brought us into being together with all our human and nonhuman brothers and sisters as part of the interconnected community of life. Such teachings offer an antidote to the prevailing wisdom and its utilitarian approach to the natural world. As followers of Jesus, we are called to love God above all and our neighbors as ourselves and to treat others as we would like to be treated. In this time of ecological destruction, this must include recognizing our other-than-human neighbors as part of our covenant community.

MARKET FUNDAMENTALISM: THE IDOLATRY OF MAMMON

Jesus points to money's invisible power. We are deluded to imagine that it is a mere passive medium of exchange, an abstract reference or token of balance. Mammon itself is a spiritual power

---

10. Rosemary Radford Ruether, *Sexism and God-Talk: Toward a Feminist Theology* (Boston: Beacon, 1993), 85.

that acts with a kind of autonomy, directing and controlling
and, finally, possessing human life. We must not be naïve in this
regard if we are to imagine and create new economic forms.

Jesus said, "You cannot serve God and mammon"[11] (Matt 6:24
NKJV), making clear that even in his day people were tempted to
serve money as an idol rather than treating it simply as a medium of
exchange. Bill Wylie-Kellermann's warning about money as a spiritual power reveals the extent to which the institutionalized power
of money has become ever stronger in this era of advanced global
capitalism. Many human beings, corporations, and even governments serve this idol, which may ultimately possess them.

God's wisdom contrasts with today's dominant view based on
valuing everything according to the market. The current system of
corporate-dominated global capitalism is an extreme expression of the
love of money, a "root of all kinds of evil" (1 Tim 6:10). The foundational belief in this age of *neoliberal* (or "trickle-down") economic
theory[12] is that society must be organized around the market,
which makes the exploitation of human labor and creation's gifts
seem inevitable. This ideology, often called *market fundamentalism*,
undergirds today's global system of unrestrained free-market capitalism and functions much as a secular religion. It is based on the
following precepts: (1) the sanctity of the market, (2) the value of

---

11. *Mammon*: biblical term for riches, often used to describe the debasing influence of material
wealth. Medieval writers commonly interpreted it as an evil demon or god. Since the
sixteenth century, mammon has been used to negatively describe the pursuit of wealth
and has been used in both religious and secular contexts. *Encyclopedia Britannica*, s.v.
"Mammon," by Melissa Petruzzello, accessed December 15, 2021, https://www.britannica
.com/topic/mammon.

12. *Neoliberalism*, also called *laissez-faire economics*, is both an ideology and a policy model
based on the value of free-market competition, free trade and unregulated capital flows,
economic growth as the way to human progress, reduced social spending, and minimal
government intervention in economic and social affairs.

self-interest, (3) the goal of generating wealth, and (4) the vision of limitless economic growth.[13] What ties these precepts together is that they all serve the false god of mammon.

These principles are foundational to the *neoliberal* ideology that promotes the "liberation" of money so that it can flow freely around the world for the benefit of those who control it. There is widespread acceptance of neoliberalism, which is also called the *Washington Consensus* because it has been embraced for decades by both major US political parties, albeit to different degrees. However this plays out in the short term, the ideology of neoliberalism is ultimately "doomed to perish" due to its limited vision and moral failures that have become ever more apparent during the pandemic. As George Monbiot points out,

> The freedom that neoliberalism offers . . . turns out to mean freedom for the pike, not for the minnows. . . . Freedom from trade unions and collective bargaining means the freedom to suppress wages. Freedom from regulation means the freedom to poison rivers, endanger workers, charge iniquitous rates of interest and design exotic financial instruments. Freedom from tax means freedom from the distribution of wealth that lifts people out of poverty. . . . What "the market wants" tends to mean what corporations and their bosses want. . . . The privatization or marketisation of public services such as energy, water, trains, health, education, roads and prisons has enabled corporations to set up tollbooths in front of essential assets

---

13. Sharon Delgado, *Shaking the Gates of Hell: Faith-Led Resistance to Corporate Globalization*, 2nd ed. (Minneapolis: Fortress, 2020), 171–73.

and charge rent, either to citizens or to government, for their use.[14]

In other words, the foundational ideology of the current global economic system is at odds with the teachings of Jesus and with what is needed for the flourishing of life. Those of us who have been socialized into the dominant culture may accept this economic ideology as a given. We hear reports of economic growth and assume it is good. But this ideological construct has been imposed by the false prophets of mammon, who serve and are served by the present historical-based system. This idolatry of money and the harnessing of its spiritual power have been exposed as serving the wealthy few at the expense of most of the earth's people, the poor, and the living systems of the earth.

Today's conventional wisdom supports the dominant view that if we work hard, we will be able to attain and maintain a middle-class lifestyle or better, that the economy can and must continue to grow indefinitely, that free trade will continue to provide us with cheap consumer goods, and that new technologies will provide solutions to all our social and environmental problems. This perspective is deeply affected by the ubiquity of neoliberal ideology, which influences our perspectives on every aspect of life.

Still, "experts" can be found to assure us that each of the above claims is true. But as the reality of humanity's current slide toward disaster becomes clear, it also becomes obvious that policies based on these assumptions will not solve our major problems. Hard work does not necessarily raise one's lifestyle because the system is designed to multiply wealth for the already wealthy. An infinitely

---

14. George Monbiot, "Neoliberalism—the Ideology at the Root of All Our Problems," *Guardian*, April 15, 2016, https://www.theguardian.com/books/2016/apr/15/neoliberalism-ideology-problem-george-monbiot.

growing economy, which demands ever-increasing consumption, debt, speculation, and the ever-expanding exploitation of creation's gifts, is impossible on a finite planet. "Free trade" is not done on a level playing field, since trade agreements are generally designed by powerful corporations for their benefit. New technologies often have unintended social or environmental impacts that cause more harm than good.

Since today's dominant economic views are pervasive, faith communities also fall prey to their ideas and values, and religion is often used to prop them up. The *prosperity gospel* is popular within some Christian and other religious circles. It teaches that God bestows favored people with material wealth, along with all its social benefits. This fits well with today's dominant economic assumptions that place full responsibility on the individual for where they fit on the spectrum of status, wealth, and power while ignoring social factors and historic inequities. Such teachings assume that wealth is a sign of God's favor and that poverty and all that accompanies it indicate personal failure of some kind.

Jesus pointed in the opposite direction. He taught his followers to depend utterly on God for their needs to be met, like the birds of the air and the lilies of the field, and to pray to God to provide their daily bread. Jesus advised his followers not to let go of attachment to earthly treasures but to relinquish such treasures altogether (Matt 6:19–21). He told the rich young man that he lacked one thing and advised him to "go, sell what you own, and give the money to the poor, and you will have treasure in heaven; then come, follow me" (Mark 10:21). The young man couldn't bring himself to do it, so he went away sad, too attached to his worldly goods to devote himself unreservedly to God. Jesus challenged the prevailing economic wisdom of his day. His teachings about money and wealth consistently upheld the values of the reign of God, for "where your treasure is, there your heart will be also" (Matt 6:21).

THE MYTH OF REDEMPTIVE VIOLENCE

Those who are freed from the fear of death, as a
consequence, are able to break the spiral of violence. . . .
The cross is the ultimate paradigm of nonviolence.

—WALTER WINK, *ENGAGING THE POWERS*

The third core assumption underlying the prevailing wisdom is that using force backed by violence to establish dominance is essential for conquering evil. This "myth of redemptive violence"[15] is a term coined by Walter Wink that describes a belief system that takes for granted that domination and violence are essential to establishing and maintaining order, with death as the final sanction. By adopting this perspective, we embody the very evil we seek to overcome. This violent ideology spills over in different forms and infects all levels of society. From children annihilating monsters on video games to air force recruiting videos that present young gamers with the challenge of high-tech precision attacks, from toy guns to mass shootings, from violent TV and movies to online platforms spreading hate, from the school-to-prison pipeline to three-strikes laws, from white supremacist violence to militarized police, from drone strikes to nuclear brinkmanship, violence and domination are taught, practiced, and reinforced at every level of US society. We are immersed in the violence of today's domination system.

The idea that domination and violence can conquer evil and establish order requires a kind of logic divorced from heart and even

---

15. Wink, *Engaging the Powers*, 141.

from common sense. It is the logic of the body count during the Vietnam War, which assumed that the United States was winning if fewer US troops died than North Vietnamese people. It is the logic of the Cold War that based security on how many tens of thousands of nuclear weapons the United States had compared to those of the Soviet Union and that developed nuclear policies known as mutually assured destruction (MAD) and counterforce (first strike). This logic has been extended to include justification for many US policies of domination, including the current development of a new generation of nuclear weapons, the lucrative business of arming the world, and the remote launching of drone attacks even in countries where we are not at war. Such policies reveal the moral bankruptcy of our current system just as surely as the cross reveals the moral bankruptcy of the ruling powers of Jesus's day.

This ideology ignores the potential for alternative ways of addressing evil through creative peacemaking and nonviolent action as modeled by Jesus, who inspired the organized nonviolent resistance campaigns of both Martin Luther King Jr. and Mohandas Gandhi. Rabbi Michael Lerner, of the Network of Spiritual Progressives, has suggested that the United States initiate a "Global Marshall Plan" by investing in peacemaking efforts and bringing ecologically sustainable development to poor nations in the effort to build a more just and peaceful world.[16] But there is no room for this kind of creative proposal in a system that assumes that domination backed by violence is the only way to conquer evil and bring order.

In life, Jesus preached and demonstrated God's compassion, offered forgiveness, and advised his followers to do the same. With his resurrection, God validated his message and nonviolent way of life, bringing hope to both victims and perpetrators for forgiveness,

---

16. "Global Peace Plan," Network of Spiritual Progressives, accessed December 15, 2021, https://spiritualprogressives.org/visionary-strategies/global-peace-plan/.

transformation, and reconciliation. The death and resurrection of Jesus exposed the futility and moral bankruptcy of the powers, which depend upon domination and violence to establish order and control, for God "disarmed the rulers and authorities and made a public example of them, triumphing over them in [the cross]" (Col 2:15). Evil is conquered not by violence but by love.

THE SPIRITUALITY OF AN EPOCH

Whether one is oppressed or privileged, structures
and spirits like white supremacy, patriarchy,
domination are within us, embedded invisibly in
our psyches. Name them and pray them out.

—BILL WYLIE-KELLERMANN, *PRINCIPALITIES IN PARTICULAR*

The "wisdom of this age" is based on the values of status and hierarchy, the idolatry of money, and belief in redemptive violence. These largely unconscious views are at odds with Jesus's values; they express the opposite of his vision of the world as God created it to be. Fortunately, we do not need to fall prey to these delusions. The presuppositions that underlie this prevailing wisdom are false.

In biblical terms, such falsehoods originate with *the father of lies* (John 8:44) and are circulated by the *prince of the power of the air* (Eph 2:2). These terms are metaphors for the principalities and powers, similar to the "devil" who tempted Jesus. This metaphorical language expresses aspects of peoples' experiences about the mystery of evil.

The *devil* or *Satan* has been understood in many ways, including the following: (1) as part of God's heavenly council, the prosecuting attorney who accused Job before God (Job 1:7–12); (2) a personal spirit (perhaps embodied) that tempts people to take a path contrary to what their conscience or their faith tells them is good and right; (3) a malevolent adversary intent on harm "like a roaring lion . . . looking for someone to devour" (1 Pet 5:8); (4) the demonic ruler of this world (John 12:31; Luke 4:5–6); and (5) the ruling authorities of this world, including the spiritual forces of evil that animate them: "For our struggle is not against enemies of blood and flesh, but against the rulers, against the authorities, against the cosmic powers of this present darkness, against the spiritual forces of evil in the heavenly places" (Eph 6:12).

When tempting Jesus, the devil claimed that he was in control of "all the kingdoms of the world" (Luke 4:5–6). Some have said that this was simply a lie he was telling Jesus, but other biblical passages back him up in this claim (John 12:31; 1 Cor 2:8). Walter Wink points to human responsibility by explaining this in terms of human choice and involvement with the demonic powers:

> When . . . Satan declares that he can give Jesus all the kingdoms of the world and their glory, he is not lying; "for it has been delivered to me, and I give it to whom I will." God *permits* Satan such power but has not handed it over to him; *we have delivered it*, as a consequence of all the consciously or unconsciously evil choices we have individually and collectively made against the long-range good of the whole.[17]

Wink also demythologized the term *Satan* by making the case that it represents the dominant milieu of a culture at a particular time in history:

---

17. Wink, *Unmasking the Powers*, 24.

Satan is the real interiority of a society that idolatrously pursues its own enhancement as the highest good. Satan is the spirituality of an epoch, the peculiar constellation of alienation, greed, inhumanity, oppression, and entropy that characterizes a specific period of history as a consequence of human decisions to tolerate and even further such a state of affairs.[18]

These words characterize the time in which Jesus lived, when Rome dominated Judea and the Roman army occupied Jerusalem. Satan as the "spirituality of an epoch" also characterizes our age and the current US-based global empire, which assumes American exceptionalism and "idolatrously pursues its own enhancement as the highest good." The present global culture of unrestrained free-market capitalism promotes overconsumption, creates extremes of wealth and poverty, desecrates creation, and glorifies violence. The "alienation, greed, inhumanity, oppression, and entropy" that characterize this specific period of history are made possible by the personal decisions of many individuals to "tolerate and even further such a state of affairs."

This sinister, even demonic, spirituality is not vague or amorphous but is embodied by representative human beings and by concrete institutions and systems that dominate our world—that is, by the rulers of this age and those who have given themselves over to them. As institutional powers, some churches align themselves with the status quo and base their teachings on the very values that Jesus rejected. Fortunately, other churches are encouraging members to think critically and to take communal actions that challenge the powers and that lay the foundation for a hopeful future.

---

18. Wink, *Naming the Powers*, 25.

Many Christians are engaged in denominational efforts and participating with ecumenical and interfaith organizations in critiquing the underlying values of the current system, challenging the dominant worldview, resisting idolatrous institutions that harm people and the earth, and supporting movements for social and ecological transformation. As followers of Jesus, we are challenged to identify the "structures and spirits" of domination that are within us and to "name them and pray them out," and we are invited to join the growing number of people who share the values of inclusion, equity, and nonviolence and who are working to build a more compassionate, just, and peaceful world. Surely this is what it means in our time to follow the one who came so that we "may have life, and have it abundantly" (John 10:10).

THE ANTI-IMPERIAL WISDOM OF GOD

> The anti-imperial meaning of Good Friday and Easter
> are particularly important and challenging for American
> Christians. . . . We are the Roman Empire of our time,
> both in our foreign policy and in the shape of economic
> globalization that we as a country vigorously advocate.

—MARCUS J. BORG AND JOHN DOMINIC CROSSAN, *THE LAST WEEK*

The wisdom of God is anti-imperial. It reveals the futility of the wisdom of this world. Worldly status does not confer virtue. Wealth does not signify divine favor. Might does not make right. This is still a subversive message. This is still good news.

In closing this chapter, we return to the story of the police clearing peaceful protestors at Saint John's Church for a presidential photo op with the Bible. To those who live by the Spirit, the words of Bishop Mariann Edgar Budde ring true: "We of the Diocese of Washington follow Jesus in his Way of love. We aspire to be people of peace and advocates of justice. In no way do we support the President's incendiary response to a wounded, grieving nation. In faithfulness to our Savior who lived a life of nonviolence and sacrificial love, we align ourselves with those seeking justice for the death of George Floyd and countless others through the sacred act of peaceful protest."

Those of us who seek to follow Jesus are offered the gifts of the Spirit, including discernment, which enables us to discern truth from falsehood and good from evil and to perceive "God's wisdom in a mystery." That wisdom of God was taught and exemplified by Jesus of Nazareth, whose Spirit is with us, guiding and teaching us still. Jesus promised his followers that "I will give you words and a wisdom that none of your opponents will be able to withstand or contradict" (Luke 21:15). May it be so, as we move from personal and societal bondage into freedom, following Jesus in the direction of the promised reign of God. We turn now to the powers that dominate the world in our time, the rulers of this age.

CHAPTER 7
INSTITUTIONALIZED DOMINATION

THE RULERS OF THIS AGE

The Bible from beginning to end is a sustained protest
against the domination systems of the ancient world.

—MARCUS J. BORG, *CONVICTIONS*

THE PREVIOUS CHAPTER addressed "the wisdom of this age"—that
is, the assumptions, concepts, values, and belief systems that make
up the dominant spiritual and cultural milieu of our time. This
chapter focuses on "the rulers of this age" (1 Cor 2:6–8), the representative human beings and dominant institutions and systems
that govern, express, and enforce the prevailing wisdom. According
to Walter Wink, "This overarching network of powers is what we
are calling the Domination System. It is characterized by unjust
economic relations, oppressive political relations, biased race relations, patriarchal gender relations, hierarchical power relations, and
the use of violence to maintain them all."[1] Together, the political,
economic, military, and ideological powers that make up today's
domination system demonstrate, promote, and reward the pursuit
of status, wealth, and dominating power.

These three values are related to "the three evils" that Martin
Luther King Jr. identified: "the evil of racism, the evil of poverty,

---

1. Walter Wink, *The Powers That Be* (New York: Galilee Doubleday, 1999), 39.

and the evil of war."[2] In his 1967 speech "Beyond Vietnam," he called these same three evils "the giant triplets of racism, extreme materialism, and militarism." He said, "We must rapidly begin the shift from a thing-oriented society to a person-oriented society. When machines and computers, profit motives and property rights, are considered more important than people, the giant triplets of racism, extreme materialism, and militarism are incapable of being conquered."[3] More recently, author/activist Bill Wylie-Kellermann has named these three evils "white supremacy, predatory capitalism, and omnicidal militarism" as yet another way to express how they manifest today.[4]

Racism describes the systemic evil of a hierarchical society mired in white supremacy, which bestows privileges enjoyed by those who are white and discriminates against people of color. Poverty, the inverse of wealth, is created by the endless growth required by the extreme materialism of predatory capitalism, which creates massive wealth for those on the top tiers of the economic ladder but corresponding misery and want for those at the bottom. Contemporary war fighting and the buildup of weapons of mass destruction are expressions of omnicidal militarism, which enforces today's domination system through militarized police and the global projection of military power. While human history is littered with tragedy—and indeed, evil—today's complex global network of interconnected institutions is overseeing the undoing of creation. This system represents a threat to human civilization and to earth's natural systems that dwarfs anything humanity has faced before.

<hr>

2. Martin Luther King Jr., an address at the Hungry Club Forum, May 10, 1967, https://www.theatlantic.com/magazine/archive/2018/02/martin-luther-king-hungry-club-forum/552533/.

3. Martin Luther King Jr., "Beyond Vietnam," Martin Luther King, Jr. Research and Education Institute, Stanford University, accessed December 15, 2021, https://kinginstitute.stanford.edu/king-papers/documents/beyond-vietnam.

4. Bill Wylie-Kellermann, speaking in a Zoom meeting on "the powers," February 11, 2021.

I write about these dangers not to drive people to hopelessness or despair but to point in the direction of hope in action. We cannot move in a direction based on truth unless we expose the lies upon which our now global civilization is built. The purpose of this chapter is to identify "the rulers of this age," describe their dehumanizing inner and deadly outer effects, and facilitate a conversation about how to engage them. This will set the stage for the final chapters of the book, which challenge us to live into the faith of Jesus as authentic human beings.

THIS PRESENT DARKNESS

Put on the whole armor of God, so that you may be able to
stand against the wiles of the devil. For our struggle is not against
enemies of blood and flesh, but against the rulers, against the
authorities, against the cosmic powers of this present darkness,
against the spiritual forces of evil in the heavenly places.

—EPHESIANS 6:11–13

In August 2020, I went to a march for racial justice in my small Northern California hometown of Nevada City. We all wore masks. I planned to stay socially distanced at the back of the march, but it became impossible when a group of ruffians without masks blocked our path and began to assault us. They wore white nationalist and Trump insignia, yelled racist and homophobic slurs, used flags as weapons, punched people, pushed people down, and destroyed property. Several wore crosses. One wore a T-shirt that said, "I stand for the flag, I kneel for the cross." They pursued us and yelled in our faces, "Get the f— out of our town!"

After the assault, the newly formed local Patriots Pushing Back group bragged on Facebook that law enforcement had been on their side. It had seemed to be so. Police officers had walked behind the aggressors and at times had walked with them. They had refused to respond to pleas for assistance from those who were being assaulted or witnessing assaults. Instead of separating the two groups or arresting those who were violent, police escorted the self-described "patriots" as they pursued peaceful protesters down the street.

We experienced this frightening eruption of hate in our small community, but it was not an isolated incident. Groups of white supremacists had recently roughed people up in nearby towns and cities as well. My sister who lives in the South commented ironically, saying, "Welcome to North Carolina," where widespread racism is assumed, at least by those who admit it. Organized hate is also here where I live in California, embedded in our communities.

It feels as if a cloud of darkness has descended upon the land, a spirit of evil fueled by hate that is circulating and spreading like the fires and smoke consuming our drought-damaged forests during California's now nearly year-round fire season. The evil of racism has plagued the United States from the beginning of its history. It is indeed our country's "original sin."[5] Nationalism, white supremacy, patriarchy, and heterosexism are deeply interwoven in US society, as are other forms of institutionalized discrimination. But organized white supremacist groups, many of them armed, grew stronger after the election of Barack Obama, our first Black president, and surged during the presidency of Donald Trump, inspired by his racist words and discriminatory policies.

Overt white supremacist violence escalated around the country during and after the 2020 election, culminating (so far) in the insurrection at the Capitol on January 6, 2021. Many were shocked at how unprepared the Capitol Police were, but extremist groups

---

5. Jim Wallis, *America's Original Sin: Racism, White Privilege, and the Path to a New America* (Grand Rapids, MI: Brazos, 2016).

that supported Donald Trump had been organizing the event on social media for weeks, with many signaling their plans for violence. Armed militia groups had been staging threatening events around the county for months, including at state capitols. Organizations that monitor hate groups and even the FBI had been noting the increase in hate crimes and warning about the growing threat posed by domestic terrorists, especially white supremacist groups and armed right-wing militias.

The 2020 virtual Republican National Convention should have been a wake-up call that violence would likely be used to prevent the peaceful transfer of power if Trump lost the election. Speakers at the convention used racist dog whistles, words intended to stoke fires of fear, hate, and violence that fueled his right-wing base but that people who are unattuned to covert racism cannot hear. They put forward a vision of a second Trump administration that was truly terrifying, demonstrating support for racism, xenophobia, violence, and authoritarianism. Speakers consistently used Christian language to sanctify their views, not only distorting but inverting the message of compassion and inclusion that Jesus proclaimed.

But where does such distortion originate—at the top or at the bottom of society? In the power structures themselves or in the people? Another way to ask the question is this: Why did I begin this chapter on the rulers of this age with the story of an assault by violent aggressors at a peaceful protest in a small Northern California town? Wouldn't it make more sense to start at the top of this country's power structure, with the leaders and policy makers, those in authority who have power to make change?

I started here to show that the values and mindset expressed and demonstrated by those at the top of institutional power are shared and practiced by people at the bottom, for the powers and principalities can only prosper with human participation. I start where I live, in a divided community struggling with the realities we face in this fearful time of social breakdown. As in Jesus's time, some people experience this time as "the end of the age" (Matt 24:3). Some fear the end of the United States as they know it, as demographics shift, resulting in a white minority, and some vow to fight it in any way possible, up to and including violent revolution or civil war. Some warn against a fascist takeover of government as voting rights and the structures holding democracy together are threatened. Others believe it is the "last days" before the end times, when things will get worse before Christ comes again. Still others see (and some seek to remedy) the existential global threats of climate change and nuclear disaster. Social, economic, or environmental collapse seems imminent as Covid-19 variants, economic woes, rising temperatures, extreme weather, systemic racism, and violence continue to decimate families and communities. Fear, tension, anger, and distress abound, contributing to the unrest experienced by so many. Similar dynamics may be at play as in Jesus's time, when the Jewish people were hoping for a messiah who would overthrow Rome and reestablish Jerusalem to its former glory, as some people have looked to Donald Trump as a messiah figure who will "Make America Great Again."

While primary responsibility falls upon those with institutionalized authority and responsibility to work for the common good, the current dysfunction is shared by people at every level of society. The Hebrew prophets primarily challenged kings, priests, and false prophets to repent from idolatry and injustice but also the Hebrew people. Jesus, too, spoke to those in positions of authority but also to the people themselves. While those with leadership responsibility have influence and decision-making power, each of us is responsible for the choices we make. The forces of this present darkness are intertwined; they are present in our psyches and at work at every level of society. So whether we start at the top of the social hierarchy or at the bottom, clearly our struggle against the "rulers, the authorities, the cosmic powers of this present darkness, against the spiritual forces of evil in the heavenly places" is a spiritual struggle that will require prayer as well as action on multiple levels.

THE POWERS THAT BE

For to survive in the mouth of this dragon we call america,
we have had to learn this first and most vital lesson—that
we were never meant to survive. Not as human beings.
And neither were most of you here today, Black or not.

—AUDRE LORDE, "THE TRANSFORMATION OF
SILENCE INTO LANGUAGE AND ACTION"

At this point we step back and take a closer look at the concept of the principalities and powers, how they have assumed so much power over human beings, and why this concept is important to this book.[6] We look specifically at the interlocking network of institutions, structures, bureaucracies, and ideologies that make up the overarching global system that dominates the world in our day, referred to as the domination system. As explained earlier, these powers include not only their obvious outer manifestations but also their inner dimensions—that is, they are not only physical powers but also cosmic or spiritual.[7] To reiterate N. T. Wright's definition of the dominant powers, "When Paul speaks of the 'rulers and

---

6. In *Shaking the Gates of Hell*, I write comprehensively about the biblical and theological roots of the concept of the powers and principalities and about the interlocking network of institutional powers that dominate the world today.

7. "The New Testament also speaks of cosmic powers at work in the world, who stand in opposition to God, but whose power has already been broken and subordinated to the power of God made manifest in Christ." Achtemeier, *Harper's Bible Dictionary* (Rom 8:35; 1 Cor 15:24; Eph 1:21; Col 2:15; Pet 3:22), 816.

authorities,' he means both the visible rulers, the Herods, the Caesars, the governors, and the priests, and the 'invisible' rulers, the dark powers that stand behind them and operate through them."[8]

These ruling powers are meant to serve a positive purpose by bringing order to life but are sinful ("demonic") to the degree that people give ultimate loyalty to these less-than-ultimate institutions, loyalty that is solely due to God. Together they dominate our cultural, social, economic, and political lives. By reflecting and reinforcing this world's values and systems of thought, these institutional powers cause great harm. At the same time, this structural disorder is reflected and reinforced by individuals, for the powers are present in our psyches, and we are part of the whole.

We human beings participate in institutions that pretend to be limitless. Today's domination system and the institutions that comprise it have taken on a life of their own and function according to their own imperatives—that is, to survive and extend their power—but to do this, they depend on human support and participation. Speaking metaphorically, they conscript human beings into service, demand allegiance, pretend to be ultimate, and insert themselves into the place of God in people's lives. As we give ourselves over to these idols, we take on their values and strengthen the institutions to which we submit. By investing these social inventions with our energies and loyalties, we identify with their illusion of transcendence over natural limits while offering our bodies in their service. Through this process, today's dominant institutions have established supreme dominance over human civilization and over nature.

The most obvious manifestation of the current domination system is the interlocking network of global bureaucracies, national

---

8. Wright, *Day the Revolution Began*, 77.

governments, transnational corporations, and other institutions that make up the overarching system of corporate globalization. Proponents claim that the ongoing advance of unrestrained free-market capitalism and the incorporation of all countries into this system is a natural and inevitable process. It is not. The system is designed to support not the common good but the good of those for whom it is designed. It runs by its own imperatives—the survival and growth of the system itself. For this reason, we can say with Audre Lorde, "We were never meant to survive. Not as human beings."

We are all in relationship with these dehumanizing powers—Stringfellow would say as victims or as intended victims. For instance, all of us are impacted by racism: "For white citizens to be blinded to [systemic racial injustice in the United States] is a victimization of them as human beings—consigning them to a delusive state where conscience is dead—just as much as the more blatant and public dehumanization visited upon blacks."[9] Whether we realize it or not, we are impacted by the current milieu of spiritual confusion, moral paralysis, violence, and chaos, which are among the dehumanizing inner effects of the principalities and powers.

It is difficult to understand these contemporary powers that continue to crucify Christ in our day and to discern how we can faithfully engage them. If our struggle is "not against enemies of blood and flesh" but against the powers and principalities, what is the nature of our struggle? The idea of the demonic, which we discussed briefly in the last chapter, seems antiquated. People may become mentally ill, but they don't really become "possessed"—or do they? How are these ancient biblical terms to be understood in this postmodern age? We will look now at today's media as a case study of a contemporary institutional power.

____

9. Stringfellow, *Ethic for Christians*, 87.

> In effect, [social media] take on a life of their own and
> become agents determining important aspects of our
> social reality. Social world-makers, if you like. . . . Fake
> news playing to those who "like" fake news. It's the
> conversational core of a political base, as it were.
>
> **—BILL WYLIE-KELLERMANN, *PRINCIPALITIES IN PARTICULAR***

In the previous chapter, we explored the concept of demonic powers, which has been interpreted in many ways over the centuries. In the Bible, they are often personified. In this twenty-first century, a more apt metaphor than "prince of the power of the air" may be "prince of the power of the airwaves," referring to the media. The media as a power demonstrates that the demonic is not abstract but embodied, manifest, and expressed through institutions, systems, technologies, images, ideologies, or other tangible structures.

According to William Stringfellow, when people relinquish their human faculties by giving themselves over to these idols, they become dehumanized and possessed by them. Take, for example, institutionalized racism and white supremacy. While these principalities are manifest in dominant organizations and even at the highest levels of government, they are also embodied in smaller groups and individuals and expressed through white fragility or white privilege, conscious or implicit bias, racial discrimination, outright hate, racially motivated violence, or uncritical acceptance of the (racially unjust) status quo.

The insurrectionist white supremacists who stormed the US Capitol on January 6, 2021, were incited by former president Donald Trump and his supporters with vitriol, lies about election fraud, false promises, and threats to both Democratic and Republican officials who did not support attempts to overthrow election results. Social media posts went viral, spewing lies, hate, and preposterous conspiracy theories that many people still believe, including some in Congress. Many who responded to Trump's call to come to Washington, where "it will be wild," and to march on the Capitol believed that they were following the orders of their leader. Some expected Trump to declare martial law and believed that the Capitol Police and National Guard would join them to stop what they saw as an illicit process of confirming Joe Biden as the winner of the presidential election. Were they simply deluded? Acting on their own volition as free and independent thinkers? Rather, they may have been predisposed or vulnerable to racist ideology, captured by an idea that possessed them, enthralled by an authoritarian president to whom they gave unquestioning loyalty, and caught up in a mob mentality that reinforced the momentum once they got to the Capitol. This is an example of a demythologized understanding of possession today.

The media has some responsibility for the January 6 insurrection. It is an example of a contemporary institutional power that influences cultural attitudes. It is often through the media that society's dominant ideas take hold and are reinforced in people's minds. Personified as a creaturely power, we can imagine the media as a colossal beast with billions of differentiated tentacles seeking to reach into the lives of everyone on earth, track and transmit messages, and call each person by name. Cultural content is relayed through these tentacles—that is, through the airwaves and other transmitters of electronic connectivity—both shaping and expressing public opinion.

The prevailing wisdom is incarnate in the media, including the internet, influencing people, making converts, and keeping people enthralled. There is danger here, especially when the idol of money determines what is relayed. Today's mainstream media, dominated by large for-profit corporations, give life to this beast by using messaging, advertising, and programming to shape public opinion in ways that increase corporate profits and reinforce the values of status, wealth, and dominating power. In today's vitriolic social and political climate, fake news and conspiracy theories abound, distorting reality not just in the echo chambers of the internet but also on many television channels and radio stations. Such programming reaches into most homes and influences not only the public but also elected officials at the highest levels of government.

Fortunately, some news media hold to standards of truth based on evidence and identify opinions as distinct from fact. Rigorous, evidence-based investigative journalism continues to uncover facts that have been hidden. For anyone who knows how and is willing to do the hard work of searching for reputable sources, facts can be verified. Tragically, many prefer to remain in "the shallows"[10] of the internet and to believe whatever is circulating in their social media bubbles.

When commercial media give priority to the most profitable programming, what is transmitted is what pays. In this time of such misleading phrases as "alternative facts" and competing charges of "fake news," this becomes even more dangerous. In our current system, the internet, too, is a profit-making enterprise. Companies use algorithms designed to keep people online for hours and to analyze what messages people "like" or forward so they can send targeted ads, programs, or messaging to potential customers. This includes the targeting of young teens with idealized images of attractiveness that reduce their self-esteem and leave them feeling depressed. When false images, distorted values, fake news, conspiracy theories, scandal, and hate are what sell, much of the material that comes

---

10. Nicholas Carr, *The Shallows: What the Internet Is Doing to Our Brains* (New York: W. W. Norton, 2020).

across the airwaves (on television, radio, computer, or smartphone) is focused on the most superficial, shocking, inane, or hateful events or statements, fostering outrage and propelling itself forward in additional news reports, reactionary comments, and endless paralyzing analysis. Biases are reinforced. These messages cannot be separated from the people or institutions that relay the messages. As Marshall McLuhan famously said, "The medium is the message."[11]

The World Wide Web, together with the internet that hosts and transmits web content,[12] illustrates the idea that the powers and principalities are not disembodied spirits but incarnate in some way in the world. At one point in my use of computers, I wondered about the nature of the "Cloud," where so much web content is stored. Then I realized that (of course), such content is not just floating around in the air in some disembodied cloud; it is stored in vast complexes of expensive, energy-consuming computers in specific locations. These massive computers are interconnected, allowing content to be stored and shared from person to person or from group to group. Ideas, images, news, personal messages, propaganda, and other content is accessed, analyzed, clarified or distorted, and transmitted from computer to computer. Some messages go viral, bringing good or evil impacts beyond the control of any human being.

As this technology evolves, it incorporates ever more creative forms of artificial intelligence (AI), such as interpretive language skills, voice recognition and verbal response, automated financial transactions, surveillance and tracking, high-speed trading, and multiple other features based on algorithms that function at an

---

11. "The Medium Is the Message by Marshall McLuhan," Animated Book Review, *Eudaimonia*, December 7, 2016, https://obtaineudaimonia.medium.com/the-medium-is -the-message-by-marshall-mcluhan-8b5d0a9d426b.

12. "Worldwide Web vs Internet—What's the Difference?," Newsround, BBC, March 11, 2019, https://www.bbc.co.uk/newsround/47523993#:~:text=The%20world%20wide%20 web%2C%20or,emails%20and%20files%20travel%20across.&text=The%20world%20 wide%20web%20contains,roads%20like%20houses%20and%20shops.

everyday level and that many of us now take for granted. In fact, the internet functions as a form of AI itself. It is self-perpetuating and self-correcting, just as many scientists claim that advances in AI technology will soon allow robots to cross over and begin to create and improve themselves in ways far beyond what limited human beings can imagine. Although humans are involved at every level of our "wired" existence, internet communications have taken on a life of their own, including in the far reaches of the "dark web." The goal of online media platforms, like the goal of every power (figuratively speaking), is to do what they can to survive, extend their reach, and advance their power, and that is what they are doing.

Because the media as an institutional power is part of today's domination system, this discussion would not be complete without mentioning the ubiquitous surveillance apparatus that makes a mockery of the right to privacy and demonstrates how far the colossal profit-seeking beast of the media has come in reaching into our lives and in calling each of us by name. In 2013, whistleblower Edward Snowden exposed the 24–7 global surveillance of citizens undertaken by US intelligence agencies and private corporations. What has been called the surveillance-industrial complex[13] has only become more sophisticated since then. It includes governments working in collaboration with the globalized surveillance industry, which surveils us through our phone and computer activities, financial transactions, facial-recognition technologies, global positioning systems (GPS), and in other ways. The industry builds profiles on us and sells our personal information to corporations or governments. Of course, technological advances that allow for increased surveillance can be used for good

---

13. Kirstie Ball and Laureen Snider, eds., *The Surveillance-Industrial Complex: A Political Economy of Surveillance* (London: Routledge, 2019).

or for ill: to engage in fraud or detect it, to run child trafficking rings or break them up, to organize white supremacist groups planning violence or identify and disrupt such groups.

Still, online media, especially social media, is addictive (and therefore dehumanizing) by design, since that is what pays. It intentionally creates habitual patterns of use aimed at being hard to break. It is multifaceted, pervasive, and powerful, but it is just one of the interrelated institutions that make up today's domination system.

The point of this discussion of the media is to show that the "spiritual forces of evil"—that is, the demonic powers that are (metaphorically speaking) in rebellion against God—are not just disembodied spirits floating around, as first-century people (and some people today) might believe—or at least that is not what makes them so dangerous. They are embodied in actual technologies, images, ideologies, worldviews, institutions, representative human beings, or systems that have grown beyond human control and have taken on a life of their own. These powers carry and transmit the values, attitudes, goals, beliefs, and impulses that drive individuals and motivate collective action. We may think we are living as autonomous and free human beings, but to the degree that we give ourselves over to these idols, we become enslaved to them and blind to their effects. Conversely, by becoming aware of the inner, spiritual dimensions of the principalities and powers, we are able to name and confront them.

CORPORATE GLOBALIZATION

If there is an idol behind the idols of corporate globalization,
it is Mammon. Here is the spirituality that drives the logic
of growth. Capital consolidates. Money begets money.
The rich get richer. . . . And because money has this

The interrelated institutions that make up the overarching system of corporate globalization demonstrate the values of institutionalized hierarchy, extremes of wealth and poverty, and dominating power backed by violence. These ruling institutions are entrenched in a global system designed to multiply wealth, dominated by corporations, propelled by money, powered by fossil fuels, enforced by militarism, and legitimized by secular and religious ideologies that are captured by the lure of status, wealth, and worldly power. This global system, based on unregulated free-market capitalism, originated in the United States and has been exported to the rest of the world.

In this hierarchical global system, the United States claims for itself the status of preeminent nation, a beacon of democracy and economic and military power. Nationalism abounds, as the country portrays itself as uniquely deserving of favored status among nations. It claims rights and privileges that other nations are denied, such as the right to overconsume and to intervene in other nations' internal affairs. The "American way of life," based on conspicuous consumption, is held up as a model to other nations and is engineered into so-called free trade agreements, despite its ecological costs. Meanwhile, as wealth is siphoned up to the top 1 percent and public services are cut, vast swaths of the US middle class slide into poverty, and people who struggle month to month fall from poverty into destitution. While promising to bestow its benefits on those who play by its rules, the rewards of the system are vastly unequal, both domestically and abroad.

The lure of wealth, already so powerful in Jesus's day, is far stronger today when the idolatry of wealth has become so widespread. Mammon rules. The idea that "money makes the world go around" is not abstract or metaphorical—electronic transfers drive the global economy. In this globalized network of interlocking political, economic, ideological, and military powers, corporations dominate, especially big banks and financial institutions that control the flow of capital and keep the system going—and growing. The result of this system and its idolatry of money is that the worth of everything is measured according to its dollar value. The gifts of the earth, the fruits of human labor, public services, and community resources are monetized and sold to keep the stock market rising, the economy growing, and capital flowing through the global financial system as wealth accumulates among the elite. This reality has become even more stark as the world's ten richest billionaires doubled their income during the pandemic, while the income of 99% of the world's people decreased and millions fell into poverty.

Institutionalized domination and violence are apparent throughout this global system, driven by the myth of redemptive violence. The United States stands out among developed nations for its extremes of social violence. It is also the global system's primary enforcer. The US criminal justice system suppresses domestic dissent through mass surveillance, militarized police forces, a racist criminal justice system, and an inequitable and punitive legal system that incarcerates more people and a greater percentage of its population than any other country on earth, disproportionately people of color. The United States enforces the system internationally with political and economic pressure, backed up by the most powerful and expensive military-industrial complex in history, and by stockpiling weapons with the capacity to extinguish much of life on earth. Where loyalty to the system cannot be bought, it must be coerced.

As massive corporations and a relatively few superrich individuals employ vast stores of wealth and immense political power to dominate national governments, public policies become ever-more conducive to their profit-making purposes. Likewise, transnational corporations dominate global institutions and promote trade agreements that champion corporate rights and create binding rules for governments to follow. In this way, corporations create a global environment in which they can thrive. Corporate subsidies, tax breaks and tax havens, financial speculation, privatization and deregulation of public resources, usurious loans, and complex financial instruments that siphon wealth to the top demonstrate the harm of a global economic machine that is spinning out of human control. The insatiable appetite of this global system of wealth-driven corporate capitalism continues to devour the earth, turning its gifts into commodities, defiling its goodness, decimating our human and other-than-human companions, reducing prospects for future generations, and diminishing our humanity.

The institutional forces at work today are akin to those responsible for putting Jesus to death. The rulers of this age continue to enact policies that wreak havoc among human beings as ecosystems collapse, communities disintegrate, inequity grows, violence multiplies, and militarism expands. The web of life unravels as the global system of unregulated free-market capitalism consolidates its control over the planet. The multifaceted crisis we face today is the direct result of a global system that has grown beyond human control and has taken on a life of its own. To the degree that the institutions that make up this system harm human beings or destroy God's creation, they stand opposed to God and should be resisted and called to account.

When Jesus walked on earth, he challenged the domination system of his day, and it responded by putting him to death. Those of us who follow Jesus and join with others to seek peace, justice, and healing can expect the ruling powers to respond to us as they did to Jesus. The powers and principalities seek to be absolute and immortal, but only God is absolute—empires come and go. Today's dominant global system contains the seeds of its own destruction, and signs of systemic failure can be seen all around. The crucifixion of Jesus reveals their godlessness, and the resurrection of Jesus demonstrates their futility.

NAMING, UNMASKING, AND ENGAGING THE POWERS

Part of preaching the gospel for us is to confront contemporary institutions that are manifestations of the demonic.

—NATHAN RIEGER, "GOOD NEWS FOR POSTMODERN MAN"

The three books in Walter Wink's trilogy on the powers are aptly titled *Naming the Powers, Unmasking the Powers,* and *Engaging the Powers.*[14] In this and previous chapters, I have focused on naming and unmasking the powers by sharing some of what I understand about them, giving concrete examples, and passing on insights from those who have developed contemporary language for understanding them. In the coming chapters, I will explore ways of engaging them, for this is part of what it means to follow Jesus in today's world.

Engaging the institutional powers involves a struggle not simply against their harmful outward manifestations but also against our tendency to internalize their values and be swallowed up in their milieu. Our struggle against "the spiritual forces of evil in the heavenly places" is not simply external, for all of us participate to some

---

14. Wink, *Naming the Powers; Unmasking the Powers; Engaging the Powers.*

degree in the powers that are manifest in the outer world, and our inner landscape is a microcosm that encompasses the whole.

The inner, spiritual impacts of the principalities and powers result in dehumanization, so much so that Stringfellow claimed that our primary challenge is "how to live humanly in the midst of the fall."[15] Walter Wink advanced this idea by interpreting the *Son of Man* designation to describe Jesus as the *Human One*[16] and by pointing to Jesus as the one who embodied and modeled what it means to be fully human and to live as a free and authentic human being. Living in freedom with our human faculties and moral agency intact requires resistance to the constant, dehumanizing assaults by the powers and creative response when opportunities for positive change present themselves, on both personal and societal levels.

We are called to exercise our freedom in Christ as we relate to the powers, calling them back to their rightful role as servants, rather than as dominators, of life. In this way, by living in creative resistance to anything that engenders futility and oppression, grounded in God's love, and renewed and motivated by the Spirit's call, we participate in God's triumph over the powers and principalities in our time.

---

15. Stringfellow, *Ethic for Christians*, 55.
16. Wink, *Unmasking the Powers*, 173.

TRANSFORMING THE WORLD

PRACTICING RESURRECTION

CHAPTER 8
PERSONAL TRANSFORMATION FOR A TRANSFORMED WORLD

Humans are not made for "heaven" but for the new heavens
and new earth. . . . The "goal" is not "heaven," but a
renewed human vocation within God's renewed creation.

—N. T. WRIGHT, *THE DAY THE REVOLUTION BEGAN*

CELEBRATING THE JOY of Easter in our time is filled with paradox. How can we understand and celebrate the resurrection of Jesus when corporate wealth, institutional power, and ideologically driven people in high places dominate public policy and endanger the world? For the word of the cross to be relevant in our time, it must address the threat posed by the powers and principalities to human life and to creation itself.

In previous chapters, we named and exposed some of the spiritual distortions and physical harm caused by the powers. We transition now to part 4, "Transforming the World: Practicing Resurrection." Because we are called by God and empowered by the Holy Spirit to live resurrected lives, these final three chapters discuss the transformative power of God to bring light out of darkness and life out of death. Here in chapter 8, we explore biblical metaphors that describe how the Spirit-filled reality revealed by Jesus brings about reconciliation with God (atonement) and spiritual transformation. In chapter 9, we discuss how prayer and other spiritual practices enable us to experience the ongoing presence of God and empower us, no matter how deep the darkness, to follow Jesus and live resurrected lives. These topics lead into chapter 10, which points in the direction of hope in action, for the promise of the gospel is a "renewed human vocation within God's renewed creation"—that is, personal transformation for a transformed world.

As I begin this chapter, I have just awakened to a new day. I begin with gratitude—for life, this very life that includes every experience that has brought me to this moment and all that I have ever loved. Life itself is a gift. Each new day and each new moment present us with the opportunity to start over and to remember afresh who we are as members of the community of creation and as members of the family of God.

At the same time, as we consider the story of Jesus in today's context and the ways Christ is being crucified today, the burden of human wrongs feels very heavy indeed. We are enmeshed in cultures, belief systems, institutions, and systems that support the deadly status quo, many of us as victims and fewer as seeming beneficiaries. We struggle to be faithful yet are aware of ways that we are either unwilling or unable to renounce the very behaviors that contribute to harming ourselves or others. We require divine aid.

For people who place their faith in Jesus, this aid is available through the gospel, the word of the cross. This chapter explores and weighs the value of several biblical metaphors that have informed Christians about this "good news" since the time of Jesus and continue to inform us today. I contend that metaphors and interpretations that illustrate the nonviolent, inclusive, compassionate, forgiving nature of God are more valuable because they are truer to the God of love that Jesus both demonstrated and proclaimed. Seeking clarity about the meaning of the word of the cross is not simply a matter of identifying a correct doctrine, for the foundation of Christian faith is not doctrine but the lived experience of the presence of the risen Christ and lives transformed by the Spirit, as described in Scripture and attested to by witnesses throughout the ages. As people who seek to live by the faith of Jesus, the good news must equip us to call the powers back to their role to serve rather than dominate life and inspire us to participate in the ongoing story of God at work in the world.

OVERCOMING ALIENATION

The human problem is not so much "sin" seen as the
breaking of moral codes . . . but rather idolatry and
the distortion of genuine humanness it produces.

—N. T. WRIGHT, *THE DAY THE REVOLUTION BEGAN*

We begin by looking more closely at the human condition in need of transformation. In traditional Christian terms, that condition is "sin," as exemplified, for example, by the seven deadly sins: pride, envy, gluttony, greed, lust, sloth, and wrath. In modern times, this condition has been called *alienation* or *estrangement*, signifying the experience of separation from God, self, other people, and the natural world. These concepts acknowledge that human beings suffer from mental, emotional, and spiritual disorders that manifest in many ways: in guilt, shame, illness, addiction, apathy, resentment, rage, cruelty, despair, futility, powerlessness, and loss of moral agency (that is, inability to take right action).

Feminist and womanist theologians have challenged this categorization of sin as alienation or estrangement because it downplays the extent of historical and contemporary injustices, especially those against women, people of color, and nature. Womanist theologian Delores Williams explains,

This defilement of nature's body and of black women's bodies is sin, since its occurrence denies that black women and nature are made in the image of God. Its occurrence is an assault upon the spirit of creation in women and nature. Whereas theologians such as Paul Tillich spoke of sin as man's [*sic*] estrangement from God and from other humans, womanist theologians can claim that humanity in the Western world has fallen to deeper states of degradation and depravity. Western Christians, some of whom are the manipulators of technology and concepts of development, no longer have to struggle only with the despair of being alienated from God (or the ground of being). They must now struggle with the attack Western man has waged against creation itself. They must struggle against the sin of defilement (evidenced today in nature and in the history of black women)—the sin that now threatens to destroy all life on the planet.[1]

When considering sin in this light, it is clear to see that human beings are not just alienated from God but caught up in social sin and institutional evil. How does this condition arise? As described in the previous chapter, we are all profoundly influenced by the cultures in which we are socialized, by the worldviews, assumptions, and norms of our families, schools, cultures, nations and other institutions with which we interact. To the degree that we submit to these powers as ultimate and give them the loyalty due solely to God, our humanity is distorted and we reinforce social sin and institutional evil to the detriment of our souls. N. T. Wright explains,

---

1. Delores Williams, "Sin, Nature, and Black Women's Bodies," in *Ecofeminism and the Sacred*, ed. Carol J. Adams (New York: Continuum, 1993), 29.

Humans are designed to worship God and exercise responsibility in [God's] world. But when humans worship idols instead, so that their image-bearing humanness corrupts itself into sin, missing the mark of the human vocation, they hand over their power to those same idols. The idols then use this power to tyrannize and ultimately to destroy their devotees and the wider world. *But when sins are forgiven, the idols lose their power.*[2]

Living in the forgiving grace of God, the Spirit shows us another way: "Do not be conformed to this world, but be transformed by the renewing of your minds" (Rom 12:2). Many biblical phrases, stories, and metaphors describe how people experience and understand this process of conversion and renewal, often called *salvation.*

Some people might balk at this term because they associate being *saved* or *born again* with conservative or fundamentalist theologies. Likewise, the terms *justification* and *sanctification* may sound alarm bells for some who associate them with otherworldly forms of piety that are unrelated to the real problems plaguing us today. Still, these terms are ways of expressing the personal transformation that people have experienced through their relationship with God through Jesus Christ. Justification is a way of expressing an experience of being forgiven and finding self-acceptance and dignity. Being born again is a way of describing a spiritual breakthrough that frees one from the bondage of the past and enables one to get a fresh start on a new and positive footing. Sanctification describes spiritual growth, an ongoing process of inner transformation that lays the foundation for overcoming bondage to sin and for transformative actions in the outer world. Salvation can include all these things and more, depending on the person who is describing their experience.

---

2. Wright, *Day the Revolution Began*, 260.

JUSTIFICATION: A MODEL OF CRIME AND PUNISHMENT

Jesus revealed to us and gave us God's restorative justice.

For many, the cross symbolizes God's forgiveness and love. A common understanding of salvation is that "a person is justified not by the works of the law but through faith in Jesus Christ" (Gal 2:16, which can also be translated as "justified through the faith of Jesus Christ").[3] This concept of justification is represented by the metaphor of a courtroom with a merciful judge who acquits someone who deserves the penalty of death or declares that a guilty person is just (righteous) simply because they have *faith in* Jesus. I have personally benefited from this metaphor because it emphasizes that the gospel is all about grace: God loves me as I am, and there is nothing that I need to do and nothing that I can do to make myself acceptable to God. Paul Tillich describes this experience:

> A wave of light breaks into our darkness, and it is as though a voice were saying, "You are accepted. You are accepted, accepted by that which is greater than you and the name of which you do not know. Do not try to do anything now; perhaps later you will do much. Do not seek for anything; do not perform anything; do not intend anything. Simply accept the fact that you are accepted."[4]

---

3. This is similar in meaning to the alternate translation of Gal 2:20, mentioned in the introduction as "by the faith of the Son of God, who loved me and gave himself for me."

4. Paul Tillich, from *The Shaking of the Foundations* (New York: Scribners, 1948), quoted by Cynthia M. A. Geppert, "Accepting Acceptance," *Psychiatric Times* 24, no. 1 (January 1, 2007), https://www.psychiatrictimes.com/view/accepting-acceptance.

Although the courtroom metaphor for justification is meaningful to many, when taken literally and out of context, it may be interpreted in simplistic and even harmful ways. The courtroom metaphor is based on the idea of sin as a crime meriting punishment: the crime must be punished, the debt that caused the offense must be paid. In criminal justice parlance, this is a model of *retributive justice*. The problem is, as legal experts know, this punitive model does not work to rehabilitate people or bring them back into a positive relationship with society. In fact, that is not even the purpose of this model.

This crime and punishment approach may be used to promote popular interpretations of ancient atonement theories that point to a God who requires Jesus to die (as punishment or satisfaction of God's honor) as a payment for human sin. Such belief systems point to the concept of a punishing God who only accepts those who, under fear of hell, are willing to accept this idea of God, this understanding of the death of Jesus, and this view of salvation. Many who love Jesus simply accept this belief system. Some accept it reluctantly, trying to reconcile it with their experience and understanding of a God of love. Some accept it out of fear of hell. This view of God leaves some people deeply concerned about the fate of family members, friends, and neighbors who do not share their beliefs. It gives them an urgent sense of responsibility to convince other people to believe as they do to save as many as possible from the fires of hell. On the other hand, some use such beliefs to dismiss sin and avoid accountability by saying, "Christians aren't perfect, just forgiven" or to neutralize or downplay egregious harm by saying dismissively, "We are all sinners." Others use this view of a God that requires punishment to justify policies of retributive justice: harsh treatment of immigrants, scapegoating of "others," unconditional support for aggressive (and even deadly) police actions, punitive laws (including the death penalty), and military policies based on domination, violence, and war. As mentioned earlier, some, including abused women or children, may internalize this view of God and turn it against themselves.

An alternative metaphor to retributive justice is *restorative justice*, which has the goal of rehabilitation rather than punishment. Systems based on this model offer people who have committed crimes the opportunity to go through treatment or rehabilitation, to make reparations, to better themselves and equip themselves for life after incarceration through training, education, or in other ways that enable them to be restored as contributing members of society upon their release. *Transformative justice* takes this idea even further by calling for changes that would improve social conditions and reduce the prevalence of violence and other forms of harm. Compared to retributive justice, the metaphors of restorative and transformative justice are more aligned with Jesus's forgiveness and compassion and with his transformational message about the reign of God. In addition, while the metaphor of retributive justice focuses on justification of sinners as the result of Jesus's death, restorative and transformative justice seem consistent with Paul's claim in Romans 5:25 that Jesus was *raised* (rather than crucified) for our justification.

A process of *truth and reconciliation* can contribute to restorative and transformative justice. After the relatively peaceful transfer of power from the racist system of apartheid in South Africa, the African National Congress government set up Truth and Reconciliation councils to supplement and provide an alternative to the imprisonment and punishment of apartheid war criminals. These councils required perpetrators of war crimes to come forward, to publicly admit in detail what they had done, to answer questions and hear the responses of victims and their families, and to ask for their forgiveness and the forgiveness of the community. This process of truth and reconciliation has become a model that has now been used to bring a degree of reconciliation to societies around the world. It enables authorities to uncover more of the facts, to identify who is responsible, and to find out where the bodies are buried, sometimes literally. It interrupts the cycle of violence, enables victims and families to find a degree of closure, gives perpetrators who are willing to participate a way to be restored to society, and creates a process for the integration and healing of society overall.

The God that Jesus proclaimed reaches out to us, offering forgiveness, acceptance, love, and a path to transformation that may involve a rigorous process of self-searching, amends, truth, and reconciliation. This is a God of *restorative and transformative justice*. Those who hear the Spirit's call are invited into a process that involves facing and coming to terms with our past and present, our immersion in whatever culture and milieu we find ourselves, and our current participation in social sin and institutional evil. The reconciling process of salvation involves repentance (turning around) and acceptance of the apparently limitless willingness of divine love to offer us grace, accept us as we are, and free us from guilt, shame, apathy, harmful patterns, and bondage to the powers. Accepting this gracious invitation sets us free to start anew, to enter a new way of living that includes following in the footsteps of Jesus and opening to the ongoing transformation of our lives and of the world. This is a participatory process that involves actions of faithfulness on our part. It is an example of what it means to be justified *through the faith of* Jesus Christ.

We can interpret the cross of Jesus as at-one-ment
that deconstructs notions of a violent God bent on
retributive justice. We see that the justice of God
is love and that love forgives, transforms, and seeks
to create new and harmonious relationships.

—SHARON BAKER, *EXECUTING GOD*

The parable of the prodigal son takes us further in exploring metaphors that express God's freely offered forgiveness and grace. Jesus told the story of a son who asked for his inheritance while his father was still alive. His father granted his request, and the young man went to a far country where he squandered the money in loose living and ended up destitute, tending swine, longing to eat what the pigs ate. He finally came to his senses and returned home, hoping that his father would take him on as a hired hand. In poignant language, Jesus told how this loving father freely forgave the offending son even before his son could fully express repentance; he embraced him, put his best robe on him, and put a ring on his finger. The father saw his son not as having committed a crime but as having lost his way. There is no framework of crime or punishment here, no legal system, no penalty imposed by the father, not even a reduction of status in the family—just the joy of a parent for a child who has returned. This parable offers a metaphor of sin as broken relationship and of salvation as reconciliation and relationship restored.

The older brother in the parable was upset by his father's actions, and he made the case to their father against giving such special treatment to his wayward brother, just as someone who upholds the satisfaction or substitutionary model of the atonement might argue that unconditional forgiveness is not fitting for God. (There are many such people. In fact, Jesus provoked the ire of the religious authorities because he welcomed and associated freely with sinners.) Instead, the father reassured the older son of his love and of the security of his place within the family, then reaffirmed his merciful action by saying, "But we had to celebrate and rejoice, because this brother of yours was dead and has come to life; he was lost and has been found" (Luke 15:32). In this parable, Jesus points to a God who promises that however far we may go astray, God awaits our coming back and receives us back with joy. God as revealed in Jesus and as portrayed in this parable freely forgives and welcomes home prodigal sons and daughters and restores them to a place of honor. This parable has also been called the parable of the loving father because it represents God's freely offered forgiveness and grace, a message similar to that of God's restorative and transformative justice.

This is the gospel, given to us by Jesus. This image of an unconditionally loving God always ready to receive us home as beloved children is a metaphor of salvation.

The image of shepherd is another metaphor of a God of love. It recurs throughout the Hebrew Scriptures as an image of a God who protects and saves. God is presented as a shepherd who tends the flock, guides the sheep to green pastures and still waters, and even accompanies them through the valley of the shadow of death so that they may fear no evil (Ps 23). This caring God, in turn, calls lowly shepherds to lead (shepherd) the Hebrew people. Abraham, the father of many nations, was a shepherd, as was Moses, who led the Hebrew people out of slavery in Egypt to the promised land. The young David was a shepherd when the prophet Samuel found him and anointed him king of Israel.

In several New Testament texts, Jesus is presented as the good shepherd who cares for his sheep, who knows each one personally by name (John 10:3), who will never desert them "no matter how hopeless or helpless or hapless" they may be,[5] and who "lays down his life for the sheep" (John 10:11). John's Gospel differentiates between false shepherds, who come in deceptively as thieves and robbers "only to steal and kill and destroy," and the true shepherd, who comes so that the people "may have life, and have it abundantly" (John 10:10).

Notably, these metaphors are relational. Not only does the loving father in the parable miss his son, but the son also yearns for his family and travels home. In identifying with the loving father (or mother/grandmother, in my case), I understand the yearning for a lost child; in identifying with the prodigal, I am relieved to know that if I have strayed, God will receive me back as would a loving parent. Not only does the shepherd know each sheep by name, but the sheep hear and recognize the shepherd's voice (John 10:3). In the parable of the shepherd leaving the ninety-nine sheep in search of the one that was lost (Matt 18:12–13), I feel assured that God will come to seek me out if I am estranged or "lost." At the same time, I understand the shepherd's joy in finding the lost sheep, for I can see how I might risk something precious to search for someone who is dear to my heart. These metaphors represent a mutuality, a relationship of care, between God and God's creation.

5. The Reverend David Nui, in a sermon preached at Nevada City United Methodist Church in Nevada City, California, on May 3, 2020.

This cup that is poured out for you is the
new covenant in my blood.

—LUKE 22:19–20 ESV

When seeking to describe the impacts of Jesus's life, death, and resurrection, early Christians created metaphors drawn from Jewish cultic practices, including animal sacrifice. Only priests could offer sacrifices. There were varied forms of sacrifices with precise instructions for how each was to be offered, which parts of the animals would be burnt, which parts were to be eaten by priests, and which parts returned to be eaten by the ones who brought the offering. There were strict rules about sprinkling blood on the altar and smearing it on "the horns of the altar" as a form of purification: "For the life of the flesh is in the blood; and I have given it to you for making atonement for your lives on the altar; for, as life, it is the blood that makes atonement" (Lev 17:11).[6] The blood on the altar represented life, not death.

Such images may seem revolting today, but in ancient times, blood sacrifice was widespread and was seen in many religions as essential for appeasing angry gods. This idea of appeasement is foreign to Hebrew thinking. Animal sacrifice was not seen as a means for appeasing God's wrath, nor did sacrifice have substitutionary implications. Animals were not punished in place of human beings. Rather, sacrifice involved the transformation of the animal by burning it on the altar, transferring it from the physical realm to a transcendent one. God received the smoke as a "pleasing odor"

---

6. William K. Gilders, "Sacrifice in Ancient Israel," SBL, accessed December 15, 2021, https://www.sbl-site.org/assets/pdfs/TBv2i5_Gilders2.pdf.

(Lev 1:13), symbolizing the intimacy and trust of a fellowship meal shared by God and human beings.

When they performed sacrifices, ancient Israelites were bringing sacred offerings to God in gratitude and seeking to express and deepen their relationship with God. For the Hebrew people, sacrifice was a form of worship that reaffirmed their faith in God's steadfast love and faithfulness. It offered the assurance that although God's people had not been faithful to their covenant with God, God remained faithful and had provided the sacrificial system as a means through which to bring the people back into right covenant relationship (atonement) with the God who had created, redeemed, and sustained them.

Because animal sacrifice was central to Jewish worship during the time of Jesus, early Christians found many similarities between the ritual of sacrifice as a gift of the God of the Covenant and Jesus's death and resurrection. Even today, some hymns focus on metaphors based on ancient cultic sacrifice, including those with metaphors such as Jesus being "the lamb of God" or about there being "power in the blood" of Jesus. Such images provide symbolic meaning to some people and repel others. But as with other metaphors, they break down if taken literally, especially today when we are so far removed in time from the archaic concepts related to the symbol of blood sacrifice.

New Testament writers adopted the concept of *new covenant* when interpreting the meaning of Jesus's life, death, and resurrection based on Jeremiah's prophesy:

But this is the covenant that I will make with the house of Israel after those days, says the Lord: I will put my law within them, and I will write it on their hearts; and I will be their God, and they shall be my people. No longer shall they teach one another, or say to each other, "Know the Lord," for they shall all know me, from the least of them to the greatest, says the Lord; for I will forgive their iniquity, and remember their sin no more. (Jer 31:33–34)

The new covenant varied from the old in that it was an inner, spiritual reality, written on the human heart, enabling people to know and be faithful to God. The book of Hebrews covers this concept of new covenant extensively, making the case that the death and resurrection of Jesus signaled the end of the sacrificial system. The author employs the metaphor of animal sacrifice and presents Jesus as both high priest and ultimate sacrifice: "Unlike the other high priests, he has no need to offer sacrifices day after day, first for his own sins, and then for those of the people; this he did once for all when he offered himself" (Heb 7:27). The new covenant was renewed not by sacrifice but by the tangible action of the Holy Spirit through prayer, communal worship, service, and the sacramental rituals of baptism and Holy Communion.

The sacraments are forms of ritual participation in the new covenant initiated by Jesus. A sacrament is an outward and physical *sign* of an inward and spiritual grace as well as a *means* of grace that furthers the Spirit's work in our souls. Baptism represents God's universal grace, an initiation into Christian faith, the "washing away" of sins, and dying and rising with Christ.[7] In Scripture, the inner, spiritual reality is emphasized, as in 1 Peter 3:21–22: "And baptism . . . now saves you—not as a removal of dirt from the body, but as an appeal to God for a good conscience, through the resurrection of Jesus Christ, who has gone into heaven and is at the right hand of God, with angels, authorities, and powers made subject

---

7. The United Methodist denomination, among others, baptizes infants, but this does not signify the washing away of original (inherited) sin. Rather, it represents God's universal grace and inclusion of all people, including infants, into the Christian community. Infants are part of the original blessing of creation, which God calls "good."

to him." Note that this passage claims salvation (and a good conscience) not through Jesus's death but through his resurrection and links it with his victory over the powers.

Holy Communion was and still is practiced regularly in Christian worship as a reenactment of Jesus's last meal with his disciples, humble acceptance of his invitation to partake of the sacrificial gift of his body and blood in the bread and wine, a celebration of the new covenant, a reminder of the presence of the risen Christ that binds us together, and a foretaste of the joy of the great heavenly banquet that is to come. The words of institution before Communion make clear that this symbolic ritual represents a sacrifice on the part of Jesus and our acknowledgment of his death as an act of self-giving love. This sacrament indicates that there is, indeed, a sacrificial aspect to Jesus's death, an understanding that in some way, Jesus died "for us," as discussed in chapter 1. This becomes very personal as Jesus says, "This is my body, which is given for you. Do this in remembrance of me" (Luke 22:19). Jesus explicitly invokes the concept of new covenant when he offers the wine as "the new covenant in my blood" (Luke 22:20).

The key question about cultic metaphors of sacrifice for us today is how we understand Jesus's death as a sacrifice. I have made the case that God did not orchestrate Jesus's death to make possible God's forgiveness of sin. But there are other ways to understand sacrifice that do make sense. We can grasp its meaning by reflecting on common human experiences, such as when parents caught up in today's poverty-generating system work two or even three jobs to make sure their children have food on the table and a roof over their heads; when a passerby rescues a drowning person but, in doing so, succumbs to the current; when people take an unpopular stand for justice even when they face threats of violence; when a teacher in our violence-ridden society is wounded or dies trying to protect students from an active shooter. Under extremely adverse and even dangerous circumstances, people may risk their well-being or even their lives out of concern for others. Such actions are not predetermined or compelled or based on obedience but freely offered. These are real and costly sacrifices, pure gifts. Jesus made his own choices throughout his life based on faithfulness to God and concern for others, including that final choice to stay faithful despite the danger, a choice that finalized his course toward death and resurrection.

FREEDOM IN CHRIST: ENSLAVEMENT AND LIBERATION

> The cross is no theological invention but the world's
> answer, given a thousand times over, to attempts
> at liberation. Only for that reason are we able to
> recognize ourselves in Jesus's dying on the cross.
>
> **—DOROTHEE SOELLE, *SUFFERING***

First-century Christians drew from liberation themes in the Hebrew Scriptures to describe the liberating power of the crucified and risen Jesus, especially from the Exodus experience of Israel's deliverance from slavery in Egypt. This central story of liberation from bondage helped form the social consciousness of the Hebrews, which resulted in laws that translated their historical experience into concern for the poor, oppressed, weak, and dispossessed (Deut 15:12–18).[8] As we have seen, Jesus himself often drew from themes of liberation, such as when he proclaimed "release to the captives" and stated his intention "to let the oppressed go free" (Luke 4:18).

New Testament writers emphasized God's ongoing providential actions, God's actions as liberator, and God's steadfast love and

---

8. Achtemeier, *Harper's Bible Dictionary*, 559.

faithfulness despite the people's intransigence and saw these themes as having both personal and social implications. The review of Israel's history in Hebrews, including the Exodus story, points to Jesus as high priest, fellow sufferer, and liberator: "Since, therefore, the children share flesh and blood, he himself likewise shared the same things, so that through death he might destroy the one who has the power of death, that is, the devil, and free those who all their lives were held in slavery by the fear of death" (Heb 2:14–16). This freedom from the fear of death is personal, but its implications are social: without fear of death, the powers and principalities cannot frighten us into submission.

In the Gospel of John, Jesus speaks of God's saving power in the context of personal bondage, saying that "everyone who commits sin is a slave to sin" (John 8:34), and links liberation to truth, saying, "If you continue in my word, you are truly my disciples; and you will know the truth, and the truth will make you free" (John 8:31–32). In Galatians, Paul writes, "For freedom Christ has set us free. Stand firm, therefore, and do not submit again to a yoke of slavery" (Gal 5:1). Paul's writings emphasize salvation as Christ's liberating power to save us from bondage to sin (Rom 6:20), bondage to decay (Rom 8:21), and bondage to the law (Rom 7:6). Because we are "in Christ," we live no longer by the law but by the Spirit: "Now the Lord is the Spirit, and where the Spirit of the Lord is, there is freedom" (2 Cor 3:17). Such passages speak to our human condition of alienation as well as to those "deeper states of degradation and depravity" into which we have fallen and point us in the direction of freedom from bondage of every kind.

Today's liberation theologians speak from their own contexts, drawing from both the Hebrew Scriptures and New Testament to profess God's liberating actions in the lives of individuals and in the social/political arena. Reflecting on these themes requires critical thinking about current events that draw from faith perspectives developed in contexts of oppression. A primary emphasis of Latin American liberation theology is "God's preferential option for the poor," first articulated in the landmark book *A Theology of Liberation* by Gustavo Gutiérrez.[9]

Liberation theologies empower movements for justice by recognizing both individual agency and social responsibility among all people, regardless of status, wealth, or worldly power. This does not mean that all liberation theologians will interpret Scripture in the same light. For example, theologians with Indigenous roots, along with their allies, may not see God's providential action in the history of the Israelites entering the "promised land," when they "dispossessed the nations that God drove out before our ancestors" (Acts 7:45). We need to consider our social and political context while reading Scripture and listen to people whose social location might be different, especially those whose experiences and insights might shed light on stories of oppression that have been falsified, glossed over, or ignored, and on how that history is playing out today.

Considering the cross in the context of liberation theology returns us to themes we explored in chapter 3, of Christ's presence in the midst of the extreme injustices and sufferings of the world and the challenge to followers of Jesus to respond accordingly. In *Getting the Poor Down from the Cross: Christology and Liberation*, liberation theologian Jon Sobrino wrote about God's identification with the poor and oppressed people of the world in the context of the ongoing crucifixion of Christ: "The cross is not a metaphor. It signifies death and cruelty, to which Jesus' cross adds innocence and defenselessness. To Christian theologians, the cross brings us back

---

9. Gustavo Gutiérrez, *A Theology of Liberation* (Maryknoll, NY: Orbis, 1973).

to Jesus of Nazareth. He is the crucified one. By calling the poor of this world the 'crucified people' they are not only rescued from their anonymity, but they are granted maximum dignity."[10]

Sobrino also reminds us that it is through our relationship with those who are victims of injustice, poverty, and oppression that we deepen our relationship with Christ. We are called to act in solidarity with Christ by "taking them down from the cross." By doing so, we act in gratitude for all that they have given us: "Without knowing it, because of who they are and because of the values they possess, they save us, humanize us, and pardon us. By carrying their reality, a heavy cross, we feel carried by them. They are a blessing."[11]

AN ECONOMIC METAPHOR: REDEMPTION AND RANSOM

Redemption uses an ancient financial custom to signify
that divine mercy springs people free from sin of all kinds,
personal, interpersonal, social, and institutional; delivers
them from death and fear of death; and liberates them from
bondage to be in turn persons of redeeming grace toward
others. . . . Rather than detailing a mechanism by which this
happens, the metaphor gratefully celebrates the result.

—ELIZABETH A. JOHNSON, *CREATION AND THE CROSS*

One of the earliest ways that Christians understood salvation was through the metaphor of *redemption*. To *redeem* has many different meanings, including to "buy back," to "free from captivity by

---

10. José María Vigil, *Getting the Poor Down from the Cross: Christology and Liberation*, 1st English digital ed. (version 1.0), International Theological Commission of the Ecumenical Association of Third World Theologians (EATWOT), May 15, 2007, 309, https://liberationtheology.org/library/EATWOTGettingThePoorDown.pdf.
11. Vigil, 309.

payment of ransom," to "make good," and even to "atone for."[12] For early Christians, the term *redemption* expressed the belief that humans are powerless over sin, "sold into slavery under sin" (Rom 7:14), and that we need to be set free. As with other metaphors that made it into the New Testament, early Christians drew from the Hebrew Scriptures and from the realities of their daily lives. For instance, if an Israelite lost everything and fell into slavery, a family member had the right to "redeem" that person by buying their freedom. If someone lost their house or land, family members could redeem their property by buying it back.

In addition to laying out these laws, the Hebrew Scriptures also speak of God as the *Redeemer* of Israel, for having rescued the people again and again throughout their history. Although the New Testament nowhere refers to Jesus as Redeemer as many Christians do today,[13] early Christians projected the idea of redemption onto God's saving action in Jesus, since it seemed to express what God had accomplished in his life, death, and resurrection. God had once again redeemed God's people, freeing them from bondage (Mark 10:45; Eph 1:7; Rom 3:24). To some, the death of Jesus ("the precious blood of Christ" in 1 Pet 1:18) was the metaphorical "cost" of redemption, validated in the resurrection.

One way early Christian theologians spoke of redemption was through the metaphor of *ransom*. As mentioned in chapter 2, this metaphor is related to the *Christus Victor* model of atonement in that it represents the victory of God over the evil forces of the universe. Origen, a theologian born in the second century, explained it like this: The human race has surrendered itself to the devil, primarily through original (inherited) sin. God has the power to liberate us from this bondage but will not infringe on our freedom

---

12. *Merriam-Webster's Collegiate Dictionary*, 11th ed., 1042.
13. Achtemeier, *Harper's Bible Dictionary*, 857.

of choice to do so; therefore, God sent Jesus (who was both truly God and truly human) as a representative of humanity to die as a ransom to set people free. Fourth-century church father Gregory of Nyssa expanded this theory by using the metaphor of Jesus as bait on a fishhook. Because Jesus was human, the devil was tricked and took the bait, killing Jesus, but because Jesus was also divine, his resurrection brought about victory over all the forces of evil and exposed the apostasy and the futility of the demonic powers. Walter Wink explains,

> When they tried to destroy him [the authorities] in fact stepped into a divinely set trap. "The devil saw Jesus as his prize, snapped at the bait, and was pulled out of the water for all to see" (Luther). As a result, it is the Powers themselves who are now paraded, captive, in God's victory celebration. The cross marks the failure, not of God, but of violence.[14]

This mythical representation of atonement as ransom in early Christian writings breaks down when attempts are made to take it literally. Arguments arose, including debates about who received the ransom payment: God or the devil. If God, did God pay a ransom to God? If to the devil, why did the all-powerful God have to set a trap or pay the devil anything? These questions do not bother us today because most of us no longer take these images literally. Jesus said that he came to give his life as a ransom for many, but that doesn't mean that he literally gave himself up to be crucified in order to buy our souls from God or the devil. This is one ancient metaphor for salvation among many.

---

14. Wink, *Engaging the Powers*, 140.

For Christians, the words *redemption* and *salvation* are now almost interchangeable. In the text from 1 Corinthians 1:30, Paul includes the concept of redemption but does not explain how it works. He tells us that God "is the source of our life in Christ Jesus, who became for us wisdom from God," as well as our "righteousness" (we are not just declared righteous but made righteous), our "sanctification" (the process through which we are made righteous), and our "redemption" (salvation, as described through varied metaphors). All these are included in our being brought into at-one-ment, which is accomplished by the grace of God alone. Through the faith of Jesus, we relinquish the claims of the self, realize that our life is part of the divine life, and acknowledge that God is all in all.

FAITH REQUIRES AN OPEN MIND

It is worth repeating a point made earlier, namely, that the church has never officially defined any one specific way of understanding salvation, never opted for one theological theory over another. New creative initiatives are possible and even necessary for a vibrant faith in our day.

—ELIZABETH A. JOHNSON, *CREATION AND THE CROSS*

In this chapter, we have explored some of the many life-giving metaphors that New Testament writers used to portray the impacts of Jesus's life, death, and resurrection on people's lives. This leads to a discussion on prayer in the next chapter that puts "life in Christ Jesus" at the fore, followed by the final chapter, which covers meaningful ways to follow Jesus, engage the powers, and live into the promise of the gospel as symbolized by the cross.

Each of the metaphors explored in this chapter and throughout this book can be traced back to the Scriptures, traditions, rituals, teachings, and laws of the Hebrew people. New Testament writers drew from them to express varied ways to understand the gospel message as symbolized by the cross. It is important not to take these metaphors literally or mistake symbols for reality. We are not required to jump through dogmatic hoops to enjoy the spiritual treasures that come through a relationship with Jesus Christ. There will always be people, religious or otherwise, who will tell others what they should think. Do not be fooled. A spiritual path is based not on dogma but on openness to the Spirit's guidance, inspiration, and transformation. Faith requires an open mind. We can appreciate each of these metaphors as varied expressions of the "wisdom of God in a mystery," consider how well they portray the God of love revealed by Jesus, and decide whether they accurately express the gospel in a way that is true and relevant to the needs of our world today.

Our understanding, the choices we make, and the actions we take under the influence of the Spirit are limited, human, finite, and often fall short of the mark. Nevertheless, the gifts that come our way through the journey of faith go far beyond those offered by any formula and beyond anything that we could have worked out on our own. Fortunately, God's restorative, transformative justice is always at work. Like the prodigal in Jesus's parable, we are always welcomed home.

CHAPTER 9
PRACTICING PRAYER
THE DEPTHS OF GOD

Let these lessons of the cross help us to see our way to accept
your calling, no matter how treacherous the way in which
it leads. For ours is to follow in Christ's Way, which is your
Way; and which by grace might one day be our Way.

—BRET S. MYERS, "A PRAYER FOR THE DAY OF CRUCIFIXION"

EACH YEAR DURING the season of Lent, Christians around the world
reflect on Jesus's temptations in the wilderness, his journey to the
cross, and his crucifixion. These reflections are a form of spiritual
practice in themselves as well as spiritual preparation for the joy of
Easter.

Several years ago, on a beautiful spring morning during Lent,
after focusing on these things in prayer, I rode my bike down Red
Dog Road to town. I stopped when I saw a class of young children on a field trip, walking from school to nearby Pioneer Park.
Suddenly, I saw a vision: there was my five-year-old granddaughter, Terra, reaching out her arms for a hug with a big smile on her
face, calling, "Grammy!" She seemed to have a bright aura reflecting light. (Remember, this is my granddaughter I'm talking about.)
Terra stayed right there on the sidewalk like she was supposed to. I
crossed the street, introduced myself to her teacher, then opened my
arms and gave Terra the big hug she was waiting for. That image of
Terra standing with a smile and arms outstretched is still with me.

The next time I preached an Easter sermon, I included this story. The text was about Jesus appearing to Mary Magdalene on that first Easter morning. Mary did not recognize Jesus at first; she thought he was the gardener and only recognized him after he spoke her name: "Mary!" (John 20:11–16). I saw a similarity in the two stories: I did not really see Terra there in front of me until she reached out her arms and called "Grammy." When I did recognize her, it was as if my beloved granddaughter was an icon of God.

Resurrection is God's action on that first Easter morning, as the people who had loved and followed him realized that in some mysterious way, he was still with them. Resurrection also takes place in those moments when we experience the Spirit's power and our eyes are opened in new ways to the presence of the risen Christ in our midst.

Throughout this book, we have explored God's presence in human suffering and in creation, considered questions of God's nature and will, and looked at some of the many ways Christians have understood sin, idolatry, and the principalities and powers. We have explored the life-giving story of Jesus and various biblical metaphors that help us understand the saving power of the gospel and its meaning for us today in our personal lives and relationships and in the larger patterns of history.

Here we go further with these themes and integrate them by pointing to participation in the story of the life, death, and resurrection of Jesus through prayer and by showing how prayer informs our actions in response to today's challenges. Prayer brings the story of Jesus home to us in our own experience and integrates all the disparate dynamics of our lives into a single whole. This creates an opening for God's wisdom to break through as an alternative to the wisdom of this world that undergirds today's domination system. Prayer provides a foundation for following Jesus as we seek to embody his teachings, speak truth to the world's power structures, and join with others to build the foundations for a more compassionate world. We begin by considering the theme of *participation*.

PARTICIPATION: LIFE IN CHRIST JESUS

For Christians, there is no greater privilege than
participating in the life of the triune God: Father, Son,
and Spirit. This is what it means to be "in Christ."

—MICHAEL J. GORMAN, "PARTICIPATION"

Participation involves reflecting on the varied aspects of the biblical stories of Jesus in our present circumstances, opening ourselves to his Spirit, learning from him, and identifying with him in his attitude, actions, and orientation toward God as we seek to live in ways that are consistent with his example. The story of Jesus's life and teachings, death and resurrection becomes our story, or rather, we become part of his story as it is incorporated into our being. Paul Gorman explains, "This participation is not an empty mysticism, nor is it a self-centered spiritual journey. Rather, it is both individual and corporate, both spiritual and missional. It is to participate fully in the fullness of God."[1]

Paul speaks of this reality as "life in Christ," which means living in the presence of the risen Christ and participating in God's ongoing actions in the world. To clarify, Marcus J. Borg says, "The old Paul had died, and a new Paul had been born whose life was 'in Christ,' to use one of his most frequent phrases. So also, he referred to other followers of Jesus as having died and risen with Christ. Indeed,

---

1. Michael J. Gorman, *Participation: Paul's Vision of Life in Christ* (Cambridge: Grove Books Ltd., 2018), 20.

this metaphor was the foundation of Christian identity, carrying the same meaning as John's language of being 'born again.'"[2]

Here is how I introduce this concept in *Shaking the Gates of Hell*:

> This state of being is expressed in many ways in the New Testament: as living in fellowship with Christ, belonging to Christ, being one with Christ, putting on Christ, and so on. But the bottom line is this: I have new life in Christ because I live in Christ and because Christ is alive in me. I experience this new life to the degree that I surrender my self-will and say yes to this unmediated fellowship with God through Jesus Christ. I live in faith that I am forgiven, accepted, and loved to the degree that I allow forgiveness, acceptance, and love for myself and others to flow through me. I experience hope to the degree that I plant seeds of hope by taking positive action in the world. Freedom, too, comes to me, but also through me, to the degree that I live not by the law, according to human constructed rules and regulations, but by the Spirit. For life in the Spirit is not characterized by moralist legalism, but by compassion and creativity.[3]

For Paul, such claims are central to the gospel because the presence of the risen Christ is the basis for Christian life. He said, "It is no longer I who live, but it is Christ who lives in me. And the life I now live in the flesh I live *by the faith of* the Son of God, who loved me and gave himself for me" (Gal 2:20; my italics). As mentioned earlier, living "by faith in Jesus" or "by the faith of Jesus" are both accurate translations. I am using "by the faith of Jesus" here to emphasize the participatory nature of life in Christ.

2. Borg, *Convictions*, 146.
3. Delgado, *Shaking the Gates of Hell*, 312–13.

To participate in this way, we need to be familiar with the story. In Christian community, this familiarity usually comes about through Scripture, sermon, Bible study, and ritual. It is important to keep an open mind and leave room for the Spirit rather than limiting the message of the gospel by insisting on taking the Bible literally or believing a certain doctrine. When I introduce a Scripture passage before preaching, I say, "listen *for* the word of God" rather than "listen *to* the word of God." The Bible itself claims not that it is the word of God but that Jesus is the word of God (John 1:1, 14). It is the Holy Spirit that brings alive the written words of Scripture so we can hear the living Word that has power to comfort, inspire, and guide us today.

In a similar way, through the sacraments, the Spirit brings the stories of Jesus to life *for us*. As mentioned earlier, baptism has varied meanings, but a primary understanding of baptism is that it represents a dying and rising with Christ, as when Paul says, "Do you not know that all of us who have been baptized into Christ Jesus were baptized into his death?" (Rom 6:3). Likewise, the sacrament of Holy Communion is a remembrance and reenactment of Jesus's "last supper," through which we gratefully acknowledge and humbly receive the blessings of his sacrificial death "for us" while acknowledging our unity in the body of Christ. As with baptism, Holy Communion is participatory: "The cup of blessing that we bless, is it not a sharing in the blood of Christ? The bread that we break, is it not a sharing in the body of Christ? Because there is one bread, we who are many are one body, for we all partake of the one bread" (1 Cor 10:15–17). The sacraments point directly to the meaning of participation in the life, death, and resurrection of Jesus, bringing these themes alive in our own experience. In a similar way, other practices with roots in the biblical stories come alive with new meaning for us in our present circumstances.

Participation both begins and ends with prayer. Prayer orients us toward the Spirit, and listening to the Spirit is itself prayer. Prayer enables us to gauge what is true and what is false, what is loving and what is hateful, what is kind and what is cruel, what is precious and what is worthless. It is through prayer that we experience the assurance of God's love and discern our gifts and our call. Prayer is a means of opening to the deep wisdom that comes from God.

TAUGHT BY THE SPIRIT

Now we have received not the spirit of the world, but the
Spirit that is from God, so that we may understand the gifts
bestowed on us by God. And we speak of these things in
words not taught by human wisdom but taught by the Spirit,
interpreting spiritual things to those who are spiritual.

—1 CORINTHIANS 2:12–13

At its most basic, prayer is conversation, sometimes with words and sometimes without. Conversing with God, whether silently or out loud or in a journal, may help us find clarity. As in any relationship, it is important to take time to listen. Listening to God is a primary form of prayer, although God often "speaks" not in words but in silence through the inclinations of the heart.

In fact, prayer doesn't have to consist of words at all. Why limit what we consider prayer? Music, art, dance, yoga; an appreciation of the beauty of creation or a deep connection with another person; sorrow, joy, tears, laughter—all these things and so many more may touch us deeply and take us to a place of awareness of the divine. Surely God knows the prayers of our hearts before we speak, yet invites our prayers, and (because we do not know how to pray as we ought) "that very Spirit intercedes with sighs too deep for words"

(Rom 8:26). Even our sighs can be a form of prayer, reminding us that the Spirit is alive in each breath as we go through the day.

In prayer we are "taught by the Spirit." There are countless books on prayer, formulas for praying, prayers to memorize, communal prayers, prayers of praise, confession, thanksgiving, intercession, and petition. But we don't need to know how to pray; we learn how to pray by praying. At times I have begun my prayer with the words "teach me to pray" or just "teach me," and such prayers never fail to be answered. By simply sitting with this request, we pray even as we learn how to pray.

Still, when one of Jesus's disciples asked him to "teach us to pray" (Luke 11:1), he taught them what has become known as the "Lord's Prayer," the "Our Father," or the "Abba Prayer." In Matthew, this prayer that Jesus taught his disciples appears as part of the Sermon on the Mount (Matt 6:9–13):

> *Our Father in heaven,*
> *hallowed be your name.*
> *Your kingdom come.*
> *Your will be done,*
> *on earth as it is in heaven.*
> *Give us this day our daily bread.*
> *And forgive us our debts,*
> *as we also have forgiven our debtors.*
> *And do not bring us to the time of trial,*
> *but rescue us from the evil one.*

This beloved prayer begins with Jesus addressing God as "Abba," which is usually translated as "Father" but is better translated as "Daddy." With this address, Jesus demonstrates his intimate relationship with God as a personal, loving parent and invites his followers to claim this relationship with God as their own. The body of the prayer begins with the words "Hallowed be your name," which points to and magnifies the mystery of the God whose unfathomable holiness and all-embracing love both pervade and encompass all creation, yet to whom we can turn with our every need.

This central prayer of Christian faith holds up a contrasting vision between the world as it is, dominated by the wisdom and the rulers of this age, and God's intended world. It gives us a simple frame for prayer that expands our personal prayers to encompass the manifestation of God's reign and God's will here on earth: "Your kingdom come. Your will be done, on earth as it is in heaven." If we request this in prayer, from the heart, it implies that we intend to orient ourselves in this direction, to relinquish self-will and commit ourselves to working to make it so. Christians around the world pray these words, yet how many of us pray and live and work as if this is the prayer of our hearts? This request is at the core of intercessory prayer, for in so many ways, the prayers that we lift up to God for individuals and for particular situations are dependent upon and representative of the condition of the society and world in which we live. By keeping this in mind, our prayers expand to include the well-being of the whole creation. We hold others and the whole world in the light of God's love.

As we make this prayer that Jesus taught our own, its simple request for "daily bread" is an acknowledgment of our dependence on God, who "gives to all mortals life and breath and all things" (Acts 17:25). We ask only to be forgiven as we ourselves forgive, which we can only do by the Spirit. In this prayer, we acknowledge the fragility of our faith, our tendency to turn to our own way when faced with temptation, and our absolute need for God to "deliver" us from "the evil one"—that is, the demonic in all its forms. This is a prayer for salvation.

It is also a prayer of participation. Crossan explains, "We cannot pray the Abba Prayer . . . by ourselves or from ourselves. We can only pray it by, with, and through the Holy Spirit. Better: only the Holy Spirit can pray it in us, for us and through us. Better still: it is a collaborative prayer between—in this order—God's divine Spirit and our human spirit."[4] He adds, "The Spirit of God prays in us and for us; the cry of that Spirit in us is 'Abba, Father!'"[5]

This is not Jesus's first or last teaching on prayer. He encourages people to be persistent, like someone knocking on a friend's door at midnight asking for bread (Luke 11:5–8). He warns against praying for show so that others will be impressed, like the hypocrites who "love to stand and pray in the synagogues and at the street corners, so that they may be seen by others" (Matt 6:5). Instead, he counsels, "Pray to your Father who is in secret; and your Father who sees in secret will reward you" (Matt 6:6). Many of Jesus's teachings, including his parables, either relate to or can be applied to prayer. But it is the Lord's prayer that generations of Christians around the world and through the ages have participated in saying, often together, continuing through today.

Referring to this prayer, Crossan poses the question, "Is Christ the incarnation and revelation of a nonviolent or a violent God?" He concludes, "Since Jesus the Christ was clearly nonviolent (thank you at least for that judgement, Pilate), we Christians are called to believe in a nonviolent God."[6] He challenges us to "think about Jesus as creator of the Abba Prayer and to ask ourselves: Do we find any divine violence in it? Or do we find in it—and in the life that produced it as its summary—a nonviolent vision that is still the last

---

4. John Dominic Crossan, *The Greatest Prayer: Rediscovering the Revolutionary Message of the Lord's Prayer* (New York: HarperOne, 2010), 24–25.

5. Crossan, 25.

6. Crossan, 187.

best hope for our species and our earth?"[7] I am convinced that it is the latter. This brings us back to acknowledging that the gospel has both personal/spiritual and social/political meanings. By integrating these two aspects of the gospel, we allow prayer to inform our actions in the world.

Just as important as praying for guidance in what to *do* is praying for insight into who we *are*. We are children of God and children of the earth, fully embraced by God and the universe. We are called not to be someone or something else or better or more perfect but to humbly face and accept ourselves as we are—with all our human limitations, our past, our shortcomings, and even our participation in evil structures—in an attitude of repentance while opening ourselves to God's transforming work in our souls. Some ways to facilitate this opening are through reflection, meditation, and contemplative prayer, which cultivate an ongoing sense of the presence of God. Such practices enable us to have the spaciousness in our hearts and lives to rise in courage, pick up our cross, and follow Jesus, embodying the values he taught and demonstrated, resisting the current unjust order, and engaging actively in the struggle for a more compassionate world.

REFLECTION, MEDITATION, AND CONTEMPLATIVE PRAYER

> If you had not given me the grace during my nightly
> vigils to drink the stillness and to submerge myself in
> it, letting it pervade me through and through, how
> could I guard that inner stillness without which one
> can hear neither human beings nor you, O Lord.

—HÉLDER CÂMARA, "MEDITATION TWO"

---

7. Crossan, 188.

When the devil tempted Jesus in the wilderness, he responded, "One does not live by bread alone, but by every word that comes from the mouth of God" (Matt 4:4). Meditation, reflection, and contemplative prayer are formal ways to listen to God. Such practices serve as both preparation for and counterpoints to action in the world. In prayer, we seek and receive insight, perspective, and guidance for our work in the world and grow in our ability to intuitively know what words to say and what actions to take. We process experiences, recognize dead ends, and learn to make course corrections, especially if we share our experiences and listen to others with whom we share the spiritual journey. Ongoing prayer also helps prevent burnout and sustains us for the long haul.

Spiritual practices are efforts to make ourselves available to the Spirit and open to receiving God's grace, but it is God who initiates this process by giving us the desire to make such efforts. Still, we must choose whether to say yes and to cooperate with the Spirit's invitation and call. Making time for regular prayer may seem counterintuitive when considering the grave challenges facing us in our personal lives and in the world. It takes courage grounded in faith to renounce frantic activity and focus on being rather than doing. There is so much work that needs to be done. But for people who seek to follow Jesus, I know of no shorter or more direct way.

Here I point to the mystics, who have kept such traditions alive and can help orient us to the ongoing practice of contemplative prayer. Over the years, a regular practice may include many different forms of prayer and degrees of connection. Even a sense of the absence of God may be part of the spiritual journey.

The "stages" of the contemplative life, which are similar in varied spiritual traditions, have generally been described as *purgation*, a process of relinquishing harmful patterns that interfere with spiritual awareness; followed by *illumination*, which is characterized by increasing insight and realization; and culminating in *mystical union*, the experience of direct communion with spiritual truth, ultimate reality, or in Christian terms, God.[8] These stages are not necessarily consecutive because everyone's process of spiritual growth is different. They are not a blueprint but are better understood as a cumulative report of countless people's experiences of spiritual transformation. God's work in the human heart cannot be defined or limited or mapped out: "The wind blows where it chooses, and you hear the sound of it, but you do not know where it comes from or where it goes. So it is with everyone who is born of the Spirit" (John 3:8). Spiritual experiences can be described, but descriptions only amount to a "finger pointing at the moon" from a particular context. No one can claim an objective view.

There are countless ways to practice reflection, meditation, and contemplative prayer. *Mindfulness* is a process of releasing thoughts and fostering awareness of body, mind, and spirit in the present moment. Also called *attentiveness* or *centering prayer*, it "puts a different relationship to time at the core of meditative exercises" by "putting down roots in the here and now."[9] Mindfulness may include focused breathing and/or paying close attention to whatever one is doing throughout the day. Some people focus on silence, attuning themselves to the Spirit. In Christian terms, this has been called "practicing the presence of God."[10]

One way to deepen our practice of prayer is to reflect on the mind of Christ, which is not just an abstract principle but a lived experience, a tangible sense of the timeless reality of the depths of God. Cultivating awareness of the ever-present mind of Christ includes

---

8. F. C. Happold, *Mysticism: A Study and an Anthology* (New York: Viking Penguin, 1963), 56.

9. Dorothee Soelle, *The Silent Cry: Mysticism and Resistance* (Minneapolis: Fortress, 2001), 177.

10. Brother Lawrence of the Resurrection, *The Practice of the Presence of God, English Translation* (Washington, DC: ICS, 1993).

living in a way that reflects the life and Spirit of Jesus and provides a safeguard against the faulty idea of a violent God. For those of us who believe that the personality and love of God are revealed in the non-violent Jesus, our understanding of God must be consistent with the biblical view of his life and teachings. Taking the Bible literally has no place here, but the overall tenor and scope of Scripture, especially the stories of Jesus, point to a God of mercy and love.

There are further guideposts for exploring the path of contemplative prayer as cultivated by the mystics. *Cataphatic* mysticism (also described as the *via positiva*, or "positive way") includes forms of meditation and prayer that incorporate imagination, symbol, and metaphor. This points to an almost unlimited range of creative possibilities to incorporate into prayer, such as spending time in the natural world, focusing on an image, or entering imaginatively into a biblical (or other) story.

Apaphatic mysticism (the *via negativa*, or "negative way") includes forms of meditation and prayer focused on silence, nothingness, or emptiness, which have been described as entering the "cloud of unknowing," as enduring "the absence of God," or as experiencing "the dark night of the soul."[11] Sometimes such experiences come uninvited, perhaps triggered by painful events in our lives or in the world.

REFLECTING ON THE CROSS

The tears you shed, my sorrowful friend, are purer than the
laughter of him that seeks to forget and sweeter than
the mockery of the scoffer. These tears cleanse the heart of the

---

11. Erik Studt, "Seeking the God Beyond: A Beginner's Guide to Christian Apophatic Spirituality," review, *Thinking Faith, Jesuits in Britain*, accessed December 15, 2021, https://www.thinkingfaith.org/articles/seeking-god-beyond-beginner%E2%80%99s-guide -christian-apophatic-spirituality.

blight of hatred, and teach man to share the pain of the
brokenhearted. They are the tears of the Nazarene.

Reflecting on the cross is a way of opening to the world's suffering and to the pain and pathos of God. It carves out a space for holding a sense of God's love and intention for the world while at the same time facing the reality of suffering, sin, and evil in the world as it is. This integrated dual focus puts things in perspective and is an antidote to being paralyzed by grief or entranced by the intrigue and drama that pass today as "the real world."

I often use Scripture as a focus in prayer. Passages I have used when reflecting on the cross include the following: "You have died, and your life is hidden with Christ in God" (Col 3:3); "always carrying in the body the death of Jesus, so that the life of Jesus may also be made visible in our bodies" (2 Cor 4:10); "for I decided to know nothing among you except Jesus Christ, and him crucified" (1 Cor 2:2). At times I repeat these or other passages as mantras, returning to them as silent prayers throughout the day.

In prayer related to the cross, I face what happened to Jesus not because of some transaction between God and humankind but because of the way he lived his life and faced death and because his living presence is still here, illuminating all who seek communion with him. Reflecting on the crucifixion and the events leading up to Jesus's death means not glorifying his death or absolving those responsible but remembering that he was crucified for cultivating a way of life and creating a community based on alternative values that directly challenged the values (and laws!) of the ruling powers, which, for that very reason, had him put to death. It means facing the painful story of his execution at the hands of a murderous system that included official representatives, religious collaborators, a public that could be manipulated, and friends who betrayed, denied, or abandoned him. It also brings to life the countless others who have been subjected to persecution and death over the years by similar systems of worldly power.

Reflecting on the death of Jesus and all the other unjust deaths throughout history brings us face-to-face with our complicity and our rock-bottom poverty of spirit. We may even experience what seems to be the absence of God, as Jesus did as he hung on the cross, crying out, "My God, my God, why have you forsaken me?" (Mark 15:34). As we reflect on our own personal failings and our complicity in unjust systems, we discover our moral bankruptcy, emptiness, and powerlessness to control the outcome of events. We recognize that our wisdom and strength are inadequate to the task of personal and social transformation, so we surrender ourselves to God, whose wisdom and power are shrouded in mystery. Our ego stops trying to justify and defend itself. We die to ourselves. We enter the darkness, the depths, the journey of emptiness and loss and letting go, the dark night of the soul. Deeper, into the depths of spirit and matter, into the silence and music of the spheres, into the dark. Surrender of self, but not submission, led by the Holy Spirit, trusting the unknown, abandoning ourselves to love. Paradoxically, it is by entering this very darkness that light dawns and hope is reborn: "Blessed are the poor in spirit, for theirs is the kingdom of heaven" (Matt 5:3). This is an example of the *via negativa*, the way of nothingness. It is the Way of the Cross, which has both an inward and an outward dimension.

By prayerfully entering into communion with Jesus in his life and in his death, I indicate my desire and willingness to follow him, to live according to his values, and to risk sharing his fate. These practices enable me to accept and, through prayer, to practice my own death and release the claims of the self that keep me conformed to contemporary culture. At the same time, the biblical witness and ongoing tangible presence of the Holy Spirit assure me that death is not the end of the journey. Holding space for this story and the ongoing story of the world's suffering brings home the painful reality of Jesus's time and of ours. It enables us to glimpse the extent of the world's pain and see it in the context of the compassion of God. In words from "Kindness," a poem by Naomi Shihab Nye,

Before you know kindness as the deepest thing inside,
you must know sorrow as the other deepest thing.
You must wake up with sorrow.
You must speak to it till your voice
catches the thread of all sorrows
and you see the size of the cloth.
Then it is only kindness that makes sense anymore.[12]

Reflecting on the cross draws us into the sorrow and kindness of God. We are saved for kindness—the only thing that makes sense anymore.

Facing death is part of what it means to be human and aware of our mortality. The ongoing cycle of life and death is integral to life as we know it here on planet earth. The resurrection of Jesus is a foretaste and a sign that death is not the end, that in some mysterious way, life goes on beyond the grave. Still, the primary focus of Christian faith is not life after death, but eternal life here and now. Life in Christ enables us to live in defiance of death, which appears not only at the end of life but also in our everyday lives: in the loss of loved ones, in communal tragedies, in injustices that diminish

---

12. Naomi Shihab Nye, "Kindness," poets.org, accessed December 15, 2021, https://poets.org/poem/kindness?gclid=Cj0KCQiA3smABhCjARIsAKtrg6I8yaxuOiTOT5nH4bNDlDCrzyh70X3-c8y83snWyit3EBZWiCFit0oaAmQuEALw_wcB.

us, in depression, in human bondage to sin, in the death of nature. Death comes in many guises, and the powers have myriad ways to magnify and inflict death.

Those of us who have heard the gospel know that the death of Jesus is not the end of the story. Through regular reflection and prayer, we gradually adjust to the silence and spaciousness, the emptiness and fullness of God. We come to realize that even when reflecting on the crucifixion, we do so in the presence of the risen Christ, who is always with us, even when God seems absent or when we question our capacity to endure. When I enter into communion with the crucified Jesus, I also commune with the risen Christ. For, as Jesus said, "He is God not of the dead, but of the living" (Mark 12:27).

Living in Christ enables us to resist and offer life-giving alternatives to the death-dealing stratagems of the powers, as Jesus did. This is the good news of the gospel: that even when facing death, despite death, in defiance of death, God comes to us in Jesus, raising us to new life and enabling us to participate in the life of God. Such experience itself is resurrection.

PRAYER AND RESISTANCE

Being-at-one is not individualist self-realization but moves
beyond that to change death-oriented reality. Being-at-one
shares itself and realizes itself in the ways of resistance.

—DOROTHEE SOELLE, *THE SILENT CRY*

Prayer and resistance go together. In prayer we release burdens too heavy to carry alone, assimilate actions we have taken in the world, and receive clarity and inspiration for acts of mercy, justice, and nonviolent resistance to the powers. In our actions in the world, we express the love and insights we have received in prayer. Prayer is a way of deprogramming from the "wisdom of this age," which expresses and underlies the powers of this world, and of attuning ourselves to the wisdom of God.

In her book *The Silent Cry*, Dorothee Soelle updates the conversation about the stages of spiritual life for contemporary times. She says, "As in the journeys of former times, the stages of today's journey flow one into the other. The three stages are as follows: to be amazed, to let go, and to resist."[13]

By *being amazed* Soelle means the *via positiva*, which includes the experience of God in nature, radical amazement, bliss, and praising God. This aspect of the spiritual journey expresses the joy and jubilation that are the gifts of ongoing connection with God. It is also consistent with creation spirituality, which acknowledges the intrinsic value of creation and the revelation of the divine through the natural world. However, as Soelle points out, so much damage has been done to the earth that our ability to celebrate God through creation with our "original amazement" is hindered: "Mystical spirituality of creation will very likely move deeper and deeper into the dark night of being delivered into the hands of the principalities and powers that dominate us. For it is not only the poor man from Nazareth who is tortured together with his brothers and sisters on the cross, it is also our mother earth herself."[14]

To explain the stage of *letting go*, Soelle points to the *via negativa*, by which she means a process of relinquishing consumerism, addiction, possession, violence, and ego. This may include the experience of the dark night of the soul or a sense of the absence of God. She speaks of the bondage of the soul in today's "consumer culture of plundering" and says, "The ego turned into an addicted identity

---

13. Soelle, *Silent Cry*, 89.
14. Soelle, 92.

functions as the best guard in our jail; it controls and effectively suppresses our attempts to escape."

Soelle links letting go to *resisting*, which she names as the third stage of the spiritual journey: "To enter into the way from the ego to ego-liberation is a beginning in resistance."[15] She describes *resisting* as the *via transformativa* (transformative way), which includes compassion and justice, living in God, and changing the world. She explains her rationale for including resistance: "The concept of resistance that meets us in many places of mystical tradition is broad and diverse. It begins with not being at home in this world of business and violence."[16]

Practicing prayer in today's context enables us to face and bear what seems unbearable—that is, that the rulers of this age, the powers that be, seem to have the upper hand and are crucifying what is precious, destroying our hopes and dreams and everything that we hold dear. But the ability to bear this apparent reality—that the dominant institutions and systems of our world are moving us toward global death—depends on a stance of resistance. Otherwise, how could we simply "accept" this cruel, unjust, and unspeakable state of affairs? That would be consent and complicity. The only way to face the horror and retain our integrity is to stand in solidarity with the crucified Jesus and with contemporary victims of the powers, to follow him in nonviolent resistance, and to risk the same fate that he endured. In this context, prayer is a way of practicing resistance to the institutional powers, which lure us into conformity and threaten us with death in so many different forms.

Reflections such as these become a means of grace as we allow ourselves to be immersed in the depths of God and as we face and repent of our participation in the domination system. As we stand

---

15. Soelle, 213.
16. Soelle, 197.

in solidarity with Jesus Christ crucified, we stand in solidarity with all who suffer, especially those who suffer unjustly at the hands of worldly powers, as he did. This solidarity becomes the foundation for actions of resistance and social transformation.

THIS IS ENOUGH

A Christian is a person whose death is behind him.

—DOROTHEE SOELLE, *SUFFERING*

I close this chapter with reflections on a conversation I had with my husband, Guari, who had been talking with me about contrasting experiences of what he called "unfulfilled potential" and "the unexpected and undeserved grace of God." He linked unfulfilled potential not with promise or hope or fulfillment or accomplishment but solely with the experience of grace.

To me, that unfulfilled potential includes the sin, sorrow, and brokenness of our lives, which many have experienced especially strongly in these fraught times. The grace, amazingly, is present as well, offering and providing consolation through it all, if I am willing to face and enter the pain and go through whatever is troubling me. By facing the pain of what can feel like a death of sorts, I enter (ironically) a space where the Spirit has easy access, where I am vulnerable, open—acknowledging my (and our) needs and limitations and my sense of being at the end of the road, of having exhausted the tools and plans and resources that I have at hand. Here, in this quiet place, at my extremity, I become willing to "drink the stillness and to submerge myself in it, letting it pervade me through and through," and by so doing, I recognize again the underlying reality of life—the God of love who enfolds us all no matter what, the risen Christ manifest in both a personal and cosmic way, and the Holy Spirit revealing these mysteries and enabling our participation and, in the process, our transformation.

This is enough. This is consolation. This is mercy. The living God present in the depths of suffering. The risen Christ alive in and among us, in defiance of death. The Holy Spirit propelling us forward into the ongoing story of God's intention for the world. This is resurrection. This is eternal life.

CHAPTER 10
THE WAY OF THE CROSS

FOLLOWING JESUS INTO THE HEART OF THE STRUGGLE FOR A TRANSFORMED WORLD

Taking up one's cross refers specifically to Rome's instrument of intimidation and execution. It reminds us again that following Jesus's liberating way puts us on a collision course with oppressive regimes and institutions, which will resort to any means necessary to crush resistance. By voluntarily and deliberately facing the prospect of death, one is freed from its power as a deterrent.

—WALTER WINK, *ENGAGING THE POWERS*

IN *THE RESURRECTION of Jesus*, biblical scholars N. T. Wright and John Dominic Crossan engage in dialogue about their respective ways of understanding the historical reality of the resurrection of Jesus. While they both agree that it was "real," they disagree about whether Jesus's resurrection from the dead as portrayed in the Gospels is literal or metaphorical. Wright argues that the scriptural accounts of the empty tomb and bodily appearances of Jesus are factual accounts based on eyewitnesses to these events. Crossan, on the other hand, makes the case that Jesus's postdeath appearances came in the form of visions, as did Jesus's appearance to Paul (Acts 9:3–7), and that the Gospel stories of these appearances are metaphorical. Both scholars have well-reasoned arguments. They make good points, challenge each other, and respectfully respond. But they agree to disagree about interpretation for the sake of their agreement on a more important issue—that is, on the meaning and purpose of the gospel's *message*. Crossan explains, "We are not pro-scribed from argument and debate on the subject, but I also invite us (indeed, implore us) to move beyond mode to meaning and to take back God's world from the thugs."[1] In this context, I think of "thugs" not simply as individual people but as the forces that cause people to act in harmful ways as well as the institutions and systems that bring harm and wreak havoc—that is, the powers and principalities.

This volume does not prescribe a "mode" for reading or understanding Scripture, nor does it seek to limit its interpretation, for that is the realm of the Spirit. But I invite readers to join me in agreeing, at least, on the meaning and purpose of the gospel so that we have common ground for considering how we might follow Jesus in responding to the challenges of our time. Can we agree that the point of the gospel, both in meaning and in purpose, is to wrest control of our hearts away from dominating powers, to set us free to love God and neighbors, and to empower us to follow Jesus in the direction of the reign of God? If so, we have a good spiritual foundation for considering how we might engage in transformative action together for the sake of God's world today.

According to Mark, Jesus said, "If any want to become my followers, let them deny themselves and take up their cross and follow me" (Mark 8:34–35). This statement refers to the cross as a metaphor for "denying the ego's claim to possess this life" (Walter Wink)[2] as well as to the actual risk of undergoing suffering or even death for adopting Jesus's values and mission, sharing his passion for the vision of God's reign, and taking action in pursuit of that vision. Early readers of the Gospels, who lived during the time of Rome's

---

1. John Dominic Crossan and N. T. Wright, *The Resurrection of Jesus: John Dominic Crossan and N. T. Wright in Dialogue* (Minneapolis: Fortress, 2006), 186.
2. Wink, *Engaging the Powers*, 161.

persecution of Christians, would have understood both the spiritual and political meaning of this invitation and call.

Following Jesus means living in a way that is consistent with his teachings and example, for "whoever says, 'I abide in him,' ought to walk just as he walked" (1 John 2:6). This includes rejecting the cultural values of status, wealth, and worldly power and practicing compassion, inclusion, justice, equity, reconciliation, nonviolence, and peace, as Jesus did. This places us at odds with the dominating institutions of our day just as it placed Jesus at odds with those of his day.

Living by the faith of Jesus means that we are called to live under the influence of the Holy Spirit as he did. We are called as he was called and sent as he was sent. His mission becomes our mission. His faithfulness becomes our faithfulness. By engaging the stories of Jesus, taking them to heart, discussing them with others, and practicing what they teach, we allow the transforming power of the Spirit to convert our hearts and lives in the direction of the reign of God. We participate in the ongoing story of the life, death, and resurrection of Jesus as his story becomes our story and as we become his.

FOSTERING INCLUSIVE COMMUNITY

> Now I appeal to you, brothers and sisters, by the name
> of our Lord Jesus Christ, that all of you be in agreement
> and that there be no divisions among you, but that you
> be united in the same mind and the same purpose.
>
> **—1 CORINTHIANS 1:10**

Jesus gathered a community of people around him built upon the values of the reign of God. If he had not done so, the Christian movement would not have gotten started and Jesus would have been forgotten long ago. If he had not had followers and a popular movement behind him, the religious authorities would not have targeted him as a threat and would have dismissed him as just another lone prophet or itinerant preacher and healer. Instead, they sought to put a stop to the movement by doing away with its leader, and they thought they had succeeded. Instead, after the initial shock of Jesus's death and in light of his postdeath appearances, the disciples picked up where he had left off. Through their experience of Christ risen and present among them, they became convinced that the same Spirit that had motivated Jesus was still with them, continuing God's work through them.

Years later, in Paul's Epistles, we glimpse some of the conflicts that took place in early Christian communities. As we see in chapter 1, Paul exhorts the Corinthians to "be united in the same mind and the same purpose" (1 Cor 1:10)—that is, to be united in mutual awareness of the "mind of Christ" and in their common purpose of continuing his legacy.

We have pointed to grave divisions within Christianity in our day, foundational differences of perspectives and values that create a gulf that may seem impossible to cross. In some cases, this may be true, as exemplified by Christian symbols being used to support actions with opposite meanings, such as the Good Friday Stations of the Cross event and the Capitol insurrection mentioned in this book's introduction. Such divisions represent a profound difference in understanding about the meaning of the life, death, and resurrection of Jesus, symbolized by the cross, as well as the nature of God and the meaning and purpose of the Christian message.

But for those of us who do agree that we are called to follow Jesus's teachings and example and live in his Spirit, what does it mean to be "united in the same mind and purpose"? It does not mean that we must agree on everything. Differences of opinions need not threaten unity in churches where freedom of thought and variations in personal experiences are valued. What is important is that we find shared meaning and purpose in the message and ministry of Jesus, in our shared communion with the risen Christ, and in our mutual commitment to carrying God's reconciling love to all people and all creation so that we can work together in the direction of a transformed world.

For followers of Jesus, this means not just living as isolated individuals, for we have been "called into the fellowship of [God's] Son" (1 Cor 1:9), an inclusive community that "God has opened to people of all ages, races, and nations"[3] based on Jesus's mission and vision. As a community that magnifies and embodies the love of God in our day, we are called to use our spiritual gifts and physical resources for the good of others, especially for those in greatest need. Some such actions may create controversy. Offering food to hungry people in a church courtyard or providing shelter for unhoused people in a fellowship hall has in some places caused neighborhood uproar. Simply putting up a Black Lives Matter sign or a rainbow flag to support LGBTQ+ rights in front of a church has at times resulted in vandalism. Church members may engage in difficult discussions and may disagree on whether or how to take a stand for justice if it might make the church less comfortable for current members, damage the church's standing in the community, or risk triggering anger that could lead to destruction of church property or violence against churchgoers. Regardless of what is decided in such situations, being "united in the same mind and the same purpose" means fostering inclusive community in ways that reflect the teachings and example of Jesus. For it is Christ's living Spirit that undergirds us, tears down

---

3. Rueben P. Job, ed., "The Baptismal Covenant I," in *The United Methodist Hymnal* (Nashville: United Methodist Publishing House, 1989), 34.

dividing walls of hostility (Eph 2:14), and gives us the unity and strength to face whatever difficulties we encounter.

Fostering inclusive community includes finding common ground with people who may be different from us but who share similar values and goals. Interfaith work is an expression of confidence in the universality of the Spirit, for God is at work in all faith traditions, in all human communities, and throughout all creation. Awareness of the mind of Christ is what is left when we move beyond the judgments and cultural overlays and belief systems that divide us and recognize that what unites us all is the reality that God is the very Ground of Being. Furthermore, as Jesus pointed out, we cannot know or predict or limit the influence of the Spirit (John 3:8). John Wesley called this universal Spirit "the soul of the universe."[4]

Our community begins with those closest to us, extends outward, and is incorporated into other like-minded and like-hearted communities, creating a network of people engaged in actions that make possible the transformation of the world in a direction that is consistent with the good news of Jesus. This means we must be willing to be in coalition with all people of conscience, including people of varied denominations, faith traditions, and secular philosophies. The largest and most powerful coalitions are built around organizing diverse groups of people working together across issues and across borders in service of a world of peace, justice, and ecological regeneration.

Ongoing awareness of the mind of Christ even brings us closer to Jesus's command to "love your enemies and pray for those who persecute you" (Matt 5:44), for it enables us to recognize that all are included within the infinite embrace of God's love, even those with whom we are at odds. They may not include us within their circle

---

4. John Wesley, Sermon 23, "Upon Our Lord's Sermon on the Mount, III," in *The Works of John Wesley*, ed. Albert C. Outler (Nashville: Abingdon, 1986), 1:516–17.

of concern, but we can include them, even those who cause great harm and whose actions we must actively oppose. This is a foundational principle of the practice of nonviolence taught by Gandhi and adopted by Martin Luther King Jr., who spoke of *agape*—that is, all-inclusive, godly love. The King Center website uses King's words to define agape:

> "Agape does not begin by discriminating between worthy and unworthy people. . . . It begins by loving others for their sakes" and "makes no distinction between a friend and enemy; it is directed toward both. . . . Agape is love seeking to preserve and create community."[5]

SPEAKING TRUTH TO POWER

> As Christians, our role in society is not to wring our hands at the corruption of power or simply to pick a candidate that supports one or another supposedly Christian policy. The Christian role, as part of naming the name of the crucified and risen Jesus on territory presently occupied by idols, is to *speak the truth to power* and especially to speak up for those with no power at all.
>
> **—N. T. WRIGHT, *THE DAY THE REVOLUTION BEGAN***

It has been said that when properly preached, the gospel should "comfort the afflicted and afflict the comfortable."[6] As we have seen, compassion characterized Jesus's life. He had compassion not only for

---

5. Martin Luther King Jr., as quoted in "The Beloved Community," The King Philosophy: Nonviolence365, King Center, accessed December 15, 2021, https://thekingcenter.org/about-tkc/the-king-philosophy/.

6. This quote is often attributed to Reinhold Niebuhr, but it originated with newspaper humorist Finley Peter Dunne, who claimed that this was the role of newspapers. "Radical Preaching," *From the Daily Office*, October 10, 2012, https://www.thefunstons.com/radical-preaching-from-the-daily-office-october-10-2012/.

people who came to him but also for the crowds, for he saw that they "were like sheep without a shepherd" (Mark 6:34). He healed them, forgave their sins, and taught them gently, telling stories and interpreting them. By so doing, many who were afflicted were comforted. At the same time, Jesus revealed the wisdom of God, secret and hidden to most people because of their immersion in the dominant culture. By promoting the values of the reign of God such as inclusiveness, forgiveness, equity, and nonviolence, Jesus made visible his opposition to the reign of Caesar, thus afflicting the religious elite who saw it as their duty to dominate the Jewish people and to maintain law and order on behalf of Rome.

When Jesus preached, taught, and spoke in parables, he presented a direct challenge to the prevailing wisdom that undergirded the system of domination and transmitted the values of God's domination-free order. Such teachings highlighted the clash of kingdoms between the reign of Caesar and the reign of God. When Jesus healed or forgave people or cast out demons, the religious leaders criticized him for healing on the Sabbath, having the audacity to forgive sins, eating and drinking with tax collectors and sinners, or breaking other laws or conventions. When he demonstrated God's power to heal and renew lives in such ways, it was a way of speaking truth to power. Jesus also directly challenged those who sought to maintain the unjust order, and he refused to back down despite the cost.

Throughout the past two thousand years, many have followed his example. Oscar Romero was archbishop of El Salvador from 1977 until he was assassinated in 1980, during the time that the United States supported the right-wing government's war against leftist rebels. At first Archbishop Romero took a moderate stand, but as priests under his authority were murdered for siding with the poor, and as he witnessed the atrocities carried out by government-supported death squads and saw the suffering of the people, he was converted to their cause and began speaking out on their behalf. "You are crucified like Jesus at the cross," said the archbishop to terrorized campesinos who had survived a massacre. He spoke to the church of God's "preferential option for the poor" and proclaimed it as a calling for God's people in which the choice is clear "to be in favor of life or in favor of death. With great clarity, we see that neutrality is impossible. We serve the life of Salvadorans, or we are complicit in their death."[7] Despite ongoing death threats, in his last radio broadcast, Monsignor Romero appealed to the Salvadoran military, saying, "No soldier is obliged to obey an order that goes against the law of God. . . . I beseech you. I beg you. I command you! In the name of God: 'Cease the repression!'"[8] Just days later, he was assassinated while serving Mass.

As with Jesus, God sent Oscar Romero to El Salvador not to die but to preach and live out the gospel. Under the circumstances, compassion and solidarity made clear to him that abandoning the people and going back to Rome was not God's will. Romero was a privileged person, an archbishop, but he looked out on the crowds of the poor, suffering people of El Salvador and had compassion for them. He identified with the Salvadoran people and ultimately died for them, pointing beyond himself to Jesus. He preached Christ crucified in the context of the oppression taking place there. He could have asked Rome to reassign him, but that would have been to betray the Salvadoran people, his calling to serve the poor and oppressed, and his God. In consequence, he was killed by the death squads.

7. Vigil, *Getting the Poor Down*, 310.
8. Seàn-Patrick Lovett, "Remembering St Oscar Romero: 40 Years after His Assassination," *Vatican News*, March 24, 2020, https://www.vaticannews.va/en/church/news/2020-03/oscar-romero-forty-years-assassination-anniversary0.html.

At one point, when threatened with death, Romero responded, "If they kill me, I shall arise in the Salvadoran people. If the threats come to be fulfilled, from this moment I offer my blood to God for the redemption and resurrection of El Salvador. Let my blood be a seed of freedom and the sign that hope will soon be reality."[9] In 2018, Pope Francis called him "a martyr for the faith" and canonized him as a saint.[10] Pointing beyond himself to Jesus, Archbishop Oscar Romero followed him to the point of death, and beyond to resurrection.

There are many ways to speak truth to power: faithful preaching and teaching, organizing within congregations and denominational structures, advocating for churches to be faithful to the way of Jesus in word and deed, engaging church leaders, challenging distortions of the gospel, making public statements, or joining with others to call for peace, justice, and environmental healing. There are many creative possibilities, but taking a stand is essential. For the problem is not just active collaboration in harm being done in the name of Jesus but also passive complicity. By ignoring the distortions of Jesus's message, we dilute it, and his message of the compassionate reign of God is needed now more than ever. M. Shawn Copeland writes,

> In this sadly gray, grim, and gloomy season around the globe . . . when casual cruelty, resentment, madness, and hatred defames and demeans, chokes and assaults, shoots and destroys, criminalizes and incarcerates, deports and demonizes children, women, and men simply because of their existence—simply because of their poverty, gender, sexual

---

9. John Dear, "Romero's Resurrection," *National Catholic Reporter*, March 16, 2010, https://www.ncronline.org/blogs/road-peace/romeros-resurrection.

10. Dear.

identity, or religious practices—we who are followers of the crucified Jewish Jesus must protest the oppression and suffering of each human person and work for their flourishing.[11]

As we follow Jesus's teachings and example by speaking out and by engaging in healing and spiritually transforming ministries, we participate in helping break the chains of the powers that bind, and we pass on the invitation to others to enter a new paradigm and live in a new way. It is important, however, that we remember who we are and the context in which we live and that we recognize and repent of our complicity in the institutional and systemic powers that dominate our world. This can be a humbling experience, made possible by grace.

For instance, as a Christian, I must acknowledge Christianity's stance of domination and its complicity in historic and contemporary injustices, for the church, too, is an institutional power. Graves of Indigenous children have been discovered and are being unearthed at former "Christian" boarding schools, children who were forcibly removed from their communities. Unspeakable horrors were perpetrated by the church in its complicity with colonization and genocide. As mentioned earlier, Christianity carries the burden of being complicit and at times being the primary perpetrator of countless atrocities throughout its two-thousand-year history. If we do not acknowledge the church's role and speak out against such atrocities, we are going along through silent consent and extending the harm into today. Speaking out involves challenging churches that ignore or perpetuate historical or contemporary injustices as well as the theologies that support them.

---

11. M. Shawn Copeland, *Knowing Christ Crucified: The Witness of African American Religious Experience* (Maryknoll, NY: Orbis, 2018), xxvi.

Some US churches actively support Christian nationalism and reject the idea that the United States should explore racism, colonization, or other sins of the past. Other churches practice a form of unity based on not offending parishioners or potential church members by ignoring or refusing to address issues considered controversial. In either case, pastors who speak out on such topics risk losing the support of their congregations, while church members who speak out risk conflict and disruption of relationships with faith communities that have nurtured them and that they may call home. This may be especially risky in these times of deep social division, hate speech, online targeting, and threats of violence. Nevertheless, speaking truth to power is part of what faithfulness requires so that we are not among those who "loved human praise more than praise from God" (John 12:43 NIV).

ENGAGING THE POWERS THROUGH NONVIOLENT ACTION

The only way to promote positive social change, for a person of
faith, is to pass through the paschal mystery, just as Jesus did.
Our action and our imprisonment were not just experiences
of the cross; they were also sharings in the resurrection.

—JOHN DEAR, *THE SACRAMENT OF CIVIL DISOBEDIENCE*

On July 18, 2019, seventy-one Catholics were arrested for an act of civil disobedience in support of immigrant children while praying the rosary with several hundred other people in the Russell Senate Building at the US Capitol. They were there to protest the cruel treatment of immigrants, including the separation of children from their parents at the border.

The worshipful action included hymns, prayers, Scripture passages, and the public reading of the words of children incarcerated in facilities run by US Customs and Border Protection. Participant Rose Marie Berger described how the action culminated: "When the U.S. Capitol Police issued three warnings for us to disperse, most of those gathered stepped back behind the police line, but five stepped forward and laid down in the shape of a cross in the center of the rotunda. A cross of human bodies. Dozens more formed a eucharistic circle around this cross" and were then arrested. Berger explained that they had gathered to "pierce the veil of morally isolated political leaders who are caging immigrant children."[12] This was one of hundreds of immigrant rights marches, rallies, vigils, and prayer services that were taking place around the country at the time. The formation of a cross of human bodies in the context of this particular action clearly represented solidarity with suffering incarcerated children, support for family reunification, and resistance to the government's cruel and dehumanizing immigration policies. This is one example of nonviolent direct action that clearly represents "the word of the cross" in the context of today's powers.

Walter Wink describes such actions as symbolic "exorcisms" that expose and engage systemic evils in our midst. He said, "The seer's gift is not to be immune to the invasion of the empire's spirituality, but to be able to discern that internalized spirituality, name it, and externalize it. This drives the demonic out of concealment. What was hidden is now revealed."[13] The point of symbolic nonviolent actions such as this one is to expose the social sin and institutional evil manifested by the principalities and powers and to call them to account.

---

12. Rose Marie Berger, "A Cross of Human Bodies: How 71 Catholics Were Arrested for Protesting Immigrant Child Detention," Sojo.net, July 31, 2019, https://sojo.net/articles/cross-human-bodies.

13. Wink, *Engaging the Powers*, 95.

Following Jesus means to live out an ethic of nonviolence, compassion, equity, inclusion, resistance, risk, and trust in God. Embodying the values of God's intended world and resisting the current unjust order presents a direct challenge to today's domination system. The powers and principalities are continually at work to further their purposes and maintain their authority over human beings. They are especially brutal wherever transformational peace, love, and joy break out, threatening to undo the status quo.

Both Gandhi and Martin Luther King Jr. pointed to Jesus as a model for their practice of disciplined, active nonviolence. The purpose of engagement through actions of organized nonviolent resistance is to challenge and engage the powers, to prevent or reduce their harmful effects, and to create public pressure that will bring systemic change. According to the International Fellowship of Reconciliation, *nonviolent resistance* is "neither passive acceptance of oppression, nor a violent opposition to it. Instead, nonviolence is active. Nonviolent action implies a commitment to utilizing nonviolent and creative means (e.g. acts of protest and persuasion, noncooperation, direct action, civil disobedience, boycotts, strikes, and education) to resist violent forces in order to influence and encourage social change."[14] The practice of nonviolence can be creatively expressed in many ways, but the key is action. According to Gandhi, "Without a direct action expression of it, nonviolence, to my mind, is meaningless."[15]

The possibilities for organizing and practicing direct action expressions of nonviolence are limited only by the context and by people's willingness to assume risk. It can include a myriad of possible tactics.

---

14. "What Is Nonviolent Resistance?," Fellowship of Reconciliation Peace Presence Program (FORPP), accessed December 15, 2021, https://peacepresence.org/learn-more/nonviolence/.

15. Mary Ellen Snodgrass, *Civil Disobedience: An Encyclopedic History of Dissidence in the United States* (New York: Routledge, 2009), 645.

In *The Methods of Nonviolent Action*, Gene Sharp lists 198 methods and gives detailed descriptions and historical examples of each. He classifies them into three broad categories: nonviolent protest and persuasion, noncooperation (social, economic, and political), and nonviolent intervention.[16] Any one or more of these methods listed may be used to build a strategic campaign based on active nonviolence. This starts by laying the foundation, building an inclusive community, recognizing the importance of symbols, deciding how to frame the issues, building public support and strength as a movement, celebrating successes, and working through roadblocks. Organizing such a campaign requires discernment, consensus and cooperation, division of roles, training, and spiritual preparation. Again, to quote Gandhi, "Just as one must learn the art of killing in the training for violence, so one must learn the art of dying in the training for nonviolence."[17]

In developing a campaign based on principles of nonviolence, civil disobedience may be employed as a tactic. Such actions are likely to result in arrest because they involve the deliberate and public breaking of laws in order to challenge unjust laws or unjust systems. Actions of civil disobedience are intended to disrupt "business as usual" for the purpose of directing the attention of lawmakers and the public to a particular social issue and reframing it as an issue of conscience. An example is the action at the Russell Senate Building mentioned above, during which Catholics and their allies were arrested for breaking the law by refusing to leave the building when they were directed to do so by law enforcement. By

16. Gene Sharp, "198 Methods of Nonviolent Action," in *The Politics of Nonviolent Action* (1973; repr., Boston: Albert Einstein Institution, 2020), available at https://www.aeinstein.org/nonviolentaction/198-methods-of-nonviolent-action/.

17. Mahatma Gandhi, "Training for Non-violence," Gandhian Institutions: Bombay Sarvodaya Mondal and Gandhi Research Institute, accessed December 15, 2021, https://www.mkgandhi.org/momgandhi/chap23.htm.

forming the symbol of a cross with their bodies, singing hymns, and praying, they had framed the issue of immigration as one having spiritual and moral significance. The action had required extensive organizational work, discussions of strategy, and spiritual preparation in ways such as those listed above.

Nonviolent direct action does not necessarily mean committing civil disobedience but can simply mean taking a stand for justice in situations of risk. Oscar Romero and the priests in El Salvador followed Jesus by acting in solidarity with the poor and oppressed Salvadoran people, knowing they were risking their lives by doing so. During that war, over 75,000 people were killed, mostly by death squads, including many Christian leaders. A death squad raped and murdered three US nuns and a laywoman;[18] an elite battalion of the Salvadoran Army massacred six Jesuit priests, their housekeeper, and her daughter.[19] It was clear even then that the Salvadoran military dictatorship, backed by the United States, supported the death squads who carried out these extrajudicial killings.[20]

Another example of direct action expressions of nonviolence that do not include deliberately breaking the law but entail the risk of extrajudicial violence are actions taken by nonviolent racial justice demonstrators in today's hate-filled climate. Threats, arrests, injuries, or death may result from official police violence, especially

18. "Dec. 2, 1980: Three Nuns and Lay Worker Killed in El Salvador," Zinn Education Project: Teaching People's History, accessed February 2, 2022, https://www.zinnedproject.org/news/tdih/nuns-and-lay-worker-killed-in-el-salvador/.

19. "Murder of Jesuit Priests and Civilians in El Salvador: The Jesuits Massacre Case," Center for Justice and Accountability, accessed February 8, 2022, https://cja.org/what-we-do/litigation/the-jesuits-massacre-case/.

20. Many Salvadoran death squad officials were trained in counterinsurgency techniques in the United States at the School of the Americas at Fort Benning, Georgia. Renamed the Western Hemisphere Institute for Security Cooperation, its over sixty thousand Latin American graduates include some of the worst violators of human rights in the world, including nearly a dozen Latin American dictators. Barbara Star, "Controversial 'School of the Americas' Closes," ABC News, January 6, 2006, https://abcnews.go.com/International/story?id=81917&page=1.

against people who are Black, Indigenous, and other people of color, but attacks may also come from white supremacists and right-wing militias. Despite the risk of both official and extrajudicial violence, the Movement for Black Lives and the larger racial justice movement are growing in power today, with many more churches becoming involved. Such coalitions have taken hold around the country, including in our small rural community. People are playing catch-up and becoming aware of the extent of systemic racism and white privilege through book studies, discussion groups, and informed actions that express what it means to be an ally.

There are other social and environmental movements today that have done the necessary footwork to incorporate nonviolent direct action, as mentioned in earlier chapters. The most powerful, effective, and hopeful movements are decentralized, dependent on grassroots organizing, and made up of unified coalitions working together across issues and across regions. Some such movements are global, such as the climate justice movement, which has created organic links between climate activists and Indigenous and other at-risk communities. To the degree that such coalitions are diverse and follow the lead of vulnerable, frontline communities, they appeal to those who are most impacted and generate a sense of solidarity and positive energy for change. Such movements are not only political but also cultural. They provide a challenge to the prevailing wisdom and reframe the issues they address in the context of ethics and morality.

With so much at stake, the struggle between the powers that dominate the world and movements of active nonviolence can seem like a cosmic struggle, as indeed it is, since it takes place not only on the physical plane but also on the spiritual plane. Still, as followers of Jesus living in the presence of the risen Christ, we are called to exercise our freedom by refusing to acquiesce to the idolatrous and consolidated their rule. For if we continue along the current trajectory, a terrifying future awaits all life on earth. Under these circumstances, the practice of nonviolent resistance is critical. In the words of Dr. Martin Luther King Jr., "The way of acquiescence leads to moral and spiritual suicide. The way of violence leads to bitterness in the survivors and brutality in the destroyers. But the way of nonviolence leads to redemption and the creation of the beloved community."[21]

LIVING INTO THE VISION OF THE BELOVED COMMUNITY

Forward together, not one step back.

—SLOGAN OF THE POOR PEOPLE'S CAMPAIGN

Jesus did not just resist the temptations of status, materialism, and worldly power; he built his ministry on their alternatives: inclusiveness, equity and justice, nonviolence. Although some consider the *kingdom of God* to relate solely to end times (eschatology), Jesus also used the term to offer a vision of hope for a better world, which can be glimpsed now but is not yet fully revealed. He not only proclaimed that "the kingdom of God is at hand"; he taught people to pray for God's kingdom to come and God's will to be done on earth as it is in heaven and created a community that modeled what that would look like.

This understanding of the kingdom of God has been described in a variety of ways. Feminist scholars rarely use the term kingdom because an idealized monarchy no longer signals hope for people who strive for democracy. Elizabeth Schüssler Fiorenza uses the Greek "basileia" (usually translated as "kingdom," "realm," "dominion," or "reign") because the language is more inclusive and portrays

---

21. Martin Luther King Jr., as quoted in "Beloved Community."

the Messiah's reign as a discipleship of equals who share the vision and commitment of Jesus. Rosemary Radford Reuther uses the term "reign of God/dess," which indicates equality for women, a new form of being in community, and an end to the patriarchal insistence that God is male. Ada María Isasi-Díaz calls it the "kin-dom" of God to express an egalitarian fellowship that resembles an extended family that includes all people and all parts of creation.[22]

Walter Wink suggested that God's "kingdom" could be expressed in modern terms as "God's domination-free order."[23] Marcus J. Borg and John Dominic Crossan have referred to it as "God's dream."[24] Richard Chilson has called it "Love's Domain," "Love's Dominion," or "Love's Rule," because "the Kingdom of God is where the God who is Love rules."[25] Theologian Jürgen Moltmann reflects a similar idea by teaching that Christian hope is hope that the world can be different.[26] Or in secular terms, "Another world is possible."

Martin Luther King Jr.'s vision of the Beloved Community is yet another way of envisioning the transformation of this world in a direction that God intends. King spoke of the "Beloved Community" as an achievable vision: a society based on inclusiveness, social and economic justice, equality, nonviolence, and love of one's fellow human beings. The Forward Together Moral Movement is an example of a movement that is being built today around King's vision. Better known

---

22. Verna Elias, "From Kingdom to Kin-dom: Three Feminist Interpretations of the Kingdom of God" (MA thesis, University of Manitoba, Winnipeg, 2001), https://mspace.lib.umanitoba.ca/xmlui/bitstream/handle/1993/2728/MQ62723.pdf?sequence=1&isAllowed=y.

23. Walter Wink, *When the Powers Fall: Reconciliation in the Healing of the Nations* (Minneapolis: Augsburg Fortress, 1998), 10.

24. Borg and Crossan, *Last Week*, 213.

25. *New World Encyclopedia*, s.v. "Kingdom of God," referencing Richard Chilson, author of *Yeshua of Nazareth: Spiritual Master*, accessed December 15, 2021, https://www.newworldencyclopedia.org/entry/Kingdom_of_God.

26. Richard Bauckham, "Jürgen Moltmann," in *The Modern Theologians: An Introduction to Christian Theology in the Twentieth Century*, vol. 1, ed. David E. Ford (Campbell, MA: Basil Blackwell, 1990), 299.

as the Poor People's Campaign, it was launched by Rev. Dr. William Barber Jr. and Rev. Liz Theoharis and modeled after King's original Poor People's Campaign. This "fusion movement" began in North Carolina in response to an egregious takeover of the state legislature by reactionary forces determined to set an example for the rest of the nation by slashing services to those who were in need and by severely restricting voting rights (an effort that is currently underway on a national scale). Both efforts were focused on Black voters. These racist assaults on democracy and on the poor were met with a strong response, with regular Moral Monday demonstrations at the North Carolina State Capitol that marshaled thousands of people, many of whom engaged in civil disobedience and were arrested. The movement has now spread to other states. While there continues to be national coordination, the campaign is organized state by state. The campaign's priorities are systemic racism, poverty and inequality, environmental devastation, the war economy and militarism, and the false moral narrative of religious nationalism.

The Poor People's Campaign works with leaders of the varied faith traditions and centers the stories and leadership of those who suffer most under the weight of damaging government policies: people who are poor, people of color, and others who are vulnerable to discrimination and injustice. It is an example of a diverse coalition that does the footwork to coordinate a successful campaign, including laying the spiritual foundation, honing its (moral) message, listening and sharing people's stories, choosing songs and symbols, engaging in political advocacy, working with the press, and preparing for coordinated nonviolent direct actions. The slogan that animates this movement is "Forward together, not one step back."

In some ways, "Beloved Community" is a way of talking about the long-held Christian teaching that God's reign is already present here among us but not yet fully realized. King declared, "The end is reconciliation; the end is redemption; the end is the creation of the Beloved Community. It is this type of spirit and this type of love that can transform opponents into friends."[27] Yet for King, the Beloved Community was not an abstract hope but a "realistic, achievable goal that could be attained by a critical mass of people committed to and trained in the philosophy and methods of nonviolence."[28] As explained by the King Center: The Beloved Community connotes a global vision in which "poverty, hunger, and homelessness will not be tolerated because international standards of human decency will not allow it. Racism and all forms of discrimination, bigotry, and prejudice will be replaced by an all-inclusive spirit of sisterhood and brotherhood. . . . Love and trust will triumph over fear and hatred. Peace with justice will prevail over war and military conflict."[29]

Clearly, this vision is far from being fulfilled. Yet the late John Lewis, civil rights hero turned congressional representative, spoke of how this vision for the future broke into the present when he was part of the civil rights movement as a young man:

> And you live as if you're already there, that you're already in that community, part of that sense of one family, one house. If you visualize it, if you can even have faith that it's there, for you it is already there. And during the early days of the movement, I believed that the only true and real integration for that sense of the beloved community existed within the movement itself. Because in the final analysis, we did

27. "Why Beloved Community?," Cooperative Baptist Fellowship, September 14, 2017, https://cbfva.org/beloved-community-2017-2018/beloved-community-introduction/.

28. "Beloved Community."

29. "Beloved Community."

become a circle of trust, a band of brothers and sisters. So it didn't matter whether you were black or white. It didn't matter whether you came from the North to the South, or whether you're a Northerner or Southerner. We were one.[30]

It is easy to become disheartened when we consider the extent of personal and social sin and the extremity of systemic evil. Building an inclusive community motivated by the Spirit and oriented toward hope that "another world is possible" may seem daunting, but solidarity and moral clarity encourage us to stay the course. There have been profound social transformations in recent years that demonstrate the possibility of the coming of a new consciousness, a new understanding of what it means to be human, and new ways of living that out.

I keep my eyes open for where the Spirit is moving in the arena of social movements. When an uprising of people power breaks out, I want to be there to give my support. These moments in history do come. Social changes do not always come gradually but sometimes come at critical times of upheaval when people catch hold of a Spirit that makes possible what has previously seemed impossible, when the groundwork that has been laid bears fruit. I continue to look with hope toward a new Great Awakening of people from varied spiritual, religious, and philosophical traditions, rising up just in time to claim and live out what is best in humanity, for the sake of the whole creation. The movement in this direction is already underway in people's dedication and actions taken and sacrifices made for a compassionate and livable world, in

---

30. John Lewis, "We Are the Beloved Community," *On Being Project* podcast, July 5, 2016, https://onbeing.org/programs/beloved-community-john-lewis-2/.

people's uprisings, and in movements for peace, justice, and environmental healing that are gaining momentum as the global crisis deepens.

RESURRECTION: THE COURAGE TO RISE

Christ was not merely raised up by God. He himself rose.

—JÜRGEN MOLTMANN, *JESUS CHRIST FOR TODAY'S WORLD*

By our own strength alone, we are not able to change ourselves at a deep level or to bring about the social transformation that is needed, but the Spirit empowers us to practice the faithfulness of Jesus, to resist the powers and their deadly effects, and to pray and work to create communities that demonstrate the reign of God in our midst. In these ways, we bring hope to seemingly hopeless situations and begin to see signs of resurrection all around. In Greta Thunberg's words, "Once we start to act, hope is everywhere."

Even as the death-dealing powers continue their assaults on creation, Christ is risen and the Spirit is alive wherever compassion and justice reign: in peoples' hearts, in social movements, in transformed people and societies. Living a resurrected life means joining in solidarity with all who seek justice, peace, and healing, especially those who are most vulnerable. By courageously following Jesus, we participate in the ongoing resurrection through actions that reflect the love that brought us into being, the love that can't be extinguished by any empire, the love at the heart of the universe. Those of us who choose to bear the cross of Jesus must join with those who are already giving themselves to this sacred struggle for the new world that is possible. By doing so, we demonstrate God's love for creation and embody hope for the world.

God rejoices with us when we rejoice, weeps with us when we weep, showers both the just and unjust with all the blessings of creation, and calls us to embody love in this world. Jesus did just that. Those of us who follow him are called to do so fully and completely, renouncing fear and paralysis, living in the power of the Spirit of the risen Christ, rising in courage, and heading straight into the heart of the struggle for a transformed world.

CONCLUSION
THE CROSS

WHICH SIDE ARE YOU ON?

And we shall be asked where we stood, whether we shared
the suffering or aided those who caused it. Suffering
tolerates no neutrality, no Pilate-standpoint.

—DOROTHEE SOELLE, *SUFFERING*

IN REFLECTING ON the cross, it becomes clear that superiority and hierarchy are drained of promise. The market, after all, has no power to save. The myth of redemptive violence is shown for the sham that it is. Lives built on these values are the cause, not the cure, of the violence, injustice, unnecessary suffering, and death that we see all around. The result of all the seeking after status and wealth and dominating power is right there on the cross: in the death of Jesus, in the many forms of death inflicted on God's beloved children, in the death of nature. We know that violence is all around us, and even within us, but for us "it is finished," as Jesus's last words on the cross resound. We have hit bottom. It is done. We humbly renounce supremacy, wealth, violence, and domination. In dying and rising to new life in communion with Christ, we place ourselves on the other side, the nonviolent side, of the cross.

This concluding chapter issues a challenge. In *The Nonviolent Atonement*, J. Denny Weaver claims that "as Christ-identified people, we have been invited by God to change sides and to stand with Christ, on the side of the reign of God that confronts and is ultimately victorious over the forces of evil that killed Jesus."[1] Changing sides requires a choice. When reflecting on the cross, which side are you on? Are you on the side of the status quo, complicit with the powers and principalities of this world? Do you stand with Caiaphas, who argued in favor of sacrificing a precious human life for the sake of security and expediency, and with others who condone such practices today? Or are you on the side of Jesus, who risked everything for the sake of the world that God loves so much, defying fear, creating life-giving community, resisting empire, and trusting God to his last breath?

Although the rulers of this age are not the same individuals or institutions that crucified Jesus, their stratagems are the same. They still tap and harness human energy and demand loyalty that only God deserves in order to survive and extend their power. They still dominate the public sphere and render invisible those whom they consider expendable. They still use violence to eliminate those who oppose them.

Do we identify with the ruling powers or the suffering ones? Do we identify with and enter into fellowship with the poor, oppressed, and dispossessed peoples of the earth? Do we join with the rest of creation, groaning to be released from the bondage and oppression caused by personal and institutional sin? In communion with Christ, crucified and risen, we become aware that we exist as part of a network of relationships and that we are responsible not just for ourselves but also for how we relate to other members of our human family, the community of life with which we are interconnected, the earth that nurtures us, and the institutions and systems in which we live.

---

1. J. Denny Weaver, *The Nonviolent Atonement*, 2nd ed. (Grand Rapids, MI: William B. Eerdmans, 2011), 98.

The cross becomes a symbol of resistance and transformation for those who identify not with the rulers of this or any age, not with the official representatives of empire who erected the cross of Jesus and who today erect other means of torture and death, but with the One who endured suffering and death at the hands of the powers and who rose despite the powers. By acknowledging our complicity in the personal and systemic "sin of the world," we see how Jesus bore that sin by undergoing suffering "for the sake of the world" and how he continues in solidarity with all who suffer and continues to bear that sin through every act of violence committed today. For it is God, transcendent but also immanent, who is crucified even today as institutionalized idolatry and injustice dominate our world. It is God—that is, divine love incarnate in humanity and in all creation—who "pays the price" and "bears the curse" for the sins of the world.

The crucifixion of Jesus is not just something that happened long ago; it is an ongoing story about the struggle between good and evil, the triumph of God over the powers of darkness, the redemption of human life, and hope for creation. Jesus's death is redemptive for us if we see ourselves not as the privileged beneficiaries of his expedient and predetermined death but simply as members of the human family and as members of the community of life on this fragile planet earth. As we place ourselves on *this* side of the cross, aligning ourselves humbly with those who endure suffering while repenting and making amends for the ways in which we ourselves inflict suffering, we die to our claims of power and privilege and rise in empowerment and courage for the sake of a better world. It is time to choose. Now is the moment to decide.

ONCE TO EVERY MAN AND NATION

1 Once to every man and nation
Comes the moment to decide,
In the strife of truth and falsehood,
For the good or evil side.
Some great cause, God's new Messiah,
Offering each the bloom or blight;
And the choice goes by forever,
Twixt that darkness and that light.

2 Then to side with truth is noble,
When we share her wretched crust,
Ere her cause bring fame and profit,
And 'tis prosperous to be just;
Then it is the brave man chooses,
While the coward stands aside,
Till the multitude make virtue
Of the faith they had denied.

3 By the light of burning martyrs,
Christ, Thy bleeding feet we track,
Climbing up new Calvarys ever
With the cross that turns not back;
New occasions teach new duties,
Time makes ancient good uncouth;
They must upward still and onward,
Who would keep abreast of truth.

4 Though the cause of evil prosper,
Yet 'tis Truth alone is strong;

Though her portion be the scaffold,
And upon the throne be wrong:
Yet that scaffold sways the future,
And, behind the dim unknown,
Standeth God within the shadow,
Keeping watch above His own.[2]

---

2. James Russell Lowell, "Once to Every Man and Nation," 1845, *Hymnary.org*, https://hymnary.org/text/once_to_every_man_and_nation. I retain the original language, although some hymnals substitute "all" for "man" to be inclusive. This was a favorite hymn of Dr. Martin Luther King Jr. It originated as part of an 18-stanza poem called "This Present Crisis," which Lowell wrote to protest the expansion of slaveholding states by annexation of the new Southwest Territory through the Mexican War. James Russell Lowell, "The Present Crisis," *Academy of American Poets*, *Poets.org*, accessed February 2, 2022, https://poets.org/poem/present-crisis.

SUGGESTED READING

Aulén, Gustaf. *Christus Victor: A Historical Study of the Three Main Types of the Idea of the Atonement.* New York: Macmillan, 1969.

Bakan, Joel. *The Corporation: The Pathological Pursuit of Profit and Power.* New York: Free Press, 2005.

Baker, Sharon. *Executing God: Rethinking Everything You've Been Taught about Salvation and the Cross.* Louisville: John Knox, 2013.

Ball, Kirstie; and Laureen Snider, eds. *The Surveillance-Industrial Complex: A Political Economy of Surveillance.* London: Routledge, 2019.

Barber, William J. *The Third Reconstruction: How a Moral Movement Is Overcoming the Politics of Division and Fear.* Boston: Beacon, 2016.

Berkhof, Hendrik. *Christ and the Powers.* Scottdale, PA: Mennonite, 1977.

Boff, Leonardo. *Passion of Christ, Passion of the World.* Maryknoll, NY: Orbis, 1987.

Bonhoeffer, Dietrich. *The Cost of Discipleship.* New York: Collier, 1961.

————. *Letters and Papers from Prison.* Edited by E. Bethge. Translated by R. H. Fuller. 4th ed. London: SCM, 1971.

Borg, Marcus J. *Convictions: How I Learned What Matters Most.* New York: HarperOne, 2014.

————. *Jesus, a New Vision: Spirit, Culture, and the Life of Discipleship.* San Francisco: HarperSanFrancisco, 1987.

Borg, Marcus J., and N. T. Wright. *The Meaning of Jesus: Two Visions.* New York: HarperCollins, 1999.

Brock, Rita Nakashima, and Rebecca Ann Parker. *Proverbs of Ashes: Violence, Redemptive Suffering, and the Search for What Saves Us.* Boston: Beacon, 2001.

Brother Lawrence of the Resurrection. *The Practice of the Presence of God, English Translation.* Washington, DC: ICS, 1993.

Campbell, Charles L. *The Word before the Powers: An Ethic of Preaching.* Louisville: Westminster John Knox, 2002.

Carr, Nicholas. *The Shallows: What the Internet Is Doing to Our Brains.* New York: W. W. Norton, 2020.

Cone, James. *The Cross and the Lynching Tree.* Maryknoll, NY: Orbis, 2011.

Copeland, M. Shawn. *Knowing Christ Crucified: The Witness of African American Religious Experience.* Maryknoll, NY: Orbis, 2018.

Crossan, John Dominic. *God and Empire: Jesus against Rome, Then and Now.* New York: HarperCollins, 2007.

———. *The Greatest Prayer: Rediscovering the Revolutionary Message of the Lord's Prayer.* New York: HarperOne, 2010.

Crossan, John Dominic, and N. T. Wright. *The Resurrection of Jesus: John Dominic Crossan and N. T. Wright in Dialogue.* Minneapolis: Fortress, 2006.

Dahill, Lisa E., and James B. Martin-Schramm. *Eco-reformation: Grace and Hope for a Planet in Peril.* Eugene, OR: Cascade Books, 2016.

Dalferth, Ingolf U. *Crucified and Resurrected: Restructuring the Grammar of Christology.* Ada, MI: Baker, 2015.

Dear, John. *The Sacrament of Civil Disobedience.* Baltimore: Fortkamp, 1994.

Delgado, Sharon. *Love in a Time of Climate Change: Honoring Creation, Establishing Justice.* Minneapolis: Fortress, 2017.

———. *Shaking the Gates of Hell: Faith-Led Resistance to Corporate Globalization.* 2nd ed. Minneapolis: Fortress, 2020.

Foster, Richard J. *Celebration of Discipline: The Path to Spiritual Growth*. San Francisco: HarperSanFrancisco, 1988.

Gorman, Michael. *Cruciformity: Paul's Narrative Spirituality of the Cross*. Grand Rapids, MI: William B. Eerdmans, 2001.

Gottlieb, Roger S. *A Spirituality of Resistance: Finding a Peaceful Heart and Protecting the Earth*. New York: Crossroad, 1999.

Greider, William. *One World, Ready or Not: The Manic Logic of Global Capitalism*. New York: Touchstone, 1997.

Guðmundsdóttir, Arnfríður. *Meeting God on the Cross: Christ, the Cross, and the Feminist Critique*. Oxford: Oxford University Press, 2010.

Gutiérrez, Gustavo. *A Theology of Liberation*. Maryknoll, NY: Orbis, 1973.

Hall, Douglass John. *The Cross in Our Context: Jesus and the Suffering World*. Minneapolis: Fortress, 2003.

Hansen, James. *Storms of My Grandchildren: The Truth about the Coming Climate Crisis and Our Last Chance to Save Humanity*. New York: Bloomsbury, 2009.

Happold, F. C. *Mysticism: A Study and an Anthology*. New York: Viking Penguin, 1963.

Harper, Fletcher. *Greenfaith: Mobilizing God's People to Save the Planet*. Nashville: Abingdon, 2010.

Hayes, Richard B. *The Faith of Jesus: The Narrative Substructure of Galatians 3:1–4:11*. Grand Rapids, MI: William B. Eerdmans, 2002.

Hedges, Chris. *American Fascists: The Christian Right and the War on America*. New York: Free Press, 2006.

Horsley, Richard. *Abingdon New Testament Commentaries: 1 Corinthians*. Nashville: Abingdon, 1998.

Jersak, Brad, and Michael Hardin, eds. *Stricken by God? Nonviolent Identification and the Victory of Christ*. Grand Rapids, MI: William B. Eerdmans, 2007.

Johnson, Elizabeth A. *Creation and the Cross: The Mercy of God for a Planet in Peril.* Maryknoll, NY: Orbis, 2018.

Keller, Catherine. *God and Power: Counter-apocalyptic Journeys.* Minneapolis: Fortress, 2005.

Klein, Naomi. *This Changes Everything: Capitalism vs. the Climate.* New York: Simon & Schuster, 2014.

Korton, David C. *The Great Turning: From Empire to Earth Community.* San Francisco: BerrettKoehler, 2006.

Mayer, Jane. *Dark Money: The Hidden History of the Billionaires behind the Rise of the Radical Right.* New York: Doubleday, 2016.

McLuhan, Marshall, and Quentin Fiore. *The Medium Is the Message: An Inventory of Effects.* New York: Bantam, 1967.

Moe-Lobeda, Cynthia D. *Resisting Structural Evil: Love as Ecological-Economic Vocation.* Minneapolis: Fortress, 2013.

Moltmann, Jürgen. *The Crucified God.* New York: Harper & Row, 1974.

———. *Experiences of God.* Philadelphia: Augsburg Fortress, 1981.

Moore, Kathleen Dean. *Great Tide Rising: Towards Clarity and Moral Courage in a Time of Planetary Change.* Berkeley: Counterpoint, 2016.

Nagler, Michael N. *Is There No Other Way? The Search for a Nonviolent Future.* Berkeley: Berkeley Hills, 2001.

Patterson, Stephen J. *Beyond the Passion: Rethinking the Death and Life of Jesus.* Minneapolis: Fortress, 2004.

Pope Francis. *Laudito Si, Encyclical on Climate Change and Inequality: On Care for Our Common Home.* New York: Melville House, 2015.

Ruether, Rosemary Radford. *Sexism and God-Talk: Toward a Feminist Theology.* Boston: Beacon, 1983.

Sharp, Gene. *The Politics of Nonviolent Action.* 1973. Reprint, Boston: Albert Einstein Institution, 2020.

Snodgrass, Mary Ellen. *Civil Disobedience: An Encyclopedic History of Dissidence in the United States.* New York: Routledge, 2009.

Soelle, Dorothee. *The Silent Cry: Mysticism and Resistance.* Minneapolis: Fortress, 2001.

———. *Suffering.* Philadelphia: Fortress, 1975.

Stiglitz, Joseph. *Globalization and Its Discontents Revisited: Antiglobalization in the Era of Trump.* New York: W. W. Norton, 2017.

Stringfellow, William. *An Ethic for Christians and Other Aliens in a Strange Land.* Waco, TX: Word, 1973.

Thurman, Howard. Deep River *and* The Negro Spiritual Speaks of Life and Death. Richmond: Friends United, 1975.

———. *Sermons on the Parables.* Edited by David Gowler and Kipton E. Jensen. Maryknoll, NY: Orbis, 2018.

Tinker, George E. *Spirit and Resistance: Political Theology and American Indian Liberation.* Minneapolis: Augsburg Fortress, 2004.

Trelstad, Marit, ed. *Cross Examinations: Readings on the Meaning of the Cross Today.* Minneapolis: Augsburg Fortress, 2006.

Wallis, Jim. *America's Original Sin: Racism, White Privilege, and the Path to a New America.* Grand Rapids, MI: Brazos, 2016.

Weaver, J. Denny. *The Nonviolent Atonement.* 2nd ed. Grand Rapids, MI: William B. Eerdmans, 2011.

———. *The Nonviolent God.* Grand Rapids, MI: William B. Eerdmans, 2013.

Wiesel, Elie. *Night.* New York: Hill & Wang, 1972.

Wink, Walter. *Engaging the Powers: Discernment and Resistance in a World of Domination.* Minneapolis: Fortress, 1992.

———. *The Human Being: Jesus and the Enigma of the Son of Man.* Minneapolis: Augsburg Fortress, 2002.

———. *Naming the Powers: The Language of Power in the New Testament.* Minneapolis: Fortress, 1984.

———. *Unmasking the Powers: The Invisible Forces That Determine Human Existence*. Minneapolis: Fortress, 1986.

———. *When the Powers Fall: Reconciliation in the Healing of the Nations*. Minneapolis: Augsburg Fortress, 1998.

Wright, N. T. *The Day the Revolution Began: Reconsidering the Meaning of Jesus's Crucifixion*. New York: HarperCollins, 2016.

Wylie-Kellermann, Bill. *Principalities in Particular: A Practical Theology of the Powers That Be*. Minneapolis: Fortress, 2017.

INDEX

prayer, 207–27. *See also* contemplative
    prayer; Lord's Prayer
preaching, 8, 27, 78, 89, 179, 211,
    235, 238
prevailing wisdom, 14, 39, 41, 137,
    139–40, 142, 148, 153, 155,
    161, 171, 236, 245. *See also*
    conventional wisdom; wisdom of
    this age
Prichard, Chet, 17
prince of the power of the air, 155, 170
prince of the power of the airwaves, 170
prosperity gospel, 39, 74, 152

racial justice, 77, 138, 143, 163,
    244–45
racism, 2, 9, 12, 77, 138, 142–44,
    161–62, 164–66, 169–70, 240,
    245, 248–49
ransom, 10, 60–62, 202–4
reconciliation, 10–11, 33, 70–71, 79,
    83–85, 88, 96, 109–10, 113,
    183, 190–92
redemption, 10, 26, 36–37, 41, 57,
    61, 83, 202–5, 249, 255
reflection, 41, 207, 216–18, 223,
    225–26
reign of God, 11, 14, 17, 20–21, 27,
    29, 40, 49, 63, 78, 102, 108,
    110, 114, 123–25, 133, 135,
    159, 190, 230–31, 236, 238,
    247, 251, 253. *See also* kingdom
    of God
repentance, 33, 191–92, 216
restorative justice, 188, 190
resurrection of Jesus, 3, 6–7, 17, 22,
    25–26, 40–41, 55, 64, 155,

179, 183, 197, 208, 211, 222,
    229–32, 260
resurrection ongoing, 3–4, 25, 38, 251
retributive justice, 189–90, 192
Rieger, Nathan, 179
risen Christ, 4, 22, 34, 43, 185, 198,
    208–10, 223, 227, 233, 245, 252
Rohr, Richard, 63–64
Roman Empire, 31, 37, 58, 118, 134,
    158
Rome, 14, 16, 31, 80, 119–20, 126,
    134, 157, 166, 229–30, 236–37
Romero, Oscar, 236–38, 244
Ruether, Rosemary Radford, 146–48,
    247
rulers of this age, 14–15, 40, 61, 113,
    140, 157, 159, 161, 163, 165,
    178, 214, 225, 254. *See also* powers
    and principalities; powers that be

sacraments, 197, 211. *See also*
    baptism; Communion
Saint John's Church, 137–38, 158
salvation, 7–8, 10, 17, 53, 59–62, 64,
    77, 88, 95, 110, 187–89, 191–93,
    198, 200, 202, 204–5, 214, 259
sanctification, 36–37, 41, 187, 205
Satan, 155–57
satisfaction, 51–54, 59, 62, 131, 189,
    193
Sessions, Jeff, 72–73, 76
Shaking the Gates of Hell, 150, 167,
    210, 260
sin: as alienation, 157, 185, 200; as
    crime, 189; as depravity, 186;
    forgiveness of, 34, 37, 40, 63,
    125, 130, 236; as idolatry, 187;